Cost-Benefit Analysis
of Manpower Policies

This project was prepared under a contract with the Department of Manpower and Immigration authorized by the Treasury Board of the Government of Canada by Minute 681341 and under Contract No. 81-53-68-41 for the Manpower Administration, U.S. Department of Labor, under the authority of the Manpower Development and Training Act. Researchers undertaking such projects under government sponsorship are encouraged to express their own judgement. Interpretations or viewpoints stated in this document do not necessarily represent the official position or policy of the Canadian Department of Manpower and Immigration or of the U.S. Department of Labor.

Cost-Benefit Analysis
of Manpower Policies

Proceedings of a North American Conference

EDITORS:

G. G. Somers & W. D. Wood

Under the Auspices of

CENTER FOR STUDIES IN VOCATIONAL
AND TECHNICAL EDUCATION
THE UNIVERSITY OF WISCONSIN

INDUSTRIAL RELATIONS CENTRE
QUEEN'S UNIVERSITY

Sponsored by

CANADIAN DEPARTMENT OF MANPOWER
AND IMMIGRATION

UNITED STATES DEPARTMENT OF LABOR

PRINTED AND BOUND IN CANADA BY HANSON & EDGAR, LTD.

EDITORS' FOREWORD

The decade of the 1960's has witnessed an exceptional growth of manpower policies in Canada and the United States. Although these policies had their origin in the early years of the decade, amidst substantial unemployment and claims of long-run structural imbalance, they continued to expand in a period of high-level employment and inflationary pressures. As the 1960's approach their end, there is a growing need to evaluate public and private manpower programs. Have they contributed to long-run growth? Have they eased unemployment, poverty, and structural imbalance? Can they reduce inflationary pressures?

In keeping with current trends in a number of government agencies, cost-benefit analyses have increasingly been used to evaluate operating programs in the manpower field. It was against this background that the North American Conference on Cost-Benefit Analysis of Manpower Policies was conceived in order to bring together academic and government researchers and policy-makers in this area. Papers were prepared for presentation at the Conference on both the theoretical and practical issues involved in applying cost-benefit analysis to manpower programs.

Why Cost-Benefit Analysis?

In utilizing cost-benefit calculations to evaluate manpower policies, economists are simply plying their trade. The textbook definition of Economics — a study of the allocation of scarce resources to satisfy human wants — is clearly applicable to the analysis of public and private expenditures designed to increase the employment and income of workers. It is understandable, then, that the papers and discussions presented in this volume should be largely in economic terms, and that the participants, mostly economists, should generally accept the basic rationale of cost-benefit analysis in the manpower field.

There is, however, a significant volume of criticism of the cost-benefit approach even in these proceedings and even among economists. For Neil Chamberlain, the underlying premises of the approach are open to serious question. William Dymond and Robert Levine, viewing the matter from the viewpoint of government agencies engaged in manpower policy, find that the practical application of cost-benefit analysis to specific programs and policies leaves much still unknown and may lead to false conclusions.

The growing use of the Planning-Programming-Budgeting (PPB) system in evaluating public expenditures has been accompanied by a growing understanding of the complexities of the process, of the institutional, methodological and conceptual hurdles facing the cost-benefit analyst. Some have cited these obstacles in concluding that this system cannot achieve reliable results and should therefore be abandoned. Many of these impediments are discussed in this volume in general terms as well as in reference to specific manpower measures. They have recently been well summarized by Robert Haveman in a report of the Joint Economic Committee of the U.S. Congress:

- The failure of many agency heads to demand program analysis or to use it in decision-making when it was available;
- The lack of interest in (and sometimes opposition to) the system by important congressional committees and congressmen;
- The failure of much legislation to clearly stipulate program goals and objectives and to provide funds for the collection of follow-up data and other program appraisal information;
- The existence of private interest groups which anticipate that hard and quantitative program evaluation will endanger the size or existence of expenditures which benefit them;
- The constraints on substantive and time-consuming policy analysis imposed by the annual budget cycle and process to which the PPB System is tied;
- A serious scarcity of analytical personnel in the PPB offices of civilian agencies;
- A basic resistance by many Federal employees to economic analysis and the difficult job of program evaluation;
- The lack of professional agreement on certain basic analytical issues, such as the appropriate public interest rate for discounting long-lived public investments, the development of shadow prices when outputs are not marketed, the evaluation of public expenditures in regions or periods of less than full employment;
- The lack of adequate data from which to develop measures of the social benefits of outputs and social costs of inputs.

In spite of these reservations and obstacles, the use of PPB and cost-benefit analysis of public expenditures will inevitably grow. As a number of political figures have recently affirmed, "any administration needs techniques of program analysis and evaluation if it is to make effective decisions on resource allocation". A quantitative evaluation of benefits and costs of alternative programs is surely required for rational decision-making in government planning.

Thus the proponents and critics of cost-benefit analysis tend to pass like ships in the night. While the former stress that the cost-benefit approach is simply an application of economic theory to government planning, the latter emphasize its limitations, noting that the present imperfection of the art can lead to abuse. It is suspected that both sides might agree that cost-benefit analysis is a growing and potentially powerful tool for the evaluation of public expenditures, but that its limitations must be recognized and that its theoretical and technical aspects require considerable improvement.

The Application to Manpower Policies

The arguments of the critics of cost-benefit analysis assume special force when applied to manpower policies. They feel that evaluation of programs to aid the disadvantaged in terms of society's monetary benefits and costs alone is inappropriate: non-monetary considerations should also be taken into account. Although it is generally recognized that non-pecuniary factors affect social welfare, such factors are seldom incorporated into cost-benefit models. The critics, therefore, feel that cost-benefit analysis concentrates on the quantitative to the exclusion of the qualitative, thereby sacrificing worthy programs on "a cross of gold".

Surely the answer to these fears is that cost-benefit analysis is not a complete approach to program evaluation and that its limitations are and should be recognized by the best practitioners of the art, as well as by the consumers of their output. Cost-benefit analysis cannot and should not purport to establish the goals of manpower policy. These are likely to be determined by non-economic as well as by economic factors. Similarly, no knowledgeable student of manpower policy would underrate the importance of non-economic benefits in evaluating alternative programs for achieving society's goals. The cost-benefit calculus is only one piece of evidence in the appraisal process, and it may not be the most significant piece of evidence. In this respect the critics perform a valuable service in reminding the analyst of the limitations of this evaluative technique. It would be unfortunate, however, to scrap a promising tool of economic analysis simply because it requires the assistance of complementary tools, and simply because the incautious fail to recognize its limitations.

The methodological and conceptual problems — dealt with in considerable detail in these papers — are at the same time less serious and more serious than the general philosophical issue discussed above. They are less serious because they can be treated as technical problems of research methodology. Like all such problems, they are troublesome and undermine some of the current findings. But progress made in the technology of data-gathering, analysis and research offers hope that continued advances will be made, thereby furthering the usefulness of cost-benefit analysis. In the short-run, however, the methodological disagreements among cost-benefit analysts pose real obstacles to a coordinated and persuasive evaluation of manpower policies. In this sense they are more serious than the problems stressed by the "philosophical" opponents of the cost-benefit approach. The papers in this volume help to clarify the issues in dispute and to reduce the area of disagreement.

The Papers

The first section of the volume is devoted to theoretical and methodological aspects of cost-benefit analysis which is essentially a technique for investment appraisal. It consists of measuring the benefits and costs of an investment and comparing them: if the benefits exceed the costs, the welfare of the investor is increased. Where alternatives are available the appropriate investment is indicated by the highest benefit/cost ratio.

Before comparison of benefits and costs is possible, the units in which benefits and costs are measured must be commensurable. The problem of reducing various kinds of benefits and costs to a common scale of measurement is one of the most difficult issues faced by the cost-benefit analyst, and one which receives a good deal of attention in a number of the papers. Incommensurability in cost-benefit analysis can take a number of forms. In the first place, a type of incommensurability is inherent in all investment analysis: from the definition of an investment, we know that benefits accrue and costs are incurred at various points in time. Economists argue that, for purposes of comparison, such values should be adjusted, by means of a discount rate, to a common point of time — usually the present. Where society is regarded as making the investment and reaping the benefits, the social discount rate is the appropriate factor of adjustment.

A second type of incommensurability may occur when the group of individuals to whom benefits accrue is not identical with the group which incurs the costs. If the investor is indifferent to any redistribution of income caused by the action in question, this type of incommensurability does not arise. If, on the other hand, redistribution is one of the stated objectives of the action, the analyst requires to know how the investor weighs benefits for various groups.

Burton Weisbrod's paper is directed mainly at the problem of incommensurability where redistribution of income is one of the objectives of a manpower program. He feels that the lack of private activity in the manpower field indicates that these programs are likely to be judged inefficient when only the "economic" benefits and costs are taken into account. It does not follow, however, that an inefficient manpower program is necessarily "undesirable". It may have favourable income redistribution consequences, and it may redistribute income in a manner which is socially preferable to the alternative of transfer payments. We must find some way in our evaluation of manpower programs of making the income redistribution consequences commensurable with the allocative consequences. The sum of these two types of benefits may then exceed the costs of the manpower program.

While André Raynauld agrees with this alternative rationale for manpower programs, he is not convinced that manpower programs are necessarily inefficient. *A priori,* nothing can be said; and the lack of private activity can be attributed to a malfunctioning private market. It is, after all, only the existence of market imperfections which yields manpower programs any kind of positive benefits at all. Raynauld points out that a possible alternative to manpower programs is an increase in aggregate demand. This also has its price tag in terms of inflation and other costs. We should ask ourselves how we can compare the two alternatives.

Commensurability is also the focus of John MacDonald's paper. He feels that the question, "cost and benefits for whom?", cannot be avoided, but that the evaluation of effects which are not measured in monetary terms is not the province of the econometrician. Cost-benefit analysis allows the economist to *identify* costs and benefits to different groups; the problem of *commensurating* them should be left to the political scientist or the sociologist to solve.

While costs usually appear to be more easily identifiable than benefits, Richard Judy warns the analyst against basing his cost calculations on accounting criteria of the cost of inputs. All cost measurement in cost-benefit analysis should be based upon the notion of forgone opportunities or opportunity cost. If market prices are to be used as indexes of social opportunity cost, the analyst should take into account violations of the theorems of welfare economics which accredit prices as a measure of costs. In addition, the use of market prices as measures of opportunity costs involves the assumption that redistribution effects involve no benefits or costs, an assumption which Weisbrod challenges.

Like the distribution of costs and benefits among individuals, the distribution of costs and benefits over time poses difficult theoretical problems. The three contributors to the Conference who examined this problem were in agreement that where society is the investor, benefits and costs to society must be brought to a common point in time by means of the social discount rate. However, two contrasting approaches to calculating this rate emerged.

Kenneth Arrow starts from the premise that we cannot use the market rate of return on capital as a measure of its opportunity cost because of market imperfections. Assuming that the market structure is otherwise perfect, are there values of the range of policy instruments open to the government which can achieve a simultaneous optimization of present and future investment decisions? In order to answer this question, Arrow examines the effects of an income tax, a consumption tax and savings tax, and a consumption tax and borrowing, upon the allocation of resources in an economy in steady-state growth. He concludes that, in the circumstances posited, optimality can be achieved; but if monopolistic price distortions, excise taxes, or a corporate income tax are introduced into the analysis, the calculation of the social discount rate becomes far more complicated.

Arnold Harberger and Grant Reuber point out that we have to estimate the social opportunity cost of funds in the presence of such imperfections. They feel that an approach aimed at a general equilibrium solution is likely to be non-operational and that a partial solution is more practicable: in other words the kind of question the analyst should ask is simply "Does the action in question increase or decrease utility?".

Harberger suggests that the analyst should identify the source of the funds to be used by a public project. Taxation and domestic borrowing are the two main sources, but, as Reuber points out, the international sector is an important source of funds which has been neglected in the cost-benefit literature. The social discount rate can be obtained as a weighted average of the marginal rates of productivity of capital in the various sectors from which investment is displaced, and of the marginal rates of time preference applicable to the various groups whose saving is stimulated by the additional government borrowing. The weights are, for each tax bracket, the elasticity of supply of savings with respect to their rate of yield, and for each investment sector, the elasticity of the investment schedule with respect to the cost of capital. A weighting system is also derived to measure the social opportunity cost of foreign exchange. In principle, all these weights can be obtained from market observations.

Turning from theoretical considerations, the second section of the volume examines the application of cost-benefit analysis to various types of manpower programs. These programs include occupational training of adult workers sponsored by the U.S. Department of Labor under the MDTA, ARA, and earlier schemes; programs aimed at reducing poverty by training disadvantaged workers; and the Canadian Manpower Mobility Program.

Problems of measurement again occupy much of the contributors' attention. Einar Hardin's survey of cost-benefit studies compares the concepts, methods, and findings of analyses of occupationally oriented, institutional training programs from three points of view — society, the individual trainee, and the government. Hardin attempts to put the results of these analyses on a comparable basis, and finds that, in every case, the investment in training is more profitable to society than an alternative investment in physical resources yielding 10 per cent.

From society's point of view, it is usually supposed that the impact of training upon national product can be inferred from the impact of training upon earnings. The impact of training upon earnings is estimated by comparing the after-training income of trainees with the income of a control group. Glen Cain and Robinson Hollister identify two types of control groups: the before-and-after comparison in which the trainees serve as their own control group; and the with-and-without comparison in which the control group consists of non-trainees identical with the trainees in all respects apart from the training variable. They prefer the latter comparison. David Sewell claims that only one of the studies cited by Hardin does not rely on a comparison between trainees and those who did not apply for training. Non-applicants may not satisfy the requirement of a control group — that they be identical with trainees in all respects other than the training variable. In particular the fact that they are non-applicants may indicate that they have a lower level of ability and intelligence than the applicants. If this is the case, the computed benefits from training include the returns to ability and intelligence also.

Hardin points out that the connection between earnings and national product may be weakened by a number of factors: these include differences between wages and employee compensation, external, vacuum, displacement, and multiplier effects. Sewell focuses upon two of these — the vacuum and displacement effects. He suggests that a distinction between the wage and the employment components of the effect of training will help us to distinguish between these effects. Training which has an employment effect alone may owe its results to displacement effects, and hence the benefits for the individual trainee are not paralleled by an increase in national output. Training which results in a wage effect, on the other hand, has enabled the trainee to move to a higher productivity job, and hence national output has been increased.

When the discussion was opened to the floor, Gösta Rehn enlarged upon the indirect effects of training outlined by Hardin. These effects illustrate a third type of incommensurability in cost-benefit analysis — where an effect is known to exist but its precise influence cannot be identified or measured. Rehn supported the view stressed by MacDonald, Parnes, and McKechnie that no policy conclusion should be drawn without taking the indirect effects into consideration. He feels that the following are of particular importance: multiplier effects, where training opens up bottle-necks in the supply of particular skills; complementarity effects, where the filling of a vacancy through training leads to increased employment of auxiliary labour; and profit effects, where the worker's move to a higher productivity job is not reflected in higher wages because of market imperfections. Rehn emphasized that the first two effects are conceptually disinct from the Keynesian multiplier.

Ernst Stromsdorfer argues that when the impact of the Keynesian multiplier is being measured, only an increment to the multiplier impact can be ascribed to the manpower investment since the multiplier effect is not unique to manpower programs. Stromsdorfer finds it difficult to rationalize reports of negative benefit-cost ratios for some MDTA programs. If the trainee's marginal productivity actually deteriorated during training, this could be regarded as a positive cost rather than a negative benefit; if all other benefits were zero, the benefit-cost ratio would be zero rather than negative. He expands upon two problem areas not covered by Cain and Hollister: the problem of valuing the capital stock used in manpower programs, and the problem of allocating the capital costs over successive cohorts of trainees. Since the physical capital costs are small relative to other opportunity costs, the valuation of capital stock will not be important as a source of error.

Cain and Hollister's paper reflects their view of the place of cost-benefit analysis in the decision-making process. If cost-benefit analysis is to aid the decision-maker it should focus upon variables which are within his ability to control, and upon programs which are replicable with respect both to techniques and participants. In this latter respect, Sewell argues, the programs examined by Hardin are non-replicable since they tended to focus upon the "cream" of the human material available for training; today's MDTA program, on the other hand, concentrates upon disadvantaged members of the labour force. The result of cost-benefit analysis, Cain and Hollister argue, will generally be modification of a program rather than approbation or rejection.

Robert Jenness shares Cain and Hollister's view of the place of cost-benefit analysis in decision-making. He argues that "one-shot studies" do not provide the type of information needed for the efficient allocation of public resources in the manpower field. Cost-benefit studies are useful to government departments principally as monitoring instruments. Jenness's manpower mobility model takes the economy as its frame of reference and the family as its unit of analysis. It attempts to provide an *a priori* benefit-cost ratio for any proposed investment in relocation; the benefit-cost ratio is estimated from information about the personal characteristics of the individual involved, the area to which he wll move, and the type of job he will fill. Subsequently the *a priori* expectations are replaced by *a posteriori* estimates derived from follow-up data, and the original benefit-cost ratios are revised. In this way, the model provides a continuing flow of incremental benefit-cost ratios which tell the program administrators which kinds of clients have the greatest likelihood of success, and which destination areas or jobs provide the highest returns.

Both Graeme McKechnie and Herbert Parnes feel that the mobility model has some ingenious approaches to some of the problems encountered in measuring program benefits, but both express reservations about the nature of the data used. While McKechnie welcomes the use of the family as the unit of analysis, he feels that errors are likely to result from the use of a "before-and-after" rather than a "with-and-without" comparison. Such errors, will, however, be less serious than those resulting from Jenness's use of averages, imputed averages, expected wages, and probabilities computed from averages. While a personality coefficient and a mobility coefficient would be useful as a screening device for selecting candidates for mobility assistance, McKechnie is of the opinion that Jenness's method of calculating these coefficients is inadequate.

Parnes feels that the effort to avoid overstating benefits by calculating the probability that the worker would have moved irrespective of the mobility program is a good feature of the model. Like McKechnie, however, he is worried about the omission of a host of secondary or indirect benefits and costs, and about the crude estimates for some of the factors which are included. Jenness argued that for practical application of a mobility model, its variables must be subject to measurement. Parnes counters this by saying that where the nature of the problem precludes precise quantification of the benefit-cost ratio, we should not try so hard to produce one; the danger is not so much in wasting effort, but that the expenditure of so much effort will make us determined to use the result. Parnes feels that the chief contribution of cost-benefit analysis to sound policy decisions lies in the comprehensive view of the issue that it engenders rather than in the benefit-cost ratios it produces.

An examination of the contribution of cost-benefit analysis to public policy decisions can profit from the experience of those who are engaged in formulating and administering manpower policy. Robert Levine, who looks at manpower programs in the context of the U.S. War on Poverty, is not inclined to minimize the consequences of devoting a large amount of effort to producing precise benefit-cost ratios. At present cost-benefit analysis cannot be regarded as a major influence on policy: it is a very partial tool in the decision-making process whereas the decisions which have to be made are at a fairly high level of aggregation; secondly, it is subject to the difficulties of constructing control groups, predicting program results, and comparing results for different programs. Levine feels, on the other hand, that it will do no harm for the planners to experiment with refined techniques like cost-benefit analysis as long as the effort to produce satisfactory benefit-cost ratios does not delay the implementation of an anti-poverty program. His own anti-poverty strategy is a negative income tax backed up by a hierarchy of manpower programs aimed at the various needs of the poor. He feels that there is no way of measuring precisely the needs of the poor for manpower programs, but that we will have to feel our way to an optimum program-mix.

William Dymond also draws upon his practical experience in formulating policy and administering manpower programs. He agrees that cost-benefit analysis has a number of disadvantages for the policy-maker: the exclusion of "non-economic" variables imposes constraints upon the use of cost-benefit models in a decision-making context; the analysis has difficulty in coping with the question of income distribution; and it is difficult to attain consistency in the assumptions and techniques used in comparing one program with another. He supports Cain and Hollister's view that cost-benefit models are more useful for improving the effectiveness of a single program (by necessitating a clear articulation of program objectives and methodology) than for making comparisons between programs. Dymond cites the Canadian Manpower Mobility Program and the Occupational Training for Adults Program as examples of the use of cost-benefit models as program monitors; cost-benefit analysis coupled with a systematic process of data collection has helped to identify the program candidates and program components which yield the highest return to resources invested.

When we apply techniques of investment appraisal to social expenditures upon education and training, we are, implicitly at least, treating people as part of society's capital stock. There is, Neil Chamberlain points out, a presumption that the rate of return on investment in human capital can be compared with rates of return on other forms of investment to determine priorities. The analyst cannot argue that this approach is value free since the price and income data upon which the calculation of a rate of return depends is based upon the existing system of social, legal, and political relations. It is clear, therefore, that this data cannot be used to calculate the rate of return on an investment aimed at changing the shape of society, a consideration which is often relevant to educational programs. In the existing system we cannot identify producers with consumers since rewards are distributed by a social process. When the analyst computes a rate of return, he cannot avoid the question "Return to whom?". It is then not permissible to ignore "incommensurable values". When incommensurabilities are present which arise out of values which people are not prepared to compromise, or out of an identification with a class interest or a status category, the rate of return cannot be "objective". Where these elements are absent, cost-benefit analysis may be useful. Chamberlain, however, concluded on a warning note by suggesting that human capital analysis cuts too close to personal integrity and life style.

In conclusion, the papers and discussions in this volume will be found to serve two important purposes in the cost-benefit and manpower fields. First, they provide a theoretical appraisal of a potentially powerful tool of economic analysis — one which is being increasingly used to evaluate a wide variety of public expenditures. Secondly, these papers demonstrate the strengths and weaknesses of this economic tool in evaluating some of the most important manpower programs of the past decade. Accordingly the editors feel that as a theoretical study and as a practical manual this publication will be useful to researchers, policy-makers, and administrators in the manpower field.

Acknowledgements

The Editors wish to express their sincere appreciation to a number of organizations and individuals who have so generously and kindly contributed to the success of the North American Conference on Cost-Benefit Analysis of Manpower Policies, and to the publication of the Proceedings. First, we are indebted to the two sponsoring government agencies whose financial support made the Conference and the publication of the Proceedings possible. In the course of planning the Conference, we also benefited greatly from the co-operation, counsel, and encouragement of a number of officials in the sponsoring agencies, particularly Miss Betti Goldwasser, Chief, Cost-Benefit Staff, Manpower Administration of the U.S. Department of Labor, and Dr. William Dymond, Assistant Deputy Minister and Dr. Duncan Campbell, Planning and Evaluation Branch of the Canadian Department of Manpower and Immigration. No words can adequately convey our appreciation to the outstanding panel of speakers and discussants for their excellent papers and for preparing these for publication. We are grateful to Mrs. Karen Kruger of the Wisconsin Center for Studies in Vocational and Technical Education, and to Mrs. Mary Walker of the Queen's Industrial Relations Centre for their expert handling of the Conference arrangements. Finally, we wish to acknowledge our heavy debt of gratitude to the staff of the Queen's Industrial Relations Centre for handling the many details involved in the publication of this volume. We wish to thank especially Mr. Harry Campbell for his expert technical assistance at all stages of preparation of the papers for publication, Mrs. Carol Williams for her meticulous editorial supervision and proof-reading, Mr. Frank Collom for his valuable assistance in the planning and production phases, and Mrs. Gail Schlachter, now of the University of Minnesota Library School, for preparing the index.

W. DONALD WOOD, Director,
Industrial Relations Centre,
Queen's University.

GERALD G. SOMERS, Chairman,
Department of Economics,
University of Wisconsin.

LIST OF CONTRIBUTORS

ARROW, KENNETH J., Professor of Economics, Harvard University.

CAIN, GLEN G., Associate Professor of Economics, The University of Wisconsin.

CAMPBELL, DUNCAN R., Planning and Evaluation Branch, Canadian Department of Manpower and Immigration.

CHAMBERLAIN, NEIL W., Graduate School of Business, Columbia University.

DYMOND, WILLIAM R., Assistant Deputy Minister, Canadian Department of Manpower and Immigration.

GOLDWASSER, BETTI, Manpower Administration, U.S. Department of Labor.

HARBERGER, ARNOLD C., Professor of Economics, University of Chicago.

HARDIN, EINAR, Professor of Economics, Michigan State University.

HOLLISTER, ROBINSON G., Associate Professor of Economics, The University of Wisconsin.

JENNESS, ROBERT A., Planning and Evaluation Branch, Canadian Department of Manpower and Immigration.

JUDY, RICHARD W., Professor of Political Economy, University of Toronto.

LAMPMAN, ROBERT J., Bascom Professor of Economics, The University of Wisconsin.

LEVINE, ROBERT A., Urban Institute.

LITTLE, J. KENNETH, Co-Director, Center for Studies in Vocational and Technical Education, The University of Wisconsin.

MacDONALD, JOHN S., Faculty of Social Sciences, University of the West Indies.

McKECHNIE, GRAEME H., Assistant Professor of Economics, York University.

PARNES, HERBERT S., Professor of Economics, Ohio State University.

RAYNAULD, ANDRE, Professor of Economics, University of Montreal.

REUBER, GRANT L., Head, Department of Economics, University of Western Ontario.

SEWELL, DAVID O., Assistant Professor of Economics, Queen's University.

SOMERS, GERALD G., Chairman, Department of Economics, The University of Wisconsin.

STROMSDORFER, ERNST W., Associate Professor of Economics, Pennsylvania State University.

WEISBROD, BURTON A., Professor of Economics, The University of Wisconsin.

WOOD, W. DONALD, Director, Industrial Relations Centre, Queen's University.

CONTENTS

Part I

*Theoretical Aspects of
Cost-Benefit Analysis*

BENEFITS OF MANPOWER PROGRAMS:
THEORETICAL AND METHODOLOGICAL ISSUES

BURTON A. WEISBROD*

University of Wisconsin

B ENEFITS from any program may be defined in terms of the program's success in meeting its objectives. Granted the usefulness of such a definition, two questions follow: (1) what are the program objectives, and (2) how should benefits be assessed when there are multiple objectives? These are the questions addressed in this paper. Although most of what is said below is applicable to programs of any type, particular attention is directed to "manpower" programs — including private and public efforts at training and retraining of workers, at enhancing worker mobility, and at improving worker placement and job-matching efforts.

I. PROGRAM OBJECTIVES

The official announcement and program for this conference includes the following statement:

> As the 1960's approach their end, there is a growing need to evaluate public and private manpower policies. Have they contributed to long-run growth? Have they eased unemployment, poverty, and structural imbalance? Can they reduce inflationary pressures?

This paragraph sets forth, in question form, the criteria by which the organizers of this conference believe manpower programs may be evaluated. That is, the paragraph contains an implicit view that the objectives of manpower policies include (or should include?) enhancement of long-run growth, and reductions in unemployment, poverty, structural imbalance, and inflationary pressures. No doubt there are persons who would add still other objectives to the list, or who might even wish to see something deleted

---

* I wish to acknowledge the helpful comments of W. Lee Hansen.

from the list.[1] But the five stated objectives constitute a group with which many people would agree. These objectives reflect broad social concerns and, hence, have applicability as standards against which a wide range of governmental programs can be, and are, evaluated.

I would prefer, however, to state these objectives of public policy more generally and somewhat differently: government activities should be, and are, directed at (1) allocative efficiency, (2) distributional equity, and (3) economic stability. *Allocative efficiency* encompasses the objectives of long-run growth and, to some extent, structural imbalance. *Distributional equity* subsumes the goal of reducing poverty. And *economic stability* encompasses the goals of cutting unemployment and inflation.

It is noteworthy that these three groups of goals are inter-related. Programs designed to influence the allocation of resources — e.g., water-resource or manpower training programs — often affect the distribution of income. Programs intended to alter the income distribution — perhaps via manpower relocation or welfare programs — are likely to influence relative prices and, hence, the allocation of resources. And so on.

Moreover, programs may have multiple goals: manpower programs, for example, may be aimed not only at slowing inflation or reducing unemployment, but also at augmenting the flow of resources into human capital investments, and shifting the distribution of income in favor of the disadvantaged.

We turn, now, to the question of what can reasonably be expected from manpower programs — in terms of their contributions to the objectives of economic stability, allocative efficiency, and distributional equity.

II. ECONOMIC STABILITY

With regard to the effect of any government expenditure program on the levels of unemployment and prices, it is important to distinguish between effects on the level or composition of aggregate *demand,* and effects on the level or composition of resource *supply.* Manpower programs are not likely to have significant demand effects on employment and prices because the alternative to public spending on manpower programs

---

1. For example, a recent publication by the Program Evaluation Staff of the U.S. Bureau of the Budget states: "The objectives [of manpower programs] are reasonably clear and operational: to reduce unemployment, to improve earnings, to increase job satisfaction." See David Page, "Measuring the Effectiveness of Federal Manpower Programs," in *Manpower Programs: Design and Analysis* (Washington: Bureau of the Budget, 1968), p. 31.

is, presumably, increased spending on other public programs, or decreased taxes and increased private spending. Thus, it seems reasonable to assume that the aggregate *demand* for labor is essentially independent of the presence or absence of manpower programs. If such programs do bring about any reduction in unemployment they do so through the mechanism of altering the skill composition and geographical distribution of the labor *supply*.

During a period of less-than-"full" employment, it may seem clear that manpower programs can hardly fail to cut unemployment by altering the labor supply mix. But an important question is whether they can do so efficiently as compared with alternative devices for reducing unemployment — devices such as transfer payments, reduced taxes, increased spending on highways, enlarged expenditures on education, and so forth.

To repeat, even if it were a fact that manpower programs utilized unemployed resources to produce the changes in labor supply characteristics, it would not follow that the opportunity cost of those resources should be regarded as zero. Because of resource complementarities, an expansion of manpower programs would very likely utilize not only some unemployed resources but also some that are already scarce, and so the real costs would not be zero. Moreover, since numerous alternative means of utilizing those unemployed resources exist, there is little reason to assume that none of these alternatives would be adopted if expenditures on manpower programs were lower.[2] Thus, the question of the allocative efficiency of manpower programs comes to the fore; more about this in section III below.

During a period of expanding demand and rising prices, manpower programs hold out the hope of being capable of altering the quality and location of labor supply so as to raise aggregate output and thereby retard inflation. Whether such a hope is justified depends not on whether a given manpower program can alter the characteristics of labor supply — as it surely can — but what output must be given up as resources are withdrawn from alternative uses and devoted to manpower programs. The net impact of manpower programs will hinge on the direction of balance between the favorable output effects of the labor-supply changes and the unfavorable output effects accompanying the withdrawal of resources from other uses in order to devote them to manpower programs. Once

2. For further discussion see B. A. Weisbrod, "Conceptual Issues in Evaluating Manpower Training Programs," *Monthly Labor Review* 89 (1966): 1091-1097.

more the issue is the allocative efficiency of the manpower programs —
the topic to which we now turn.

III. ALLOCATIVE EFFICIENCY

This section examines the question of what favorable effects on the
allocation of resources can be expected from governmental manpower programs. A number of questions will be raised about the efficiency of these
programs in dealing with the objectives set forth in section I, above.

Do (or can) manpower programs cut unemployment? Quite probably.
If an unskilled, unemployed worker living in an economically depressed
area were trained and provided with skills for which there was an excess
demand, or were relocated to an area of excess demand for labor, surely
the likelihood of the worker finding employment would be enhanced.

But there is more involved. The issue of the allocative efficiency of
manpower programs is not a question of whether manpower programs
produce benefits, but whether the benefits exceed the costs. And the
answer to this question is far more in doubt. A simple numerical illustration may help: assume that an incremental expenditure (cost) of $2,000
on manpower training would enhance an unemployed worker's skill to a
level at which he would become employed. Assume further that in the
absence of training, the worker would not have remained unemployed
the remainder of his life, and that even with the training he will be suscept-
ible to some periods of future unemployment — the net effect of which is
to increase the discounted present value of the worker's additional lifetime
earnings (benefits) by $1,500. If the prices of inputs to the training process
represent opportunity costs, and the increased earnings represent added
value of marginal productivity, then it would not be efficient to undertake the retraining. Cutting unemployment is not in itself a sufficient condition for ensuring allocative efficiency.

The preceding discussion assumed implicitly that the favorable employment effects of manpower programs represent increases in total employment and output, not merely improvements in opportunities for one
group of workers at the expense of another. Little is known about the
extent to which manpower training, relocation and job-matching programs
have served simply to permit some workers to get ahead of others, with
little or no expansion of total employment and earnings. If — or insofar
as — manpower programs merely expand income and employment oppor-

tunities for some persons at the expense of others, the programs are clearly not economically efficient, for aggregate output would remain unchanged whereas real resources were utilized by the programs. Such a finding of inefficiency does not necessarily imply, however, that the programs are "undesirable," a point to which we return later.

Although benefits from manpower programs may come partially at the expense of non-participants, the contrary may also be true: non-participants may benefit from manpower programs. Training or relocating workers could help break resource bottlenecks, thereby expanding employment, income, and productivity among other workers.

Do (or can) manpower programs contribute to reduction of "structural imbalance" — that is, to reduction in the amount of mis-matching of the types and locations of workers who are seeking employment? As pointed out above in the discussion of economic stability, it seems clear that relocation and training of workers, and increased availability of information among employers and employees can cut unemployment. What is not clear is whether this can be done consistently with attaining other objectives such as allocative efficiency and lessened inflation. Neither of these objectives is served if the costs of reducing structural imbalance exceed the gross productivity gains that result.

Do (or can) manpower programs ease inflationary pressures? The answer is yes — or no — depending on whether or not the program brings about a more efficient allocation of resources. Given the initial aggregate supply of and demand for output, an improvement in the efficiency with which resource inputs are allocated will increase output without changing the requisite inputs, thereby cutting pressure on prices. Thus, to answer the question posed above we must determine whether manpower programs are economically efficient — generally, sometimes, occasionally, rarely.

Do (or can) manpower programs contribute to long-run economic growth? In part the answer is the same as that given in the preceding paragraph: when manpower programs are allocatively efficient, undertaking them will expand output. But even so, a once-and-for-all increase in output will not alter the long-term trend growth rate; to raise the growth rate would require *continued* improvement in the economy's allocative efficiency — that is, continued *expansion* of economically efficient programs of manpower training, mobility, and placement.

Are manpower programs more efficient during periods of low, and falling unemployment? When employment is rising, unemployment falling, and the price level climbing, the benefits from manpower programs may appear to be greater than when the variables are moving in the opposite direction. But two caveats are in order: (1) the apparently greater benefits from manpower programs during periods of economic expansion may be an illusion. Just as it is easier for those workers who have participated in manpower programs to find employment in an economic expansion, so it is easier for all other workers. It is the *difference* between the experience of similar workers who have and who have not participated in manpower programs that constitutes the benefits from the programs. The magnitudes of these differences in unemployment experience and earnings may or may not vary with the level and rate of change in economic activity; more empirical evidence is required.

(2) Even if the benefits from manpower programs are greatest when economic conditions are favorable, the allocative efficiency of these programs may not follow the same pattern. Program *costs* are also likely to be greatest during an economic expansion, as many of the resources used in manpower programs become increasingly scarce.

When the benefits from particular manpower programs are being evaluated, there is a risk of overstatement insofar as a combination of programs is actually employed while all the benefits are attributed to a single program. And such overstatement is likely to be cyclically sensitive. Manpower training and retraining programs, for example, are likely to be evaluated by comparing post-training employment and earnings records for trainees and non-trainees. Granted that the two groups are initially comparable, the point is that trainees are likely to differ from non-trainees not only because of the training but also because greater job-placement efforts have been made on behalf of the trainees. It would be the unusual training program director who failed to be energetic in placing his trainees. Consequently, the program evaluator who does not control for the additional placement efforts will inadvertently attribute to the training program benefits which may be attributable — in part or, conceivably, entirely — to the placement activities. The same is likely to be true with respect to worker-relocation programs, for these are also likely to be combined with more strenuous placement efforts.

When two or more programs are, in effect, combined, it is difficult to know how effective — and how efficient — each one is independently. In addition, the relative and absolute efficiency of different types of manpower programs may well vary with the level of economic activity. Expanded worker-placement efforts might be most efficient during periods of high level demand, whereas that might not be true (or equally true) for relocation or training programs.

IV. ARE GOVERNMENTAL MANPOWER PROGRAMS LIKELY TO BE ECONOMICALLY EFFICIENT?

This paper began by asserting the proposition that "benefits" from manpower programs refer to the achievement of program objectives. It proceeded to argue that among the objectives — and, presumably, high among them — is the search for increased allocative efficiency in the economy. Indeed, this is the chief focus of most efforts to evaluate manpower as well as other governmental programs, aside from transfers. Those who are sympathetic to the given program hope (and often believe) that a "sound" evaluation will disclose that the program is efficient in the sense that measured benefits — usually in the form of enhanced output and earnings — will exceed incremental costs.

Why, one might ask, is governmental action required if there are such efficiency benefits to be had from retraining, relocation or job-matching. Each of these activities can be, and is, carried on in the private sector: training programs are available in commercial trade schools and on-the-job training programs; relocation is a continuing phenomenon in the United States, occurring in the main without governmental involvement; and matching of jobs and workers is the business of private employment agencies throughout the country (in addition, of course, to occurring through newspapers, billboards, word-of-mouth and other formal and informal — but private — forms).

Justification — on allocative efficiency grounds — for government involvement with manpower programs (either as a provider or a subsidizer) would exist if such programs produce external real benefits: benefits that the private market fails to recognize adequately (or costs that it takes too much into account) because they are not captured either by the prospective trainee or job seeker, or by the firm producing the training or job-matching.

If a retrained, relocated or better-informed worker were to have his social marginal productivity increased by more than the increase in his wages because of benefits to third parties that were not captured by the worker, then governmental subsidization of retraining, relocation, and labor market information would have a rationale on allocative efficiency grounds. (The issue of whether such subsidization should take the form of aid to private decision-makers or governmental provision of these services is an open question.) Whether real externalities occur in meaningful magnitudes is clearly a significant question, but as with most cases of suspected externalities, it is extremely difficult to determine their presence and importance. Little hard research has been done to ascertain the facts in the case of manpower programs.

What if there were no real external benefits from manpower programs; these programs might still be justified on allocative efficiency grounds if imperfections in manpower markets — imperfections which doubtless exist — could be reduced efficiently by public but not by private authorities. Such might be the case if, for example, the transactions costs of establishing a nation-wide (or even regional) clearinghouse of workers and job availability data would be lower for a government agency than for a private employment agency. Again, whether such scale economies exist and are significant is a factual matter about which little is known.

Or capital market imperfections might retard the ability of low income or unemployed workers to borrow in order to finance taking a training course, moving to another area in search of a job, or taking sufficient time in job searching to find the "best" job available. There is little doubt that the poor and unemployed have difficulty in borrowing for these and any other purposes, and that whatever loan funds are available to them carry a higher interest rate than is the case for the more affluent. But this is not equivalent to finding capital-market inefficiency — not if, as is probably the case, the risks associated with private investments in training, mobility, and job search for the poor and unemployed are actually higher than for other investments. For insofar as the risks are higher, there is a presumptive case that the use of funds for manpower programs for the disadvantaged represents an inefficient use of resources. As with all presumptive cases, this one is rebutable: the relatively high risk that the lender will not be repaid is not necessarily equivalent to the risk that the training program, for example, will fail to raise earnings (or other benefits) by more than the marginal program cost. The private risk to the lender may exceed the social risk.[3] For example, an investment in a training program might pay off handsomely for the worker, but if he failed to repay the loan, the lender would clearly be hurt. At the quantitative level, however, little is known about such deviations between private and social risk of investments in manpower programs.

This rather rapid and sketchy survey suggests — but certainly does not demonstrate — that lack of allocative efficiency in the private sector is not likely to be an adequate justification for governmental support of manpower programs. It may be true that manpower programs do produce privately-uncapturable benefits, that information about job vacancies and worker availabilities is available in sub-optimal amounts in the private market, that there is "too little" geographic mobility of labor in search of jobs and plants in search of workers, that loan funds to finance workers who wish to build human capital via education or training — and who may have to forgo earnings or job searching to make this investment — are available in inefficiently small amounts. It may be that the private market is economically inefficient and that it significantly underproduces these commodities. But the evidence for this proposition is extremely limited.

This is not to say that private markets in the manpower area work "perfectly." Private markets do not work perfectly in any area (nor do government agencies), and so it is by no means clear that the search for allocative efficiency dictates the diversion of resources from other public and private uses to manpower programs. As long as there are real costs associated with improving the allocation of resources, it will continue to be efficient to have "imperfect" markets. The marginal costs of perfection exceed the benefits.

There does not seem to emerge a strong case for the proposition that economic inefficiency in the private sector justifies significant governmental involvement with manpower programs. That is, it seems difficult to defend the proposition that the market benefits from expanded manpower programs are likely to exceed the costs. Thus, while personal value judgments may lead one to hope that benefit-cost analyses of these pro-

---

3. For additional discussion of differences between human and physical capital, as they affect the investment process, see Lester C. Thurow, "Comments on Yoram Ben-Porath, 'The Production of Human Capital Over Time'" (National Bureau of Economic Research, Conference on Education and Income, Madison, Wisconsin, Nov. 15-16, 1968).

grams will show that the programs are efficent, as they sometimes do,[4] one should not be at all surprised to find the contrary.[5] Forces in the private market are constantly seeking profitable ways to train workers (on the job and off), to match jobs and workers, etc. The probability that governments can succeed where private markets have failed is of unknown magnitude. Yet, it is likely to be "low," except — and this is an important exception — for the cases of collective-consumption goods, from which the external (and difficult-to-capture) benefits of private provision are very large relative to the internal benefits to the provider.

Manpower training and relocation programs, however, do not appear to have a significant collective-good component. Although the provision of information about job openings and worker availability does seem to have a collective-good characteristic in that the information can be helpful to many persons simultaneously, it is interesting to note that private employment agencies are moving increasingly into the business of matching workers with jobs, and vast networks of interstate information systems are already functioning. Perhaps the private market is underinvesting in such systems, but — at least on allocative efficiency grounds — this is by no means clear.

When considering the benefits from manpower programs, it is useful to distinguish between those that accrue to workers and employers, and those that accrue to others. Indeed, we have already done so above, with the latter benefits being referred to as external. The external benefits include the technological or "real" benefits — essentially those affecting the productivity of other resources — and the "pecuniary" benefits.[6] The latter include, for example, any reductions in transfer payments resulting from improved employment conditions. In a sense these are not benefits at all; for they are benefits to one group of people that have a precise

---

4. Glen G. Cain and Ernst W. Stromsdorfer, "An Economic Evaluation of Government Retraining Programs in West Virginia," in *Retraining the Unemployed,* ed. Gerald Somers (Madison: University of Wisconsin Press, 1968), pp. 299-335; David A. Page, "Retraining Under the Manpower Development Act: A Cost-Benefit Analysis," *Public Policy* (1964): 257-267; and Michael E. Borus, "A Benefit-Cost Analysis of the Economic Effectiveness of Retraining the Unemployed," *Yale Economic Essays* 4 (1964): 371-430.
5. For example, see B. A. Weisbrod, "Preventing High School Dropouts," plus comments and rejoinder in *Measuring Benefits of Government Investments,* ed. R. Dorfman (Washington: The Brookings Institution, 1965), pp. 117-171.
6. For further discussion see B. A. Weisbrod, "Concepts of Costs and Benefits," in *Problems in Public Expenditure Analysis,* ed. S. B. Chase, Jr. (Washington: The Brookings Institution, 1968), pp. 257-262.

counterpart in losses to another group. The benefits to taxpayers are exactly equal to the losses of income from transfer payments to the former recipients. Thus, the essence of "pecuniary" benefits or losses is that they represent simply *transfers* between groups. As such they should be distinguished from *real* benefits, which expand incomes and opportunities for some people without contracting them for others. The increased labor productivity resulting from manpower training programs is a real benefit; the reduction in welfare aid to low income or unemployed persons is a pecuniary benefit (effect).

The significance of the distinction between real and pecuniary benefits lies with the point that it is not appropriate to add the two types of benefits — unless the losses associated with the pecuniary effects are also taken into account, as costs. But even this is not fully sound, unless one is indifferent to the members of the two groups between which the transfers are occurring.

Since "society" does appear to care about this distribution of income, and, more particularly, about raising the incomes of those at the bottom, it seems clear that benefits to all income groups are not equally important. Allocative efficiency is not the only justification for governmental interest in manpower programs.

V. MANPOWER PROGRAMS AND THE EQUITY OF INCOME DISTRIBUTION

Public concern about poverty and economic opportunity provides another rationale for governmental attention to manpower programs. These programs are generally addressed to the long-term unemployed, the residents of economically depressed areas, the unskilled, and so forth. The desire to alter the distribution of income in favor of these groups, by enhancing opportunities for sustained employment at relatively high rates of pay and in jobs providing opportunities for advancement, are goals of public policy to which manpower programs can contribute. Along with these goals is the goal — an aspect of the Protestant Ethic — of seeing the poor made better off *through working*.

The conjunction of these goals produces a preference for manpower programs over transfer programs even when the former is less efficient. Even if a transfer program (in cash or in goods) were 100 per cent efficient in the sense that every dollar spent benefited the poor and there were no administrative costs, there might be a preference — by either tax-payers or recipients or both — for utilizing manpower programs, even though a dollar spent on such programs might raise (the present value of) earnings by, for example, only ninety cents.[7] The point is that our social objectives include considerations not only of how *much* income everyone has, but also *how* he obtained it. And one dimension of the latter in-volves the distinction between earned income and transfers ("hand-outs").[8]

Granted that there is a social preference for assisting "needy" people to *earn* increased income rather than receiving transfer payments, the question is how strong is that preference? Is it equally strong with respect to all needy persons, and, if not, how does it vary? If there is a social prefer-ence for the 90 per cent "effective" manpower program (referred to above) over the 100 per cent effective transfer program, how far would the 90 per cent figure have to fall — how inefficient would the investment in manpower programs have to be — before the transfer route would be preferred? Upon the answers to such questions — involving trade-offs among goals — depends the overall "desirability"[9] of each of the com-peting programs.[10]

SUMMARY

Benefits from manpower programs, or any other government program, may be judged in terms of the program objectives. While these objectives are stated in a wide variety of ways, they involve generally the achieve-ment of (1) greater allocative *efficiency,* (2) enhanced economic stab-ibity (less inflation and less unemployment), and (3) improved distri-butional *equity.*

7. See B. A. Weisbrod, "Expenditures on Human Resources: Investment Income Redistribution or What," in *Federal Programs for the Development of Human Resources,* vol. 1 (Washington: Joint Economic Committee, U.S. Congress, 1968), pp. 80-83.
8. For further discussion see B. A. Weisbrod, "Collective Action and the Distri-bution of Income: A Conceptual Approach," in *Economic Analysis on Public Expenditure Decisions: the PPB System* (Washington: Joint Economic Com-mittee, U.S. Congress, forthcoming).
9. What I have termed elsewhere the "grand-efficiency" of a program. "Income Redistribution Effects and Benefit-Cost Analysis," in *Problems in Public Expen-diture Analysis, op. cit.,* pp. 177-209.
10. Social concern about the distribution of income is not limited to the *size* distribution; there are also the geographic, racial, and age distributions. And concern about the *method* of distribution is not limited to the manpower-pro-gram context; similar issues arise in connection with the distributional impact of a wide variety of public programs. A number of these issues are discussed in my "Collective Action and the Distribution of Income: A Conceptual Approach," *op. cit.*

The major point of this paper is that manpower programs may, but are not likely to, produce benefits in either of the first two forms that exceed costs. Any evaluation of a manpower program should begin, therefore, with the presumption that the program is not economically efficient in the sense that benefits in the form of increased worker productivity (as measured by earnings) exceed the real cost of the program. Perhaps the program would be found efficient if external benefits were taken into account, but measurement of these benefits is very difficult, and the active presence of private firms in providing training programs and worker placement suggests — but does not prove — that these externalities are not of major significance.

Even when manpower programs are not efficient, however, it does not follow that the programs are undesirable. For they have other virtues — particularly insofar as they have favorable income distributional consequences. They do not merely raise earnings, but they do so for a group deemed "deserving" — largely the poor and "hard-core" unemployed — and they do so in a manner that is socially preferred to transfer payment alternatives.

Thus, if government manpower programs are to be justified at all, it will often be necessary — and proper — that weight be given to their income-redistributional consequences, to their favorable effects on needy, meritorious groups of individuals. The critical question is: How much weight?

COSTS: THEORETICAL AND METHODOLOGICAL ISSUES

RICHARD W. JUDY
University of Toronto

THE CONCEPT OF COST IN COST-BENEFIT ANALYSIS

COST-benefit analysis is, or should be, the application of certain principles of micro-economics to actual problems of decision-making. Micro-economics is the science of rational choice and, as such, constitutes the theoretical basis of cost-benefit analysis. What is to be said here about the concept of cost in cost-benefit analysis is merely a restatement of some basic notions of micro-economic theory. That these principles should be familiar to every economist does not negate the value of their repetition; they have a way of being ignored in practice.

The Paradigm of Choice

Economists usually view problems of decision-making as those of constrained maximisation or minimisation. Restated, this means that the problem is to choose from feasible alternatives so as to:

    (1) Achieve the *most* of what is desired with *given quantities* of resources used, or

    (2) Achieve *given quantities* of what is desired with the *least* resources used.

Problems of choice consist of a number of aspects which can be presented as the following paradigm:

    (1) Specification of the objective function,

    (2) Determination of the constraints,

    (3) Elaboration of feasible alternatives,

    (4) Measurement of costs and benefits of feasible alternatives,

    (5) Evaluation and choice.

Each aspect deserves attention.

Specification of the Objective Function. Managers are frequently exhorted to "determine your objectives". In practice, this appears usually to mean statements of either or both of the following type:

(1) The statement of definite targets to be achieved (e.g., "reduce the rate of unemployment to 2.5% in this community").

(2) The enumeration of "goods" which are generally desirable (e.g., "the creation of a centre of scholarly excellence", "achievement of equality of educational opportunity").

Statements of the first type are more properly regarded as constraints and will be discussed below. Statements of the second type, at best, are enumerations of arguments (i.e., outputs whose maxima are sought and inputs whose minima are sought) of an objective function which is to be extremised; at worst are lists of platitudinous desiderata.

An explicit objective function requires not only a list of outputs and inputs but statements of the units in which they are to be measured. Finally, it requires a statement of the form and coefficients of the function which transforms the arguments into a scalar index of preference. This is a very tall order as well as a large mouthful.

Not surprisingly, the explicitly specified objective function is a rare species. Cost-benefit analysts often sidestep the problem of specifying the objective function by employing value measures (e.g., prices, rents) as indicators of benefits produced or received.

Determination of the Constraints. Choice of a preferred alternative must be made from a set of *feasible* alternatives, i.e., the preferred choice must be *possible*. Every decision-maker or analyst can think of highly desirable alternatives that, for one or several reasons, are simply not feasible. It would be nice, for example, to increase the research output of Ontario universities' laboratories while eliminating the investment of resources into those laboratories. Such an alternative is obviously not feasible because of constraining technological relationships between resource inputs and research outputs.

It is analytically useful to regard the demarcation between the set of feasible alternatives and all the non-feasible alternatives as being determined by *constraints*. Some of the more important kinds of constraints are as follows:

(1) *Technological contraints* are those defined by the state of technology. Only certain combinations of labour services, ma-

terials, and services of capital facilities will produce an automobile of a given quality. So also are certain combinations of instructor services, student effort and facilities services needed to "produce" a given learning outcome.

The "production function", beloved by economists, is an expression of the technological constraints that derive from a given state of technology.

(2) *Policy constraints* are imposed by superior decision-makers on subordinate ones. In Ontario, for example, the present policy is to fix the number of provincially assisted community colleges at twenty-one. Until that policy is changed, everyone must work within that constraint. Alternatives that envision more or fewer colleges are excluded from the feasible set.

(3) *Political constraints* are those imposed, or are thought to be imposed, by political conditions. For example, an alternative method of financing Ontario universities mainly from tuition fees would, at present, be thought to be politically excluded.

(4) *Organisational, constitutional and legal constraints* reflect the division of powers, interests, rights and responsibilities among institutional entities. For example, the set of feasible antipollution policies which might be adopted by the Federal Department of Energy, Mines and Resources is constrained by the powers, interests, rights and responsibilities of other federal agencies, provincial authorities, etc.

(5) *Resource constraints* express the limited availability of one or several resources required by certain alternatives. Limited budgets are a prime example of this sort of constraint.

(6) *Target constraints* express a firm commitment to achieve particular goals or targets. For example, a goal of graduating 250 medical students per year at the University of Toronto is a target constraint. This type of constraint is really an objective where the cost of under-fulfillment is implicitly infinite and the value of over-fulfillment is implicitly zero.

(7) *Imaginary constraints* arise most frequently out of people's unwillingness or inability to contemplate the unfamiliar. Habits, standard operating procedures, and rules of thumb often solidify into mental barriers. Imaginary constraints usually remain implicit, they just silently restrict the range of alternatives that are considered to be feasible.

The reduction of the set of feasible alternatives imposed by a particular constraint may be painless. The constraint may exclude alternatives that would never be chosen anyway, or the constraint may be redundant, i.e., exclude alternatives already excluded by other constraints. Painless constraints are sometimes called "non-binding" constraints and they warrant no further discussion.

If a preferred alternative is excluded from the feasible set, the constraint is indeed painful, i.e., it is a binding constraint. Cost-benefit analysts should especially be alert to the existence of binding constraints (explicit or implicit) because costs are associated with observing those constraints. This point will be taken up again below.

Elaboration of Feasible Alternatives. In a decision-making situation there are some variables whose values may be established by the decision-maker and others which are beyond his control. The first are called "decision variables" and the second we call "non-controllable variables".

An alternative is one specific set of values for the decision variables. Associated with each alternative are one or more possible outcomes. In a deterministic world of perfect certainty, there would only be one set of output variables associated with each alternative. In the real, stochastic world of imperfect certainty, several sets of output variables may *ex ante* be associated with each alternative.

A major task of the cost-benefit analyst and the decision-maker is to elaborate a menu of alternatives. It is important also to examine the results of each alternative under differing assumptions about the values to be assumed by non-controllable variables.

Measurement of Costs and Benefits of Feasible Alternatives. This is bread and butter activity for most cost-benefit analysts. Professor Weisbrod discusses benefits in his paper; costs are treated in more detail below. Professor Arrow discusses problems of discounting costs and benefits over time.

Evaluation and Choice. The rules of choice are simple in a world of perfect certainty, independent alternatives and unlimited resources. They become more complicated when uncertainty, complementarity and substitutability of alternatives and budgetary constraints enter the picture.

Cost as the Value of Forgone Opportunities

Every choice of an alternative excludes other opportunities that might have been chosen. The value of the best of these forgone opportunities is the true cost of the chosen alternative.

This basic notion of opportunity cost should underly all cost measurement performed by cost-benefit analysts. Unfortunately, one frequently encounters cost calculations which are based on accounting criteria of cost of inputs. Only under special circumstances do the opportunity cost and the accounting cost measures give identical results.

An Illustration. Let us illustrate these ideas with an example. Suppose that we were asked by he Government of Ontario to estimate the cost of a program of public support for *all costs* of post-secondary education in the province for 1969-70. What categories would probably be considered under (1) the accounting concept and (2) the opportunity cost concept?

(1) *The Accounting Concept*
   * All operating costs of universities and colleges required to accommodate the number of students expected if tuition fees were abolished.
   * Maintenance and living expenses of all students.
   * Amortisation on fixed facilities plus rental cost of all facilities leased by colleges and universities.

(2) *The Opportunity Cost Concept*
   * Stipends to students equal to the value of earnings which they would forgo by being in school.
   * All operating expenditures by colleges and universities.
   * The higher of estimated annual lease value or the annual interest on the sale value of all land, buildings and other fixed facilities of the colleges and universities.

The costs enumerated under (2) above represent the *minimum* opportunity costs of the program. A good cost analyst should next ask if there are likely to be governmental budget constraints. Suppose that he discovered that, for political reasons, a global budgetary constraint will exist for the fiscal year 1969-70. The analyst would then have to examine the forgone benefits of government programs which would have to be curtailed or eliminated because of the increased allocations to post-secondary education. If the sum of the most beneficial of those forgone opportunities exceeded the sum arrived at by the calculation of (2) above, it would represent the true opportunity cost of the proposed program.

CONCEPTUAL AND METHODOLOGICAL PROBLEMS OF COST ESTIMATION

The simple example of the preceding section provides a basis for discussing certain conceptual and methodological problems of cost measurement and estimation. These problems are grouped under the following headings:

(1) The use of prices as measures of forgone benefits,

(2) The use of incremental, average and total costs,

(3) The problem of external costs,

(4) The problem of joint products,

(5) Constraints and shadow prices,

(6) Uncertainty and irreversible decisions,

(7) The redistributive effects of public programs.

Prices as Measures of Forgone Benefits

If the analyst is taking social benefit as his maximand, he is likely to want to use market prices as indices of the social opportunity cost of using resources by the alternative being analysed. Some basic theorems of welfare economics provide a basis for believing that market prices do provide that information. On the other hand, violations of the assumptions on which these theorems are based are common and deserve some discussion.

Imperfect Competition. The basic theorems of welfare economics are developed as conditions of perfectly competitive equilibrium.

Unfortunately, our real economic systems are permeated by monopolistic and oligopolistic elements. These forces of imperfect competition cause prices of goods and resources to diverge from those that would exist in conditions of perfect competition.

The cost-benefit analyst should be alert to the existence of monopolistic pricing policies insofar as they may affect prices of inputs used by alternatives whose costs he is studying. But what should he do when he discovers their existence?

To take the earlier example, suppose that post-secondary school teachers in Ontario had organised themselves into a strong union that restricted entry into the teaching profession by demanding a doctoral degree before permission to teach could be granted. In this case, the present generation of teachers would be collecting a surplus, a rent, over what they would have received under conditions of free entry into this part of the labour market. What should our cost analyst do?

The answer in this case is that teacher salaries would represent the upper bound of the social opportunity cost of using their services. The true indicator of that cost would be the salaries at which those teachers could find employment elsewhere in the economy. The difference between the two represents the cost of accepting the teacher's monopolistic restriction of entry into their profession. It is a payment for continued observation of the constraint that the doctoral degree is a prerequisite for post-secondary teaching; such a payment for observing a binding constraint is called a rent.

Economic Transition. The theorems of welfare economics assume a state of competitive *equilibrium*. In fact, the economic system is always in a state of transition. At best, it is only *tending* toward an equilibrium. The prices that we observe are transitional prices rather than equilibrium prices. This fact should be borne in mind by the cost analyst.

It is especially important to recognise that present prices may not accurately reflect future scarcities. Since cost-benefit analysts always work on future projects, it is important to attempt to anticipate price changes in preparing cost estimates.

Induced Changes in Scarcity Relations. Cost analysts are often asked to prepare cost estimates of projects that involve massive shifts of resources from their present pattern of allocation. Such shifts may imply significant changes in scarcity relations. In such cases, it is clearly inappropriate blithely to use *ex ante* prices as indexes of the social opportunity costs of a major diversion of resources.

Suppose, in our earlier example, that covering all costs of post-secondary education (including forgone earnings) resulted in greatly expanded enrolments. This could affect wages by withdrawing members of the labour force from their former employments. In this case, the use of *ex ante* wage rates to measure the value of forgone earnings would be inappropriate.

This point is illustrated by Figure 1. Suppose supply and demand curves for labour were S^lS^l and D^lD^l respectively. The amount of labour supplied would be OA at wage OC. Suppose the more attractive stipends for post-secondary students shifted the labour supply curve to S^lS^l. The new equilibrium would supply OF labour units at wage OE. The cost of this shift is the area FHBA which differs from FGBA (the cost evaluated by *ex ante* wage OC) by the amount GHB. With linear demand and supply curves, the appropriate procedure would be to take the arithmetic mean of the withdrawn labour as valued at the *ex ante* wage and the *ex post* wage, i.e., Cost = FA (OC + OE) /2.

FIGURE 1

Adjustments to an Upward Shift in the Supply Curve

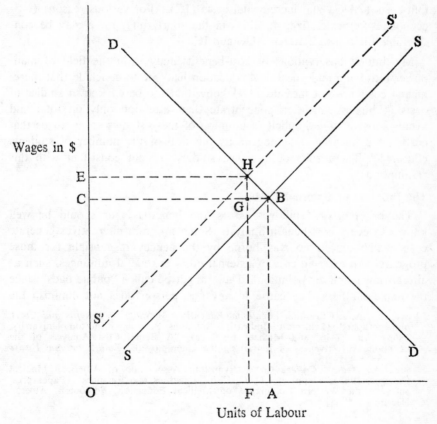

There are other problems lurking along the path of the cost-analyst who wishes to use prices as measures of forgone benefits. Limitations of time and scope do not permit their discussion here.

The Use of Incremental Costs

If we accept the opportunity cost concept, we become solely interested in costs that are *avoidable*. If there are fixed costs that must be incurred irrespective of which alternative is selected, those fixed costs have no place in our cost-benefit comparisons of alternatives. This is true even if our *budgeting* must provide for total including fixed costs.

Closely related to the idea of avoidable costs is that of *incremental* (or marginal) costs. If we are costing an expansion or contraction of an existing program, it is important not blithely to assume equality of average unit costs (AUC) and incremental costs (IC). For various reasons (e.g., economies of scale, fixed facilities in the short run), there may be considerable difference between AUC and IC.

My limited observations of cost-benefit analyses in the field of manpower retraining and vocational education lead me to conclude that incremental costs are not measured.[1] I know that the better known studies of costs in higher education concentrate their attention only on total and average costs.[2] The implicit assumption of these studies seems to be that costs are a linear and homogeneous function of the number of students educated. The results of our own studies are not consistent with this assumption.

The Problem of External Costs

The problem of "spillover" costs and benefits is or should be well known to every cost-benefit analyst. Some program alternatives generate costs which are in no way borne by the agency responsible for those programs. An extreme case of external costs is general nuisances, such as aircraft noise and air pollution. These might be called "public bads" since the unpleasantness they cause to any one person does not diminish the

---

1. See, *e.g.*, A. J. Corazzini, *Vocational Education: A Study of Benefits and Costs*, mimeographed (Princeton: Industrial Relations Section, Princeton University, 1966), pp. 27-46, and Michael E. Borus, "A Benefit-Cost Analysis of the Economic Effectiveness of Retraining the Unemployed," *Yale Economic Essays* 4 (1964): 405-415.
2. See *e.g.*, *Medical College Costs* (Evanston: Association of American Medical Colleges, 1965), 64 pp. and D. C. Fish, "Faculties and Finances" (Paper presented to the Western Conference on Medical Education, Edmonton, Alberta, December, 1965).

amount or unpleasantness that they can cause to the rest of mankind.[3] One can do little except admonish cost analysts to be alert to these externalities and to try to measure them when they are important.

The Problem of Joint Products

The name of the cost-benefit game is the attribution of costs and benefits to particular alternatives or programs. Program Planning and Budgeting (PPB) establishes programs in relation to certain objectives. Costs are then attributed to programs and cost-effectiveness analysis is invited.

So long as there exists a one-to-one correspondence between a process and an objective oriented program, no serious attribution problem arises. But when two or more objectives are furthered by the same process, we have the phenomenon of joint production.

Teaching and research are usually regarded as joint outputs of a university professor's activities. Public service and consulting are often added to the list of joint products. A professor working on a funded consulting project may be collaborating with a graduate student (teaching), expanding his own knowledge (research) and accomplishing the objectives of the project's sponsor (consulting) simultaneously. Attribution of the project cost to any one of the three ends being served is arbitrary. It is like trying to attribute the grass eaten by the sheep to the mutton or the wool.

Most attempts to allocate university costs to programs founder on the problem of joint products. Typically an inventory is taken of faculty activities. Each faculty member is asked to distribute his effort among programs, e.g., undergraduate instruction, graduate instruction, research, administration, etc. This produces, for each faculty member, a vector of proportions indicating the share of his efforts devoted to each program $A_i = (A_{i_1}, A_{i_2}, \ldots, A_{in})$, where A_{ij} is the per cent of the ith faculty member's effort devoted to the jth program. Programs costs are developed by distributing faculty salaries among costs thusly:

$$P_j = \Sigma_i A_{ij} S_i$$

where P_j is the academic salary cost of the jth program and S_i is the

---

3. A fine example of a public bad is the potential future damage caused by the increased concentration of carbon dioxide in the atmosphere resulting from the combustion of fossil fuels. Some scientists expect this to increase the heat retention properties of the atmosphere, melt the polar ice caps, raise the ocean sea level, and flood the coastal areas of the world — all this within a few decades from now.

annual salary of the ith faculty member. Other costs are allocated in rough proportion to academic salaries.[4]

This procedure simply ignores the problem of joint production which, in a good university, is a ubiquitous phenomenon. Difficulties of this kind can cause serious administrative confusion. An example of this is the dispute about which governmental agency, the federal National Research Council or the provincial Department of University Affairs, should pay for certain programs that have outputs of both research and instruction.

Fortunately, the problem is not completely intractable. Suppose that an analyst knows that two outputs, x and y, are jointly produced by a process but that he (the analyst) is interested only in increasing the output of x. Then, if he knows the value (market or otherwise determined) of y and the technology of the joint production process, he can assess the value of the by-product y associated with proposed increases in the output of x. The value of the by-product y can then be substracted from the cost of raising the level of the process to produce x. In doing this, it is very useful to work with a quantitative model of the process.[5]

Constraints and Shadow Prices

Earlier we discussed how the set of feasible alternatives is delimited by *constraints* of various kinds. To the extent that these constraints actually bind, they force the actual decision away from what otherwise would be preferable. We can measure the cost of a particular constraint by computing the sacrifice involved in observing it.

Let us return to our earlier example of the strong union of post-secondary teachers. Suppose that the constraint of the required doctoral degree effectively limited entry of otherwise well qualified potential teachers into the profession. To compute the cost of that constraint, we should estimate the savings that would ensue if it were to be relaxed and freedom of entry were established.

The analyst cannot take it upon himself actually to relax constraints that are not self-imposed — although he ought to strive to do that. He can, and should, compute the estimated cost of observing constraints that he believes are relaxable by his superiors. Decision-makers should be alert to

4. See Footnote 3, *supra*.
5. One type of such tool is the CAMPUS model developed at the University of Toronto. See "Systems Analysis of Alternative Designs of a Faculty", a paper presented at the O.E.C.D. Conference in Paris, 1968, by R. W. Judy, J. B. Levine, and R. Wilson, M.D.

constraints over which they have control and should ask for estimates of the costs of observing them. When the question is not one of completely eliminating a constraint but of relaxing it marginally, the decision-maker should expect to be provided with "shadow prices", i.e., indicators of minor relaxation or tightening of constraints.

Uncertainty and Irreversible Decisions

For few public programs is it possible to contemplate certain costs and benefits with probability one. It is a stochastic world where ignorance and uncertainty abound. This being true, the cost-benefit analyst must not pretend that he can estimate costs and benefits with perfect certainty. Neither should his boss expect it of him.

At the very least, the analyst should examine the sensitivity of his cost and benefit calculations to non-predictable and non-controllable variables. It is even better if he can place probability estimates on those variables. If he can do this latter thing, he can also tell his boss something about the probabilities attached to various net outcomes, benefit-cost ratios, etc.

It is not a part of cost measurement, but I cannot resist saying something about criteria for decision-making under imperfect certainty. If his boss does not already have an appreciation of these things, the cost-benefit analyst should attempt to provide a suitably disguised tutorial on these criteria and decision theory. It is a world of imperfect certainty and some decisions warrant an expected-value maximising approach, others a minimax approach, etc. The idea of sequential decision-making instructs us not to decide today what we can, without costs, put off until tomorrow and it guides our search for information.

A particularly important problem arises when an alternative involves an irreversible decision and potentially (albeit, with apparently low probability) very high opportunity costs. An example here might be the Glen Canyon Reservoir project which destroyed a thing of rare natural beauty and denied it permanently to teeming urban populations. Another example might be the question of permitting the use of certain insecticides or radioactive elements whose long-run, cumulative effects on the ecological cycle or genetic structure are poorly understood.

Fortunately not every analyst has to cope with the uncertainty problem in its extreme forms. Nevertheless, it arises to some degree in almost every project and should not be ignored.

The Redistributive Effects of Public Programs

An implicit assumption of using market prices as measures of opportunity costs is that any income redistribution effects of the alternative being analysed are of no interest and involve no benefits or costs. The assumption of neutral redistributive effects is not something to be taken for granted. Many public programs have redistributive effects as explicit objectives and to ignore the redistributive side-effects of other programs is contradictory.

It is still exceptional to encounter an explicit consideration of the income redistribution effects of alternative public policies. This is even true when some kind of redistribution is included among the ostensible objectives of the program. An example of this is the Ontario Student Awards Program (O.S.A.P.) which sets "equality of educational opportunity" as a principal aim. Despite the fact that nearly $40 million will be spent on O.S.A.P. in 1969-70, there are no data on recipients of these funds classified by socio-economic background. Even less, by the way, is known about the cost-effectiveness of O.S.A.P. in removing financial barriers to higher education in Ontario.

We have recently undertaken a study of the incidence of the costs and benefits, by income class of students' family income, of public aid to higher education in Canada. Preliminary results indicate (see Table 1)

TABLE 1

The Incidence of Costs and Benefits of Higher Education
in Canada, 1961-62 to 1964-65

| | Income Group of Student's Family | | | | |
	0-3,000	3,001-5,000	5,001-7,000	7,001-10,000	Over 10,000
1961-62					
Per cent of Costs	10.4	20.5	24.9	20.0	24.3
Per cent of Benefits	13.5	24.0	22.2	18.7	21.5
1962-63					
Per cent of Costs	10.0	19.9	25.2	20.6	24.6
Per cent of Benefits	13.4	24.0	22.3	18.7	21.6
1963-64					
Per cent of Costs	9.7	19.9	25.1	20.5	24.7
Per cent of Benefits	13.4	23.9	22.3	18.7	21.7
1964-65					
Per cent of Costs	12.2	21.4	24.9	19.8	21.8
Per cent of Benefits	13.3	23.9	22.3	18.7	21.8

Source: Computations by the author in a study shortly to be published.

that the redistributive effects are mildly in favour of the poorer income families. This result is contrary to common assumption and results from the fact that the taxation structure is somewhat more progressive in Canada than is the distribution of college and university students by income class of family. These results are rough and preliminary but they indicate that much can be done in this area to assess the incidence of costs and benefits by income class.

CONCLUSION

This paper has raised a number of conceptual and methodological questions surrounding the definition and measurement of costs in cost-benefit analysis. All of these problems have been raised before, especially in the corpus of micro-economic theory where the conceptual foundations of cost-benefit analysis are to be found.

The purpose of these remarks has been to emphasize certain problems of cost measurement that are often ignored in actual practice. Neat solutions to some of these problems do not exist. Cost-benefit analysis appears to be a fairly crude tool until it is compared with the available alternatives.

DISCUSSION: BENEFITS AND COSTS: THEORETICAL AND METHODOLOGICAL ISSUES

JOHN S. MacDONALD
University of the West Indies

C OST-benefit analysis for public policy and the resolution of social problems has made great advances in this last decade. Yet the method is
under mounting criticism, from inside as well as from outside this spe-
cialty. Criticisms from outside come from two different directions: human-
ists and humanitarians, on the one hand, and pragmatists and generalists,
on the other. The present commentary views these outside criticisms
from the inside. In other words, we shall try to reinvigorate some of the
early aims of cost-benefit analysis as an answer to criticisms which would
lead to the abandonment of the method.

Some five years ago, when this method was just gaining widespread
support, many of its leading protagonists saw it as a way of introducing a
humanistic or humanitarian approach to applications of theories of choice
for the commonweal. They have not, however, taken an active part in
developing social cost-benefit analysis and, instead, have become dissat-
isfied as this method has become increasingly the work of econometricians. Since econometrics concentrates on data which are already
measured in monetary terms, the complaint that cost-benefit analysis has
not incorporated a wider range of measurable indexes is not justified.
Nor can one complain that more so-called intangibles have not been taken
into account. These are not the proper business of econometricians such
as Professors Weisbrod and Judy. Why have not sociologists or political
scientists contributed more to the expansion and elaboration of comprehensive project appraisal?

The reaction of those engaged in designing or running unemployment
and manpower projects is not simply the usual impatience of politicians or
administrators with academic niceties or with long-term research. Cost-
benefit analysis means exposing the inner workings of particular branches
of an agency. The dominant econometric approach means going through
the books in detail. Moreover these details are related immediately to
external criteria. In public administration studies, the efficiency of an
agency's inner workings had generally been appraised in its own terms and
then its overall performance judged in macro-terms. Micro-analysis is
much more disturbing, even when it is wrong.

Indeed cost-benefit analysis for public policy is essentially disturbing for everybody when it is anchored to an abstract collective welfare of which no particular interest group is enamoured. The current fashion of asking "Social sciences for whom?" is especially pertinent to social cost-benefit analysis. Mr. Weisbrod's paper proposes benefits for Everyman; Mr. Judy's paper suggests benefits for The Boss. The real answer lies in between. For there is no simple consensus about the commonweal in North America, and perhaps there never was one. In any case, it is feasible to break down a project's costs and benefits according to the interest groups or sectors involved.[1] Most important, one can readily contrast Consumer and Producers/Operators. In Judy's terms, The Boss may come from any sector, but it is difficult to imagine him representing the interests of all sectors.

Typically The Boss represents Producers/Operators. This means that, once again, economics would dodge the issue of consumption. Perhaps economics should stick to choices among resources, regardless of ends. But welfare economics, one of the main inspirations for social cost-benefit analysis, has extended economics to the point of no return from the question "Production/operation for what (and for whom)?". It is so much easier to remain inside the theory of the firm, and assume away teleological variables, by believing that a public agency (Producer/Operator) can really function as a homeostatic entity unto itself. If and when the Producer/Operator sectors are in agreement among themselves about preference scales, there remains the fact that Producer/Operators are part-time Consumers, and vice versa.

The closest approximation to homeostasis and lack of external purpose is found in the arms race and the space race. The great success of war machines and aerospace systems in generating economic growth confirms the paradox that it is easier to satisfy the consumer by running an economy as if consumers were of minor importance. The people on the receiving end of a war machine are defined away as non-people, so they are not consumers, and the space race delivers products which, so far, have not been consumed on other heavenly bodies. The trouble with these extreme cases of consumer-free choice-making systems is that they

---

1. N. Lichfield, *Report and Advisory Outline Plan for the Limerick Region*, vol. 2 (Dublin: Stationery Office, 1967).
——, "Road Proposal for a Shopping Centre," *Journal of Transport Economics and Policy* 2 (December, 1968).

do not always succeed in conquering non-people or space. Also, if they succeed for long, interest groups climb aboard and, in effect, become consumers, for example, the military-industrial complex identified by the late President Eisenhower. In any event, there are always consumer sectors putting pressure on existing Producers/Operators in many other activities. So heavy defense or space expenditures cannot be relied upon to solve our theoretical problems by solving our practical problems.

The economics of consumption can be incorporated into social cost-benefit analysis by using a sectoral model. This involves calculating the number of people likely to lose or gain in each affected category of Producers, Operators or Consumers.[2] This immediately brings to mind the voting strength and political power of these sectors insofar as they are active interest groups, not mere categories. Professor Lichfield, outstanding exponent of the sectoral model, avoids the next big step of trying to incorporate the political process into the cost-benefit model, whereby he would bring his sectors to life by identifying their political weight. Instead, he lines up the various sectors and leaves politics for them (or The Boss) to decide. But some of his sectors may be politically inactive categories, which will be irrelevant to public policy, unless cultural values inspire other interest groups to take their part in case of loss. In case of ideological intervention by one interest group in favor of another sector, the former not the latter should be accounted for in tabulating costs and benefits sector-by-sector, to avoid double-counting.

It is not surprising that there has been no meeting of minds between micro-economists and political scientists about the relationship between the market place and the political arena. True, they should have much in common because economics is supposed to be the study of choice among scarce resources, while political science, they say, is the study of the art of the possible. Yet the Economic Man placed inside typical models of theories of choice is an abstraction, though a logically acceptable one for model-building. The welfare Economic Man whom we can see behind the symbolic logic of applied and micro-economics is a more exotic animal, for he does not even seek altruistic self-interest; hence the absurdity of a political cost-benefit analysis in the service of public policy.

---

2. In his Limerick Project evaluation, Lichfield deals with seven main sectors, but, in one sub-project, uses as many as 16 sectors. In his Swanley Project, he deals with 9 main sectors which he breaks down into 37 sectors. See his "Cost-Benefit Analysis in Urban Development—Swanley," *Proceedings of Regional Science Association Congress,* Cracow, 1965.

Micro-economists have commonly assumed that equilibrium-seeking tendencies of the political process compensate for the disequilibrium of the market. This is a case of "distant pastures grow greener". Neither field is in equilibrium usually.

Apart from single-minded totalitarian regimes, there has been a marked departure from the ideals and practices of the rotating two-party state. Also, the unilinear array from-right-to-left-through-center in the multi-party state has fallen in disorder. Perhaps neither system really worked before the last World War. But certainly today it is clear that interest groups are to the fore, and that their interplay is much more complex than the neatly packaged platforms or ideologies of party politics. Moreover, interest groups regularly go outside parliamentary and bureaucratic channels to get what they want, as "Black Power", "Blue Power", "Flower Power", etc., bear witness. The one-party states and one-point-one party states of the Third World have the same disorderly interplay of interest groups within the ruling party, between revolutions and coups-d'état. So the political process presents as many problems of monopoly, monopsony, oligopoly and other explosive rigidities as the market.

The identification of costs and benefits to particular sectors is no mere refinement of detail. It is necessary because there may be no equilibrium among interest groups. This immediately calls into question the use of macro-indicators of collective welfare, such as national income per head, allocative efficiency, inflation and a single discount rate. Often the question can be answered in the affirmative, with the addition of conditional clauses, such as "Slow inflation is a good measure of the commonweal, if education and other avenues of social mobility are expanded." However, in the long-run or between different contexts, the indexes of collective welfare may not remain valid.

In having to go beyond macro-indicators and analyze sectoral interests, social cost-benefit analysis is obliged to return to the comparison of alternative projects. Taking econometric macro-indicators for granted means that alternative projects do not have to be appraised because macro-indicators are supposed to reflect the balance between a proposed project and all alternatives. This line of reasoning has lead to the neglect of primary indirect and secondary costs and benefits, which do or will affect the commonweal. Consequently, cost-benefit analysis of employment projects does not take into account the monetized costs of regular crime, nor the new political forms of violence, destruction and disruption. Without going outside an econometric model, it would not be difficult to include the costs of robberies, drugs, riots, burning and looting. Logically, one might say that robbery and looting are simply re-distribution of income, and that drug-addiction is just another form of consumption, which objectively do not affect total collective welfare. But still there remain the escalating costs of encounters between demonstrators and police, national guard and army, plus the burning of ghettos. In any case, there is more than money directly involved, because the political process is based on force and the emergence of new sources of power changes the political structure itself.

The concept of interest groups, i.e., politicized sectors, is a junction point not only for welfare micro-economics and political science, but also for welfare micro-economics and sociology. Unfortunately the attitude of welfare economists to sociology often amounts to blind infatuation, once the apron strings of professional economics are loosened. It is admirable that some welfare economists go beyond their first task of identifying a single-valued, objective welfare function. But it is a mistake to replace it with the multi-dimensional value scales[3] which Professors Gross and Rothenberg[4] propose that social cost-benefit analysis transplant from sociology. For sociologists themselves have serious doubts about these schemes.[5] These multiple, incommensurable preference functions are not unsuitable because they are incommensurable, but because they are essentially static and harmonious. However, social cost-benefit analysis is supposed to inform public policy about changes which are unintentionally causing disharmony or about purposeful changes which could avoid disharmony.

---

3. F. Kluckholn, *Variations in Value Orientations* (New York: Harper & Row, 1961).
   S. Lipset and A. Solari, eds., *Elites in Latin America* (New York: Oxford University Press, 1967), Introduction.
   T. Parsons and N. Smelser, *Economy and Society* (New York: Free Press, 1965).
4. B. Gross, "The State of the Nation," in *Social Indicators,* ed. R. Bauer (Cambridge: M.I.T. Press, 1966).
   J. Rothenberg, *The Measurement of Social Welfare* (New York: Prentice-Hall, 1961).
5. M. Black, ed., *The Social Theories of Talcott Parsons* (New York: Prentice-Hall, 1961).
   M. Cross, "Cultural Pluralism and Sociological Theory," *Social and Economic Studies* 17 (December, 1968).
   F. Strodtbeck, "Considerations of Meta-Method in Cross-Cultural Studies," *American Anthropologist* 66 (June, 1964).
   D. Wrong, "The Over-Socialized Conception of Man," *American Sociological Review* 26 (April, 1961).

Moreover, the cultural value systems which are suggested for social cost-benefit analysis are exclusively homeostatic. The basic tenet is "Human behaviour is cultural, therefore culture explains behaviour." There should be no doubt that a people's behaviour is related to its cultural values and that, even in the most monetized cultures, values are multi-dimensional. Yet culture is only one aspect of the field of forces in which human behaviour takes place. The question remains: "When is culture a considerable factor, and then to what extent?" In terms of cost-benefit analysis for public policy, behaviour is a product of the interaction among cultural values, political power, and choices among alternative allocations of resources. Political power can be expressed on a unilinear scale or a series of interrelated planes, as can choices to allocate resources. The goals inspired by cultural values may be analyzed separately in all their varied dimensions. However, it is not at all necessary to hold that a theory of cultural system excludes a theory of choice, or vice versa. It is this *non sequitur* which keeps economics and sociology apart, except for occasional blind elopements which yield sterile progeny.

Cost-benefit analysis has borrowed heavily from welfare economics. It is time to ask whether the basic tenet that nobody lose or be left behind is necessary. This premise makes it impossible to do realistic project evaluation in many cases. So much economic development has taken place at the expense of some interest group, but has led to the eventual increase of collective welfare. It is odd that welfare economics excludes the notion of sacrifice, although some interest groups have put great value on sacrifice for ideological reasons. In this way, social cost-benefit analysis unnecessarily excludes most historic cases of increased welfare (perhaps all). Escape lies in two directions: net loss for a particular sector can be turned into gain, if a culture gives its ideological blessing to sacrifice; or net loss is irrelevant to public policy because the affected sector does not mobilize itself into an interest group.

There has been a marked tendency to put all but the most easily monetized variables outside the model of social cost-benefit analysis. Political and cultural factors are not subjected to scrutiny, but are treated as constraints, instrumental objectives or externalities. Yet even a strictly econometric model can cope with some more of these. There is a definite trend toward using the terms "intangibles" and "externalities" interchangeably. If intangibles are unambiguously defined as variables which have not yet been measured in monetary terms and, therefore, cannot be used inside the cost-benefit model immediately, then this usage may be a temporary expedient. It cannot be justified on other grounds because so many externalities are measurable. In any case, putting goals beyond analysis by putting them outside the model means that cost-benefit analysis would not go beyond sub-optimization and cost-effectiveness to optimization and a rate of return.

The concept of externalities is political in that it is tied to the legal framework within which a firm (agency) is held accountable for the costs and responsibilities it owes to other firms (agencies), while being permitted to recoup benefits, within a certain scope. The data for the econometrician's work are couched in terms of legitimized rights and duties, rewards and punishments, or benefits and costs, as expressed in account books, inventories, property registers, tax declarations, payrolls and such.

One of the dreams of cost-benefit analysis in the pioneer stage was to point the way toward reorganization. For it looked as if we might clarify questions about vertical versus horizontal integration, the allocation of joint costs and joint products, or optimization versus sub-optimization. These questions, which involve comparison of alternative structures of accountability and recoupability, no longer attract much attention. Shadow-pricing is another of the fundamentalist tenets of cost-benefit analysis which has fallen by the way as the method has moved its center from operations research, engineering economics and business administration toward welfare economics. The use of wages as the measuring rod of benefits generated by employment programs means the abandonment of shadow-pricing. Yet it is hard to believe that wages received by beneficiaries of an employment program constitute their value-added from the program. Shadow-pricing can scarcely be avoided when it is a way of adjusting for the very market disequilibrium which social cost-benefit analysis is supposed to correct.

SUMMARY CONCLUSIONS

The last five years have witnessed the intensification of social cost-benefit analyses which are entirely or predominantly econometric; a gain made at the expense of oversimplification. Particularly in the application of the method of anti-poverty programs in North America, there has been little analysis of incommensurables, structural rigidities, primary indirect costs and benefits, secondary costs and benefits, alternative programs, reorganization of the scope of accountability and recoupability of the Producer/Operator, and shadow-pricing.

Econometric balances are necessary, but not sufficient to social cost-benefit analysis. As it is, the method often tends to be politically naive. Since it is essentially political, it suffers more than other scientific endeavours which do not have to face public debate immediately. The remedy prescribed is to bring political power inside the model by identifying separate sectors' costs and benefits, and translating them into groups' interests.

Interest groups, being the junction point of choice among resources, power and cultural values, should be more pertinent than cultural values alone. Neither the cultural values identified by sociologists nor the monetized preference scales revealed by econometric analysis are homeostatic.

Leaving an econometric analysis in the hands of The Boss, so he can make up his mind in terms of other considerations, is passing off an intellectual responsibility for which The Boss is typically no more competent than the analyst.

The narrowness of so many recent analyses can be regarded as an initial phase of digging-in with the sharpest tools at hand. Nevertheless, a broader, more elaborate social cost-benefit analysis is needed, if it is not to be rejected by The Boss, the collectivity, or the sectors which it is supposed to serve.

ANDRE RAYNAULD
University of Montreal

COST-benefit analysis is a down-to-earth technique for decision-making and it is both excessive and dangerous to concentrate too much on the theory of it. The theoretical issues involved in the use of this technique are so wide and far-reaching that it is difficult to go into them without doing anything but cost-benefit analysis. It may even be dangerous and self-defeating to try to abide by all the theoretical requirements in concrete situations where the technique itself has no substitute since decisions are often taken and large chunks of money are often spent on no measured basis whatsoever.

Moreover I would suppose that the theoretical foundation of cost-benefit analysis is fairly well known by now. What is of more immediate interest to me is the ingenuity of researchers in translating the concrete issues into a meaningful economic framework and in devising new gimmicks to get at the significant facts. My usual concern in this field is to evaluate the short-cuts that are used to get nearer the true concepts and to examine the relative practical importance of what is included in, as opposed to what is being left out of, the analysis.

In describing my own scale of preference in this way I am giving myself a well-reasoned basis for congratulating Professor Weisbrod on his paper as well as his other publications since his very high reputation lies with those achievements I have just mentioned. In any case Professor Weisbrod must be commended for his attempt in this paper to discuss the issues in the context of manpower policies.

The paper is organised in three main parts. In part one (up to section IV, where programs are confronted with the objectives, manpower policies are presented to us as potentially inefficient in the sense of producing benefits below costs. In part two (section IV) a presumption is established against efficiency in manpower programs. Part three (section V) proposes an alternative rationale for manpower policies based on income redistribution.

Although I found the paper a solid piece of work I confess that I remain unconvinced by the main conclusions. In the first part where all the good questions are asked, the possibilities of efficient or inefficient programs are definitely left open because only the actual facts of the cases can provide the answers. It is proper and necessary to be reminded that it is not sufficient for manpower policies to reduce unemployment or structural imbalances but that they still have to do so in a cheap enough way. On the other hand this kind of argument cannot be held against manpower policies without first investigating the actual costs and benefits of given programs.

Whether or not manpower programs are efficient rests in the paper on the question posed in part two: If a public program were expected to be efficient, why is it not undertaken privately when the private sector is already active in the field? The two standard answers to such a question — externalities and market imperfections — are rejected by Professor

Weisbrod and he is led to believe that if the market does not provide the services it is probably because they cannot be profitable or efficient. The discussion in this section is again interesting but somehow it does not carry conviction.

I do not know really why private placement, training and relocation are not done on a larger scale but I certainly see a good number of unemployed around the place. I know that in Canada we have had for four years in a row, price increases of 4% a year along with 4% to 5% unemployment nationally. Assuming that this problem can be reduced to misallocation then I must presume that the markets do not function properly. Having said that I cannot deduce *a priori* that manpower programs are likely to be inefficient. I simply do not know until I measure virtue and vice whether "marginal costs of perfection exceed the benefits". Incidentally I do not see either why market imperfections cannot be taken as a presumption in favour of government action rather than against it.

Having expressed some reservations I hasten to say that I fully agree with Professor Weisbrod's redistribution rationale for manpower policies. This is in my view a perfectly valid, although probably a minimum case, for those policies.

Let me now raise the somewhat wider issues that papers by both Professor Weisbrod and Judy have led me to think about.

Especially in a redistribution framework, transfer payments and manpower programs may be viewed as alternative methods of achieving a given goal. But when you have not only multiple but also competing goals, so to speak, I wonder if the weighting system proposed by Professor Weisbrod is adequate. This is an example of the gimmicks I like. But suppose we don't want to feed people but put them to work. Then transfer payments are out of the picture in the sense that they are no longer a feasible solution. Now let us suppose that the costs of a feasible solution, moving the people to another area say, exceed the benefits. Then obviously this excess of costs over benefits is a transfer, and it is the price for achieving the goal that has been set. It is up to "society" to decide whether that price is tolerable or too high. The only other relevant question in my mind is this: is there another solution to unemployment which would be less costly to society than moving the people?

The question of relevance of goals and solutions raises important methodological issues with respect to the definition of a project.

Ideally we should have one objective and several alternatives to achieve it. Then the task is relatively easy. You choose the most efficient solution, provided that there is at least one which breaks even. Most of the time however you are given a single program to assess in regard to a large variety of goals. From my limited experience in this field I can say that a good rule of thumb is that the more numerous the stated goals are, the less efficient the program will prove to be. Professor Judy starts off his paper with this problem in mind and he keeps saying all along that feasible alternatives have to be found and examined. I am reminded of Rignar Frisch's opening remark on his report on Egypt. He said: give me a million investment projects and I will start to work as an economist, an economist that is, who is concerned with marginality.

The question of the nature of the project and its stated goals brings up the matter of the level of optimisation and second-best decision rules. The issues relating to this question have not been examined explicitly in the papers and it would perhaps be in order for the speakers to comment on this if they see fit. Divergences from a welfare maximum elsewhere in the economy are normally taken care of through corrections to market prices but in their review of cost-benefit analysis Prest and Turvey say that in practice anyone has to assume that the other is doing his job properly. Now consider the following case: a quarter of a million dollars are now being spent in a poor area of Canada to create jobs for 4% of the labour force in the region and to move 50% of it out of the region over the next ten years. In following a "let live" rule in assessing an investment project for this region, costs in the region are very low because unemployment is assumed throughout, and benefits derived by moving the people out of the region are very high because full employment is assumed throughout. If I follow common sense and Professor Judy, I would suppose that the true costs of developing a region are the foregone benefits out of the region. My own difficulties with restricted sub-optimisation are increased unduly because I have never resolved in my mind the following very simple issue: if one assumes full employment in the economy (or the rest of the economy) the contribution to employment of any project or even industry taken one at a time is zero by definition. Then if one cent is ever spent on creating a job, it is a losing proposition. This is why I find it difficult to mind my own business and leave others alone.

My next point is related to alternatives again. Given some unemployment in the economy that it is thought desirable to reduce, an obvious substitute to the introduction of manpower policies is increasing aggregate demand. It cannot be assumed any longer, if it ever was, that demand management is a free input. The trade-off technique has produced a price tag in terms of inflation and there are other costs as well in misallocation of resources and reduced long-term productivity growth. My question in this respect is how can one compare the costs in foregone consumption of a manpower program and a higher level of aggregate demand?

My last comment refers to transfer payments. It may be accepted readily that transfer or pecuniary benefits must not be added to real benefits in cost-benefit calculations. However transfer revenues do affect the private behaviour and calculations of the beneficiaries. They may have a lot to do with the alleged imperfections of the market. In certain outlying areas people may be better off being unemployed 6 to 9 months a year rather than working full time in a large city mainly because of Government allowances of all conceivable sorts. The benefits to give to the entertained lady will have to be pretty high because her forgone earnings, along with pleasure rather than work, are all the higher. In more serious words a public program to retrain or move the rich unemployed will have to be more generous because of the unemployment allowances paid than otherwise, and the program is therefore likely to appear much less efficient.

THE ROLE OF BENEFIT/COST ANALYSIS IN FORMULATING MANPOWER POLICY

WILLIAM R. DYMOND
Canada Department of Manpower and Immigration

THE role of benefit/cost analysis in policy formulation occurs in the context of governmental participation in a market economy. As a first approximation, it might be said that governments are charged with providing the public or publics with levels and kinds of services that private enterprises will not offer, curbing the abuses or discriminatory practices of private competition or managing the economy to meet goals of full employment, economic growth and price stability.

Governments have come to exert broad market power in response to the dictates and interests of the public. Historically, governments displaced private enterprise first with respect to defence and law and order, then in transportation, working conditions and labour relations, public health and safety, and finally in areas involving the quality of life, education, medical care, recreation and conservation. In all of these fields, the resource allocation decisions made by governments penetrate deeply into the pattern of choices open to men and women throughout our economy. This, in turn, places a responsibility on administrators and policy makers for weighing the costs and benefits of government programs and parts of programs and for recommending one direction rather than another.

Benefit/cost analysis has emerged as a most significant and useful tool to analyse alternative courses of action and alternative resource uses in making decisions about government programs. While it is a relatively new instrument, particularly in the field of human resource development, its origins are old and it draws on positive and normative elements from welfare, public finance and resource allocation economics.[1] The technique recognizes the many-sided effects of government activities and takes into account returns, not simply to the investor, but to all the participants in the productive process.

Moreover, benefit/cost analysis lends itself to predictive uses. That is, it will tell us the results of alternative allocations of resources within programs and to a lesser extent, as between programs.[2] This latter characteristic is particularly important when large public resources are involved and where programs once established are difficult to drastically change or eliminate. This characteristic is also important to policy makers in making a case for the use of resources for a new program or for a substantial expansion of an existing program. Tight budgetary situations, as those of you in government are aware, can often mean the allocation of scarce resources away from programs.

This brings me to the application of benefit/cost analysis in the field of human resources development. The increased emphasis on human resource development in the last decade or so has focused attention on private and public rates of return on investment in education and on the contribution of investments in the other areas of human resource development to productivity and economic growth. Partly, this thrust reflects a belated recognition of the importance which human skills played in the rebuilding of post-war Europe and in shaping the economic development of less-developed nations.[3] It is not surprising, for instance, that the Organisation for Economic Co-operation and Development has played a leading role in promoting "an active manpower policy" and in sponsoring a great deal of research and policy analysis in this field and in urging its member countries to develop an integrated set of manpower policies to complement monetary and fiscal policies.[4]

1 Stephen A. Marglin, *Public Investment Criteria: Benefit-Cost Analysis for Planned Economic Growth* (Cambridge: MIT Press, 1967), chap. 1; Otto Eckstein, *Water-Resource Development: The Economics of Project Evaluation* (Cambridge: Harvard University Press, 1961), chap. 2; and A. R. Prest and R. Turvey, "Cost-Benefit Analysis: A Survey," *Economic Journal* 75: 683.

2 W. R. D. Sewell, John Davis, A. D. Scott and D. W. Ross, *Guide to Benefit-Cost Analysis* (Ottawa: Queen's Printer, 1965), p. 3.

3 E. F. Denison and Jean-Pierre Poullier, eds., *Why Growth Rates Differ: Post-war Experience in Nine Western Countries* (Washington: Brookings Institution, 1967); and F. H. Harkison and C. A. Myers, *Manpower and Education: Country Studies in Economic Development* (New York: McGraw-Hill, 1965).

4 See O.E.C.D., *Economic Growth, 1960-1970; A Mid-decade Review of Prospects* (Paris, 1966).

It would be inaccurate for me to suggest that policy makers and administrators have welcomed benefit/cost analysis with open arms. To some extent, it is the treasuries of governments which have pushed in this direction. In illustration, the first benefit/cost model of the adult training program in Canada was jointly financed by the Treasury Board and my Department. Some program administrators have had fears that too narrow an economic interpretation of the comparative benefits and costs of programs, which have important social and human values, might undermine and distort both the objectives of programs and endanger their case for expanding them.

Many manpower and employment service activities in Europe and in North America were developed and administered by departments with strong social commitments and orientations. In fact, in Europe those agencies which are responsible for manpower programs are often a part of a ministry primarily concerned with the administration of social security legislation. Thus, the problems with which such departments of government traditionally deal lie outside the main stream of the market place or have to do with the redistribution of income. Such areas do not lend themselves easily to profit and loss calculations, optimization or marginal analysis. The rigour and quantitative bias of benefit/cost studies have led to uneasiness among program administrators (I have been aware of this in the Manpower and Social Affairs Committee of the Organisation for Economic Co-operation and Development), and such concerns are often expressed in terms of the pitfalls and shortcomings which apply to this type of analysis.

I shall leave to other parts of this Conference the technical complications, the difficulties of measuring qualitative and non-economic attributes, the choice of interest rates, the "spill-overs",, the problems of suboptimizing and the selection of satisfactory trade-off points. It is important for all of us to be aware of the limitation of this kind of quantitative analysis. These analyses assume that non-economic variables are exogenous to the analysis and proceed on the assumption that such variables remain unchanged while the economic parameters and variables within the model change. This, of course, imposes constraints upon the use of these models in a decision-making context. There are probably feedback relationships between these social and economic variables in any situation or program. It is important in the process of making assumptions that we do not assume away an integral part of the problem, that we arrive at facile conclusions, or that we parade over-simplified quantitative measures and ratios in contexts in which meaningful social and human values are equally or more important.

Such criticisms probably apply wherever economic analysis is carried out at or near the frontiers. Welfare economists have heard and echoed them for years.[5] To be fair when we look back at the development of benefit/cost studies, there have been very substantial advances in techniques and in the measurement of characteristics which once were thought to be outside the domain of economic analysis. Nevertheless, early studies skimmed the easiest items, and as we move into areas that lend themselves less easily to quantitative structuring and interpretation, the going will be more difficult. For example, although there are still considerable methodological problems, the techniques used for the analysis of education and adult training are fairly well defined.[6] On the other hand, the application of benefit/cost analysis to immigration policies has not yet made a start. The difficulty in this area is essentially on the side of measuring benefits. To determine benefits, we must push back to a theoretical analysis of the impact of immigration on the economy which, in turn, can be empirically tested. This we have not as yet done and until we have, we are not in a position to develop an effective model for the benefit/cost analysis of immigration policy.[7]

I think it is important, and I stress this point strongly, that I do not consider benefit/cost ratios alone as providing sufficient justification for choosing between programs or even for substantial alterations in existing programs. The technique is not one which will allow you to conclude that because there is a higher benefit/cost ratio in adult training as compared to a mobility program or an immigration program or an Employment Service activity, that one should put more resources into one program than into another or that one should entirely scrap programs with benefit/cost

---

5 See E. J. Mishan, *Welfare Economics: Five Introductory Essays* (New York: Random House, 1964).

6 See, for example, Einar Hardin and Michael F. Borus, "An Economic Evaluation of the Retraining Program in Michigan: Methodological Problems of Research," *Proceedings of the 1966 Social Statistics Section Meetings* (Washington: American Statistical Association, 1966), pp. 133-137.

7 There have been some writings in this area. See, for example, Solomon Barkin, "The Economic Costs and Benefits and Human Gains and Disadvantages of International Migration," *The Journal of Human Resources* 2: 495-516.

ratios less than unity. Except at the margins of resource use, programs are not substitutable for one another as they often serve different publics and in some instances, serve different functions in the economic process and in their social role.

Benefit/cost studies measure what *can* be measured, but this is *all* they do. They are certainly to be preferred over speculation or political or administrative intuition, but they are only part of a larger context. If the social benefits of a program stand very high, they can well offset low or negative ratios for the economic measures of the benefits of a program.

Such considerations are of paramount importance where governments allocate resources for the particular purpose of improving the quality of life, or raising the productive capacity of manpower. It is here that government programs fill gaps not reached by private enterprise or by the unaided actions of individuals.

It will not be news to you, particularly at this university where John R. Commons was in the forefront of the development of institutional economics, that markets operate very imperfectly in the field of human resources. Marshall pointed it out over seventy years ago when he listed the special "peculiarities" of the labour market and the many disadvantages which workers face in selling their services.[8] In the development of human resources, the net benefits may be high, but they are frequently so diffused that many single individuals cannot capture enough of them, or have a sufficiently long-term perspective, to justify the additional investment even when high and quick returns can be captured.

It is natural that private enterprise would develop the least-risk individuals and leave others to fend for themselves. Governments are then required to pick up the pieces. The need for and the development of our federal and state social security and employment service systems are witnesses to this process. In both the United States and Canada, private insurance schemes, for example, are notorious for turning away chronic care and other high-risk cases.[9] In the field of education, there are private contributory plans for parents who have university aspirations for their children, but there are no private schemes for school drop-outs who wish

8 A. Marshal, *Principles of Economics*, 8th ed. (New York, 1949), p. 626.
9 Royal Commission on Health Services, *Report* (Ottawa: Queen's Printer, 1964-1965) and C. Wilcox, *Toward Social Welfare* (Homewood, Ill.: Irwin, 1969), pp. 79-85.

to complete their education or for the rehabilitation of workers who suffer physical or cultural deprivation.

My point here is that since the responsibilities of government extend to ensuring that all citizens, however vulnerable, have reasonable access to jobs, income, education and health, benefit/cost analyses that focus solely on economic returns almost inevitably favour private rather than public activities. This is why in government programs, benefit/cost findings constitute only one test of the program's worth to be balanced against the broader humanitarian and social considerations. Despite these caveats, the fact is that most benefit/cost studies with respect to government programs in the human resource development field have turned up highly favourable results. Our own benefit/cost model of the adult training program, which is carefully developed and based on quite accurate data, has indicated a preliminary overall ratio for the program which shows that for every dollar of public funds invested, $2.50 is added to real gross domestic product.

Admittedly, some benefit/cost investigations have been pretty spurious, but on the whole, there seems to be ample evidence that the purely economic returns from programs which are directed to increasing the quality and productivity of manpower resources are indeed high. When one contemplates these results, they are not too surprising when one considers the malfunctioning of the capital market in the manpower field. If private initiative invests too much in physical resources and too little in human resources, the incremental rates of return on the latter will be disproportionately high and on the former disproportionately low.[10]

At any rate, partly because of these happy results (at least for administrators and policy makers) and partly because properly-qualified benefit/cost studies fit in well with the newer governmental program planning and budgeting techniques, much of the original apprehension over the too narrow and literal application of the technique to decision-making has abated. Thus with its limitations fully recognized, benefit/cost analysis can be an important technique for considering the allocation of funds among programs and among components of individual programs.

10 See E. F. Denison and Jean Pierre Poullier, *op. cit.*; and E. F. Denison, "Proportion of Income Differentials among Education Groups Due to Additional Education: The Evidence of the Wolfe-Smith Survey," in *The Residual Factor and Economic Growth,* ed. J. Vaizey (Paris: O.E.C.D., 1964).

Once the objectives of individual programs are clearly set forth and the benefits and costs carefully defined and measured, it is a fairly easy matter to determine whether an additional dollar will produce a greater benefit if used for one activity as compared to another. Since no one denies that a dollar should, other things being equal, go where it will bring the greatest return, it seems self-evident that a rational allocation of funds requires benefit/cost analysis. However, I hope I have made it clear that other things are never equal. Not all our values are economic, even if one adopts a purist approach. It should be recognized that funds will and should be channelled into programs that in the technical jargon are associated with "merit wants".[11] Even here, benefit/cost analysis still performs the very basically important function of pinpointing and identifying how much economic sacrifice the serving of such "merit wants" entails. Modifying the real costs in relation to the alternatives foregone, provides treasuries and policy makers with a relatively precise instrument on the economic side to weigh against the non-economic considerations. From this balance, it can then be determined whether to encourage or curb investment in one direction or another.

The proponents of benefit/cost analysis have claimed that one of its principal uses is to compare the allocation of resources as between programs.[12] While analyses of programs using comparable techniques and methodologies may be suggestive of alternative resource uses among programs, this approach must be treated with a great deal of caution. Quite apart from the impossibility of analysing all programs simultaneously in a time sense, real functional differences exist between programs.

Only rarely are the objectives and clientele served by one program truely substitutable for another. It is true that workers can increase their productivity and that of the economy either by moving geographically, industrially or by upgrading their occupational skills. Moreover, they can raise their occupational productivity either by formal education, night school, apprenticeship, on-the-job training or by full-time adult training courses given by public authorities. However, not all workers are free to choose between the programs, nor do they have access to the same range of alternatives.

11 Richard Musgrave, *The Theory of Public Finance: A Study in Public Economy* (New York: McGraw-Hill, 1959), pp. 13-14.
12 See the Survey article by Prest and Turvey, *op. cit.*

Each activity and each program tends to have its own set of candidates and beneficiaries.

Once launched, programs tend to have an organic life of their own, although time and circumstances render some of them obsolete. New programs can replace old ones, but usually the process requires that most of the clientele served by the original program be no worse off than before. Hence, where a program shows higher marginal benefit/cost ratios than a similar program at every level of service, there are limits on the choices government can make simply because the group served by one program does not coincide with the groups served by the other. This becomes an income distribution question on which benefit/cost analysis has little to say. As among programs therefore, benefit/cost analysis can give only a directional guide at the margin and even there, there must be a reasonable consistency in the assumptions and techniques used in comparing one program as against another.

Let me be more specific. Even between our own studies of two relatively complementary manpower programs — the Adult Occupational Training Program and the Manpower Mobility Program — there are different assumptions. The Training Program study, for instance, focuses on the future earnings of only the worker since the Program's objective is to deepen the individual's skills. The Mobility study, on the other hand, takes account of all the actual or imputed earnings of every family member who is moved to the new community. The Training study posits future earnings in keeping with a permanent escalation of skills, the Mobility study assumes no change of skills. Both sets of assumptions are arbitrary — designed to make the models more manageable. Workers often have to move after training in order to use their new skills; and geographic mobility is frequently accompanied by occupational change and the learning of new skills. But these contingencies would add considerable complications to the models.

Let me cite another instance. The Training model, like other training studies, makes little provision for the real economic question — what would have happened in its absence? Would some of the workers have raised their skills through other means? The mobility model on the other hand does assume that workers migrate voluntarily and lowers the benefits attributable to the program accordingly.

Most of these differences in assumptions deal with the workers' future paths of action. I suppose with sufficiently complex models, some of the differences could be reconciled. For instance, as follow-up information flows in over a long enough period we could attach probability estimates to the alternative paths. But much would remain that escapes quantification or which — because the programs serve different sets of clients — remains analytically non-comparable.

An additional factor is that some programs are functionally inter-related with each other. For example, in reaching the objective of employing surplus manpower in a depressed area, it is often necessary *both* to move and to train the redundant workers involved. In achieving an objective of re-employment for this particular group, an Adult Training Program and a Mobility Program are not substitutes for each other, but are rather components of a total process.

In practice, we have not found it possible to use benefit/cost ratios to compare programs except in the most general terms. Each program has its own set of internal and external benefits and costs and each has its own model built to fit its particular circumstances. The assumptions that underlie each model will likely differ to some extent and the measurement problems, the selection of the appropriate proxies, the state of the statistical system in relation to the program and so forth vary widely.

As a generalization, therefore, benefit/cost models are much more useful for altering or otherwise improving the effectiveness of a single program than they are for making comparisons between programs.

Benefit/cost analysis imposes a very valuable discipline on the thought and decision-making processes of administrators and policy makers. It requires a clear articulation of objectives and a precise methodology for determining exactly how these objectives are being met. It is surprising, for example, when one faces the administrators of a program with the task of making explicit their objectives for purposes of quantification that one discovers they have never really thought seriously about this question. Means and ends are often intermingled in their minds and decisions have often evolved about a program in patchwork quilt fashion without any real regard for the balance and proportioning of the parts in relation to an objective.

By identifying the amount and incidence of the benefits and costs for the economy, the administering agency, the clients of the Program and third parties, the research develops a benefit/cost model which covers the essential components of the Program and provides a structure for analytic interpretation which greatly facilitates program monitoring. In the process, cost inefficiencies are often uncovered. Clients who are marginal to the real purposes of the program are often identified, and a number of other problems and difficulties with the program are brought to light by the mere act of gathering the data and structuring the analysis for a benefit/cost model.

Policy makers are forced to think in a disciplined way about the relevancy and implications of individual sub-activities within their programs. To be effective, a benefit/cost model must provide an accurate mirror of a program in terms of its institutional structure, the clients it serves, and its financial and economic costs. When in use, it can be a valuable predictive technique by which planners can gauge the net economic impact of implementing one or other policy suggestions or of expanding or contracting certain sub-activities within a program.

The benefit/cost models of Manpower and Immigration programs which my Department has and is constructing yield overall benefit/cost ratios which provide some guidance to the allocation of resources among programs. They are, however, as I have indicated, more useful as monitors for optimizing the structure of the components of particular programs. They are efficient instruments for identifying problem areas within programs and thus for facilitating changes in the combination of factors employed or in the level and structure of services offered to the public.

Essentially, this kind of managerial approach means that benefit/cost models must provide continuing incremental data on each program. Among other things, they will combine the steady flow of information on the characteristics of workers with *a priori* or *a posteriori* probability estimates of each worker's likelihood of success in the program and the expected net benefits generated as a result of his participation in the program. In addition for each program, there is a continuing feedback of information through systematic follow-up questionnaires month-by-month. We have, for instance, initiated detailed follow-up surveys of (i) workers moved under the Manpower Mobility Program, (ii) Adult

Occupational Training Act trainees, (iii) newly-arrived immigrants selected under Canada's newly liberalized immigration program, and (iv) Canadian students at home or abroad helped through our programs to place students. Take the Manpower Mobility follow-up, for example. The initial methodology, design, interviewing and statistical tabulations were developed by consultants under the direct supervision of departmental benefit/cost experts. Questionnaires are now sent to all workers one year after their move, asking about their job, income and family adjustment, etc. since moving. Each client's reply is coded, programmed and related back to the information on his original application form. Weights to adjust for non-returned questionnaires have been worked out. Through regressions and related techniques, we can determine what personal characteristics, jobs, areas, etc., contribute significantly to the worker's likelihood of success. We also ask each worker what he thinks about the counselling and financial help he got under the Program. In this way, we get personal insights directly from the users which we might never get from our own staff, and can make changes in the administration or policy accordingly. I might illustrate this point by the kinds of outputs available from our benefit/cost model of the Occupational Training for Adults Program. The benefit/cost analyses from the model can be carried out not just for the program in general, but for the apprenticeship portion of the program, the general educational upgrading portion, the specific skills training portion, and the training within industry portion of the program. It is possible to make benefit/cost analyses of the different course groups within, for example, the skill training program. One could see, for example, that carpentry courses have a higher benefit/cost ratio than barbering courses and so one could adjust the purchase of courses accordingly. One can even theoretically get down to the level at which the benefits and costs of different barbering courses are compared so as to cut out the barbering classes which were the least efficient in an economic sense.

The same kind of analysis can be used to determine on which kinds of candidates for programs investments can most profitably be made. We can, for instance, determine whether workers in certain courses will in fact use this training, whether they increase their income over time as a result or are less likely to be unemployed. By comparing their past history with their activities and earnings after a training course or mobility grant, we can judge what kinds of workers use the programs to greatest advantage, and which constitute the riskiest investments. Does a history of broken employment, for instance, make the worker an unattractive candidate for training — particularly given his lack of options elsewhere? Do older workers do better than younger? Are married workers better motivated, judged by the results?

Even with less than three years' experience in administering our programs, we have already considerably altered the selection criteria for some to bring them into line with individual net benefit estimates. Recently, for instance, we tilted our Mobility Program in favour of older married workers with large families because they are the one's least likely to move on their own and most likely to settle successfully afterwards. We have cautioned our counsellors against unreservedly authorizing relocations to certain labour markets which our analysis revealed as high turnover areas. We have cut out training courses where workers seemed to have made little use of the skills afterwards.

In fact, the applications of what might be called micro benefit/cost analysis based on continuing program benefits and cost data, as these examples show, are almost infinite.

All of this kind of analysis and the decisions which flow from it must be undertaken with a high appreciation of the practical limitations of benefit/cost analysis as opposed to ultimate theoretical limitations. The fact is that no benefit/cost model yet devised measures precisely what it purports to measure because of the need to use proxies on (in many cases) both the benefits and costs sides of the model.

This dynamic approach allows benefit/cost analysis to be used both as a tool of economic analysis and as a technique which makes a major contribution to decision making for program administrators. It transforms the model from a static "one-shot" exercise using partial equilibrium parameters to a dynamic technique which yields a steady flow of net benefit estimates associated with different types of program candidates, destination areas, training courses and similar sub-activities. It enables administrators to gauge the economic effects of deliberate changes within the program, to eliminate high cost elements or alternatively to gauge the trade-offs associated with directing a program towards say the labour market's most disadvantaged groups.

The information these models produce should through time provide an indication of the varying levels of expenditure which are appropriate to use in manpower programs in different periods of the business cycle. I think it is clear that the economic contribution of various manpower programs will vary over the course of the business cycle. This too, is a frontier area of analysis and parenthetically, I should like to draw your attention to the OECD International Conference on Employment Fluctuations and Manpower Policy which was held in London in February of this year. In this context, I am sure that you will all find the report of this Conference, when it is published, of very substantial value.[13]

As was indicated at the London Conference, it seems fair to assume that, during periods of seasonal or cyclical slack and of higher unemployment, the benefits from manpower resource investments (being by definition, labour intensive) will rise relative to that of other programs and that they will fall relatively speaking during periods of economic buoyancy. Such findings can be confirmed (or negated) by individual benefit/cost findings over time and related to the larger macro-economic purposes associated with global, monetary and fiscal policies. In the pursuit of economic stabilization and growth, governments have an important need to identify what selective activities yield the highest incremental returns and by implication the greatest impetus to full employment and economic growth.

Those of us who are in the manpower business feel intuitively, although there is little empirical evidence, that manpower programs can make a substantial contribution to economic stabilization in a cyclical context but we have yet to completely convince the "big lever" policy makers in government. I am personally hopeful that benefit/cost analysis will make a considerable contribution to defining in an empirical way the extent and character of this contribution.

In saying that, however, it is important also to say that the benefit/cost studies will not *per se* throw much light on whether manpower programs materially reduce structural unemployment or lower the Phillips curve trade-off between inflation and unemployment.[14] They can only throw

---

13 O.E.C.D., *Papers,* International Conference on Employment Fluctuations and Manpower Policy (Paris and London, 1969).

14 A. W. Phillips, "Employment, Inflation and Growth," *Economica* 29: 1-16.

some light on when it is most useful in a cyclical sense, to raise and lower expenditures and in what directions the expenditures should flow.

Manpower programs undoubtedly contribute substantially to a nation's day-to-day resolution of the macro-economic inflation/unemployment and related trade-offs. But the measurement of that contribution requires insights other than those which benefit/cost studies provide. It is true, of course, that benefit/cost studies are designed to take account of spillovers and externalities throughout the economy, and attribute net benefits to all factors or users of a program. But their genesis is micro-economic, based on static partial-equilibrium assumptions.

It is not simply that there are too many interdependencies — that the sum of their parts undoubtedly exceeds the whole. It is rather that benefit/cost studies measure net returns over various time periods — they provide a criterion for choosing *between investment options* today and therefore are germane to the whole question of economic growth.[15] But they cast little light on the investment/savings versus consumption choice which is crucial to the short-run, unemployment-inflation problem. Other measuring instruments are necessary.

In conclusion, the value of benefit/cost analysis in the manpower field, as I see it, is primarily a rigorous analytical aid to managerial decision-making, with perhaps some clues as to the appropriate distribution of resources as between programs. It has substantial limitations particularly with respect to the collective or social responsibilities of government as a basis for the substantial revision of human resource development programs. In total, however, in my Department of the Government, we have definitely found benefit/cost analysis to be the most singularly useful analytical device yet devised for guiding our resources and for gauging the impact of our programs on the populations whom we have the responsibility to serve.

15 Stephen A. Marglin, *op. cit.*

THE SOCIAL DISCOUNT RATE*

KENNETH J. ARROW
Harvard University

1. THE BASIC ISSUES

IN the social evaluation of a competitive economy, it is customary and proper to start by using market prices as an estimate of social costs. Why then are many of us not content to use the market rate of return on capital as the measure of its opportunity cost? Several related difficulties have long been pointed out or can be abstracted from economic theory.

(1) There is not one but a whole spectrum of market rates of return. Which is the appropriate rate to use? Indeed, the spectrum is even greater than apparent, for the prevalence of credit rationing means that there are numerous shadow rates unobserved on the market. (2) Since there are very few futures or other forward markets, the welfare-theoretical argument for the allocative role of market prices, and in particular for the interest rate, is gravely undermined. Only if price anticipations were reasonably accurate would the classical case remain valid. (3) The future is risky, and existing risk-bearing markets are not, in principle, sufficiently complex and differentiated for optimal allocation. This raises the question how uncertainty is to be introduced into the evaluation of future income streams from government investment, possibly by adjustments in the discount factor. (4) I take it that government investment is primarily investment in public or collective goods, i.e., in goods which because of inappropriability or increasing returns cannot suitably be left to the market. Hence, the pricing of these goods and, by implication, the returns to public investment, cannot be fully recaptured. The problem of financing

---

* The research on which this paper is based was done at Stanford University jointly with Professor Mordecai Kurz under a grant from Resources for the Future. A full statement will appear in a joint book, *Public Investment, the Rate of Return, and Optimal Fiscal Policy*.

those investments (taxes or borrowing) then arises and its solution may in turn have repercussions on the appropriate rate of discount. (5) There is a widespread feeling that the government or the general public for which it is trustee has a special responsibility for the future. above and beyond that expressed by actors in the current market. In formal economic-theoretical terms, a full optimization over time would require obviously impossible trading between unborn and living generations. The government is then thought of as acting implicitly on behalf of the unrepresented.

The first three factors are undoubtedly very closely interrelated. Since risk-bearing is complementary to investment, the paucity of risk-bearing markets inhibits the making of forward contracts. The multiplicity of interest rates and the wide extent of credit rationing are clearly also substitutes for non-existent separate markets for insuring credit risks. There is strictly speaking no single risk-free rate of interest, so long as there is uncertainty about price movements and about the future of the rate of interest itself (variations in the rate of interest give rise to capital gains and losses). The second source of uncertainty is absent from time deposits and very nearly so from short-term bills, but unfortunately it is the long term rates that are most natural for discounting projects of long duration. Even if there were some interest rate that could be regarded as essentially risk free, it would not necessarily follow that it measures the time preference of individuals. Clearly it would be inappropriate for an individual who neither holds nor issues any of the riskless security. Further, for an individual planning over an extended period of time, the knowledge that in the future he cannot borrow at the riskless rate will affect his current consumption and portfolio decisions in complicated and not easily understood ways. There is a presumption that the riskless rate would understate the true marginal time preference.

There seem then to be three basic problems in identifying the social discount rate with market rates: (1) the divergence between private values and market behavior because of capital market imperfections; (2) the divergence between social values and private costs in the products of government investment activity; (3) the divergence between social and private values with regard to perspectives for the future. At a somewhat lesser level of generality, there is a fourth problem which has been mentioned prominently: (4) the imperfections of the capital market due to, specifically, the corporate income tax.

2. ECONOMIC POLICY IN A MIXED ECONOMY

In a perfectly and ideally centralized economy, the divergences just listed would be irrelevent; the central planning board could produce an optimum investment policy and enforce it. In the course of computing this policy, it might be useful to determine some Lagrange multipliers which can be interpreted as discount rates.

In a world with both a government and a private sector involved in economic decision-making, the problem is in principle more complicated. After all, the decisions on public investment should be made in light of those on consumption and private investment, and vice versa, both because all these activities compete for the same resources and because there are complementarity relations between public and private investment and between investment of either type today and consumption tomorrow. The government cannot directly control private investment or consumption, but it can influence them through its *instruments*, such as taxes and creation or retirement of debt. Hence, the government decision on public investment should be made jointly with a choice of instruments. Since a decision on the volume of public investment is implicitly a decision on its marginal productivity, i.e., on its rate of discount, this position is equivalent to the more usual formulation that the social rate of discount depends on the mode of financing.[1]

The clearest way of posing the issues is to regard them as the dynamic analogue of Tinbergen's theory of economic policy.[2] The government is assumed to have certain ends and to be endowed with a given set of instruments for their accomplishment. There can be calculated what may be termed the *publicly optimal policy,* the policy with regard to all variables (in this case, public investment, private investment, and consumption) which would be adopted by a perfectly altruistic government

---

1. This is the position taken by O. Eckstein in *Water Resource Development* (Cambridge: Harvard University Press, 1958), pp. 81-104; Baumol has expressed his disagreement (see W. J. Baumol, "On the Social Rate of Discount," *American Economic Review* 58: 788-802, at p. 792), but on analysis it is clear that, despite his disclaimer, the main thrust of his paper is concerned with the allocation of a fixed volume of investible resources between public and private use. The allocation between investment and consumption is ignored initially; when it is subsequently introduced (pp. 797-798) he simply notes that there are two different margins, and, "there remains an inescapable indeterminacy." This seems to be a misleading way of stating that we have a second-best problem (see below).

2. J. Tinbergen, *On the Theory of Economic Policy* (Amsterdam: North-Holland, 1952).

with unlimited powers. Then the first question that might be asked is whether or not the publicly optimal policy can be achieved by a suitable choice of values of the instruments by the government. Formally and more generally, we will say that a given allocation policy is *controllable* by a given set of instruments if there exist values of the instruments, varying over time in general, which cause the private and government sectors together to realize that policy.

The controllability of the publicly optimal policy will of course depend on the number and power of the instruments available. When the specified instruments are insufficient to control the publicly optimal policy then it is necessary to seek a "second-best" policy, the best that can be achieved with the given set of instruments.[3]

3.   INVESTMENT POLICY AS OPTIMIZATION OVER TIME

Some of the special problems in understanding the question of the social rate of discount are common to all problems of investment policy. They inhere in the stock-flow relations between capital, which determines output, and investment, which is that part of output which goes to the increase of capital. Capital is a stock, measured in quantity units; investment, like consumption and output, is a flow, measured in quantity per unit time. If there were only one commodity and one kind of capital, we would have, in the absence of depreciation, the basic relations of capital accumulation.

$$(1) \qquad \dot{K} = I \; ,$$

where K is the stock of capital, I is the rate of investment, and the dot denotes the rate of change of K over time. If Y is output and C is consumption, we then supplement (1) with the identity,

$$(2) \qquad Y = C + I \; ,$$

and with some production relation linking Y to K. In a perfectly central-ized economy, the instruments of the government at any moment of time

---

3. The theory of the second-best, developed for static problems by Meade (see J. E. Meade, *The Theory of International Economic Policy* (Toronto: Oxford, 1951-55), vol. 2, *Trade and Welfare* (1955), chap. VI) is identical with Tin-bergen's theory of economic policy when the instruments are insufficient to control the publicly optimal policy.

are C and I, to be chosen subject to (2) to maximize some appropriately chosen utility functional which evaluates the entire consumption path.

This simple formulation has significant implications for analysis. Many previous analyses have simply evaluated the direct return from government investment. More recent writers[4] have recognized that the return to government investment (the so-called "throw-off") is available for future consumption, private investment, or government investment. However, even these writers have assumed an undue rigidity in future allocations. In particular, it is sometimes assumed that the proportion of the throw-off devoted to further government investment in the future will be fixed. But this reflects an inconsistency of viewpoint. The whole purpose of investment policy is to determine optimal decisions at a given moment; but then it should also be assumed that future investment is optimal.

A consistent simultaneous optimization of present and future investment decisions requires the use of mathematical techniques which, in their modern form, are known by the names of "dynamic programming" and "optimal control theory".[5]

4. THE PRODUCTION AND VALUATION ASSUMPTIONS

We assume now that there are two types of capital, private and government, and that output, Y, at any moment is a function of the quantities of these two types of capital, K_p and K_g, respectively, and of the labor force, L. Assume further that the labor force is growing at a constant rate, π. First, suppose that constant returns to all variables prevail and that technological progress is labor-augmenting at a constant rate, τ.

---

4. See O. Eckstein, *Water Resource Development, op cit.,* and S. Marglin, "The Opportunity Costs of Public Investment," *Quarterly Journal of Economics* 77: 275-289.

5. See R. Bellman, *Dynamic Programming* (Princeton: Princeton University Press, 1957), and L. S. Pontrayagin *et al., The Mathematical Theory of Optimal Processes* (New York and London: Interscience, 1962). The only previous application of these techniques to the theory of public investment is that of Uzawa (see H. Uzawa, "An Optimum Fiscal Policy in an Aggregate Model of Economic Growth," in *The Theory and Design of Economic Development,* ed. I. Adelman and E. Thorbecke (Baltimore: Johns Hopkins Press, 1966), pp. 113-139), although they have been widely used in the theory of economic planning. For a brief exposition with special reference to economic applications, see K. J. Arrow, "Applications of Control Theory to Economic Growth," in *Mathematics of the Decision Sciences* (Providence, Rhode Island: American Mathematical Society, 1968), part two, pp. 85-119.

(1) $Y = F(K_p, K_g, e^{\tau t} L)$,

where t is time. The function F is concave and homogeneous of degree one. If we define the natural rate of growth, $\gamma = \pi + \tau$, and let,

(2) $y = e^{-\gamma t} Y, k_p = e^{-\gamma t} K_p, k_g = e^{-\gamma t} K_g$,

then as is well known we can write,

(3) $y = f(k_p, k_g)$,

where $f(k_p, k_g)$ is strictly concave.

What may not be so well known is that certain cases of increasing returns can be written the same way. Basically, it is assumed that government capital is labor-augmenting, a case which certainly covers manpower programs very well. We follow here the discussion of Levhari and Sheshinski.[6] Assume that government capital and labor cooperate, with possible increasing returns, to produce an intermediate good, which might be termed "trained labor," which, in turn, cooperates with private capital under constant returns to produce output. The production function for trained labor is in particular taken to be of the form, $H(K_g, L^\delta)$, where H is concave and homogeneous of degree one. The case $\delta > 1$ displays increasing returns.

We may generalize this formulation by assuming in addition labor-augmenting technological progress at a rate τ'. The production assumptions now take the form,

(4) $Y = G[K_p, H(K_g, L_E^\delta)]$ for some $\delta > 0$, where G and H are both homogeneous of degree one and concave, and $L_E = L e^{\tau' t}$. (This form is the most general which admits the possibility of balanced growth.) If we now define $\gamma = \delta (\pi + \tau')$, $\tau = \gamma - \pi$, and use the definitions (2), we can again arrive at (3), together with the relation, $\gamma = \pi + \tau$.

The criterion function which evaluates alternative policies is here taken to be,

(5) $\int_0^\infty e^{-\rho t} P(t) U[\bar{c}(t)] dt$,

where ρ is a discount factor for utilities (not necessarily for commodities), P is population, $\bar{c}$ is per capita consumption, and U is the current flow of utility (or *felicity*). We do not attempt a detailed defense of this criterion function here but hope that it will be accepted as plausible and add a few remarks. (1) Equation (5) does ignore distributional considerations,

---

6. D. Levhari and E. Sheshinski, "A Theorem on Returns to Scale and Steady-State Growth," *Journal of Political Economy* 77: 60-65.

from which we are abstracting. (2) The additivity over time and the stationarity of the discounting process seems eminently reasonable in the analysis of long run consequences. (3) The infinite horizon is an idealization of the fundamental point that the consequences of investment are very long-lived; any short horizon requires some method of evaluating end-of-period capital stocks, and the only proper evaluation is their value in use in the subsequent future. (4) Utility attaches to per capita consumption, since that is what the representative individual receives, but if different generations have different numbers of individuals, society should maximize the sum of discounted total utilities for all generations; otherwise, the more numerous generations are discriminated against. (5) Some government capital contributes directly to consumer satisfaction, and it would be more general to let U depend on $\tilde{k}_g$, per capita government capital, as well as $\tilde{c}$; the more general assumption is made in Arrow and Kurz,[7] but only the simpler assumption is made here.

Assume in addition that $U(\tilde{c})$ is homogeneous of degree $1 - \sigma, \sigma > O$; the family of such functions is broad and flexible. If we define,

(6) $c = P(t)\, \tilde{c}\, e^{-\gamma t} = P(O)\, \tilde{c}\, e^{-\gamma t}$,

i.e., total consumption adjusted for the natural rate of growth, then some elementary manipulation shows that,

$$e^{-\rho t}\, P(t)\, U(\tilde{c}) = [P(O)]^{\sigma} e^{-\lambda t}\, U(c).$$

where,

(7) $\omega = \rho + \sigma\tau,\ \lambda = \omega - \gamma$.

The constant, $[P(O)]^{\sigma}$ can be ignored in maximization problems, so that the criterion function can be written,

(8) $\int_0^{\infty}\, e^{-\lambda t}\, U[c(t)]\, dt$.

We assume $\lambda > O$.

By definition, we have,

$$Y = C + I_p + I_g, \quad \dot{K}_p = I_p, \quad \dot{K}_g = I_g,$$

where I_p and I_g are the rates of investment in private and government capital, respectively, and the dot over a symbol denotes its derivative with respect to time. If we now introduce the growth-normalized investment rates,

(9) $i_p = e^{-\gamma t}\, I_p,\ i_g = e^{-\gamma t}\, I_g$,

then from (2) and (6) we can say,

---

7. K. J. Arrow and M. Kurz, *Public Investment, the Rate of Return, and Optimal Fiscal Policy* (Baltimore: Johns Hopkins, forthcoming).

(10) $y = c + i_p + i_g, \; \dot{k}_p = i_p - \gamma k_p, \; = i_g - \gamma k_g$.

It is probably easiest, after these reductions, to assume that we are dealing with a stationary population and technology, with future utilities discounted at λ and both kinds of capital depreciating at a rate γ. From the preceding discussion, and, in particular, formulas (8), (2), and (10), such a static model is completely isomorphic to the dynamic one we are primarily concerned with.

5. THE PUBLICLY OPTIMAL POLICY

It is useful as a starting point to consider the inter-temporal allocation policies which would be followed by a fully centralized economy which can choose consumption and both kinds of investment. We start from some initially given quantities of the two kinds of capital. The problem then is to choose the instruments, consumption, c, and the two kinds of investment, i_p and i_g, as functions of time so as to maximize the criterion function, (8) or (5). Notice that at any moment of time the future from there on has the same structure; it is therefore clear that the choice of instruments is a function only of k_p and k_g.

An optimal policy will, under the hypotheses made, tend to a stationary equilibrium, a pair of values for k_p and k_g (the growth-adjusted stocks of the two kinds of capital); call them k_p^∞ and k_g^∞, respectively. Under the hypotheses made, if the initial values of k_p and k_g are k_p^∞ and k_g^∞, respectively then the optimal policy calls for keeping these constant; then the growth-adjusted values of consumption and the two kinds of investment, c, i_p and i_g, respectively, are also constant. However, the following discussion is not necessarily confined to balanced growth paths; the initial conditions may be arbitrary.

If the two kinds of capital are freely transferable between the two sectors, then a publicly optimal policy would regard the two kinds of capital as one. Specifically, let,

$$k = k_p + k_g ;$$

then at any given moment of time, the total k should be reallocated between the two sectors so as to maximize output. (Under the assumption made, capital can be reallocated in the future as desired; hence, maximization of current output clearly dominates any other policy.) Maximization of output requires that,

(11) $f_g = f_p$,

i.e., the familiar doctrine that the rate of return on government capital should equal that on private capital.

However, it is important to note that even when this position holds, it is not a complete description of policy; by itself it does not in any way determine the volume of investment to be undertaken. We need a complete description of the optimal policy.

In this case, the process is fairly simple. Since we are choosing k_p, k_g, to maximize output for given k, the output is now determined from (3) by,

(12) $y = g(k) = \max_{k_p + k_g = k} f(k_p, k_g)$.

From (10), we note,

(13) $\dot{k} = i - \gamma k$, $y = c + i$,

where $i = i_p + i_g$ is total growth adjusted investment. The choice of instruments, c, i as functions of time, or, better, of k, so as to maximize the criterion function (5) subject to the constraints (12) and (13) for a specified initial value of $k = k_o$ was first analyzed in a classic paper of Ramsey.[8]

Associated with any proposed consumption stream, there is an implicit rate of interest, as will be shown immediately; then an optimal accumulation policy is one for which the marginal product of capital (the same for both kinds according to (11)) equals the consumption rate of interest.

For a given consumption stream, the consumption discount factor for time t is simply the marginal rate of substitution between future and present consumption; in view of (5) or (8) it is the ratio of their marginal felicities, modified by the discount on future felicities.

Consumption discount factor = (felicity discount factor) x
(marginal felicity of future consumption/marginal felicity of present consumption).

Since the (proportional) rate of change of a product is the sum of the rates of change of the factors and an interest rate is the negative of the rate change of a discount factor,

consumption rate of interest = (felicity rate of interest) —
(rate of change of marginal felicity of consumption).

---

8. F. P. Ramsey, "A Mathematical Theory of Savings," *Economic Journal* 38: 543-559.

Let us apply this statement to (8),
rate of change of marginal felicity of (growth-adjusted) consumption

$$= \frac{1}{U'(c)} \frac{dU'(c)}{dt} = \frac{U''(c)}{U'(c)} \dot{c} = \frac{U''(c) \, c}{U'(c)} \frac{\dot{c}}{c} = - \sigma \frac{\dot{c}}{c}.$$

Thus, the rate of interest appropriate to growth-adjusted consumption is,

$$\lambda + \sigma \, (\dot{c}/c).$$

Since growth-adjusted consumption increases at a rate which is lower than that of consumption itself by γ,

(14) consumption rate of interest $= r_c = \omega + \sigma \, (\dot{c}/c)$,
from (7).

Then by the usual arguments, optimality demands that,
(15) $f_p = f_g = g' = r_c$,
i.e, the rate of interest used in evaluating either kind of investment should be that implicit in the individuals' evaluations of their changing consumption stream.[9]

A very important and not always understood implication of these elementary remarks is that the rate of investment (in this case, either type of investment) is not determined merely by the rate of interest. What (15) tells us is that it is the stock of capital at any moment which is related to the rate of interest. Changes in the growth-adjusted capital stock, i.e., investment other than that needed to maintain the normal growth of the capital stock, require changes in the rate of interest.[10]

Indeed, in (15), the line of causation in the short run goes from the existing capital stock to the rate of interest rather than vice versa. What the latter in turn determines is not consumption (and therefore investment) but the rate of change of consumption. From (14) and (15),

(16) $\dot{c}/c = [g' \, (k) - \omega] / \sigma$.

9. The above analysis of the consumption rate of interest is essentially due to Eckstein (see O. Eckstein, "Investment Criteria for Economic Development and the Theory of Intertemporal Welfare Economics," *Quarterly Journal of Economics* 71: 56-85).

10. That the concept of a schedule relating investment to the rate of interest has no meaning has been argued very ably by T. Haavelmo in *A Study of the Theory of Investment* (Chicago: University of Chicago Press, 1960), chaps. 25, 28 and 29.

This equation, together with,

(17) $\qquad \dot{k} = g(k) - c - \gamma k$,

deducible from (13) and (12), constitute a pair of differential equations governing the evolution over time of the capital stock and the consumption level. The initial stock of capital is given, but that of consumption is not, since it is an instrument.

In fact, the initial value of consumption has to be determined by the condition that the two time paths must converge to their stationary values.

These in turn are found by setting $\dot{c}$ and $\dot{k}$ both equal to O in (16) and (17).

(18) $\qquad f_p^\infty = f_g^\infty = g'(k^\infty) = \omega$,

(19) $\qquad c^\infty = y^\infty - \gamma k^\infty$

i.e., in the long run the marginal productivities of the two kinds of capital have to equal the subjective time preference parameter, investment is that needed to increase the stocks of capital at the natural rate of growth, and consumption is whatever is left out of output.

From (16) it follows that consumption is increasing so long as the rate of interest is above long-run subjective time preference; i.e., if the initial stock of capital is low, then consumption is low and gradually increases to its steady-state value as capital increases to its. The relation between investment and present and future rates of return is complex; it can be said that, to a first approximation, growth-adjusted investment is proportional to the discrepancy between the current rate of return and the steady-state time preference, ω.

To repeat, the optimal level of investment, apart from normal growth, is not determined by the rate of interest but primarily by its future changes. An interest rate determination for optimal public investment policy makes sense only when joined to an appropriate level of investment activity.

6.   CONTROLLABILITY WITH FIXED SAVING RATIO
IN THE PRIVATE SECTOR

We turn now to the controllability of the publicly optimal policy and to the possibility of being forced to seek second-best policies if the publicly optimal policy is not controllable in the sense of section 2. The possibility of controllability depends upon the workings of the private markets and upon the range of instruments open to the government.

We noted briefly in section 1 good reasons for believing that private saving behavior is not a decisive indicator of individual time preference. There is little evidence that saving is in fact responsive to rates of return, though it would be premature to say that the contrary is proved. For our purposes, we make the simple assumption that private saving is a fixed fraction, s, of disposable income.

(20) $s_p = s\, y_d$,

where s_p and y_d are the growth-adjusted values of private saving and disposable income, respectively.

We consider several alternative hypotheses concerning the range of instruments available to the government. The first case is the one which most nearly reflects actual practice; financing of government investment is accomplished through the income tax alone. Borrowing, at least in peacetime, is relatively small compared with the total budget and is primarily motivated by considerations of employment, rather than allocation, policy.[11] In this case, it is simplest to assume the absence of debt. Let x be the rate of income tax. Then,

(21) $Y_d = (1 - x)\, y$,

(22) $c = (1 - s)\, y_d$,

Private capital formation equals private saving; adjustment for growth yields,

(23) $\dot{k}_p = s\, y_d - \gamma\, k_p$,

while government capital formation equals taxes,

(24) $\dot{k}_g = x\, y - \gamma\, k_g$.

The aim of an optimal policy is to maximize the criterion function, (8), subject to the above constraints. First, we observe that the publicly

---

11. This model has been studied by Eckstein (see *Water Resource Development, op. cit.*, pp. 94-104), and subsequently by Steiner (see "Choosing Among Alternative Public Investments," *American Economic Review* 49: 893-916) and Marglin (see "The Opportunity Costs of Public Investment," *op. cit.*). Some of the present analysis was earlier presented by Arrow (see "Discounting and Public Investment Criteria," in *Water Resources Research*, ed. A. V. Kneese and S. C. Smith (Baltimore: Johns Hopkins Press, 1966), sec. 4).

optimal policy is not controllable except by chance. From (23) and (22),

$$(\dot{k}_p + \gamma \, k_p) \, /c = s/(1 - s) \, .$$

In the limit, then,

$$\gamma \, k_p^\infty \, /c^\infty = s/(1 - s) \, .$$

If the publicly optimal policy could be achieved the left hand side would have a certain value which would not depend on s; hence, equality could hold only by accident.

Since the publicly optimal policy is not in general controllable, the optimal policy sought for is a "second-best" policy. We proceed heuristically as follows. For any given initial values of k_p and k_g, there is an optimal policy, which yields a value of total discounted utility, (8), call this value $W(k_p, k_g)$. Then the shadow price in utility terms of k_p is,

$$p_p = \partial \, W/\partial \, k_p \, ,$$

and similarly for government capital,

$$p_g = \partial \, W/\partial \, k_g \, .$$

Any point of time could be regarded as the initial point, so associated with the optimal policy are two functions of time, $p_p(t)$ and $p_g(t)$, termed auxiliary variables in control theory. Hence, an addition to either kind of capital (growth-adjusted) can be valued at these rates. At the same time, a consumption, c, yields a current utility return, $U(c)$, so that the total national income in utility terms can be written,

$$H = U(c) + p_p \, \dot{k}_p + p_g \, \dot{k}_g \, ,$$

or, from (28) and (24),

(25) $H = U(c) + p_p \, (s \, y_d - \gamma \, k_p) + p_g \, (x \, y - \gamma \, k_g) \, .$

Since it is always desirable to increase H, the sole instrument, x, is to be chosen to maximize H. (Recall that c and y_d both depend on x.) Then setting $\partial H/\partial x = O$ yields,

(26) $(1 - s) \, U'(c) + s \, p_p = p_g \, ,$

which can be thought of as an equation to determine x in terms of k_p, k_g, p_p and p_g. Note that the burden of an increment of government capital, financed by taxation, falls on consumption and private saving in the proportions 1 - s and s.

It remains to determine the evolution of the auxiliary variables over time. The equations used are the analogues in utilities and auxiliary variables of the usual equilibrium condition for the holding of an asset:

the marginal productivity plus capital gains must equal the rate of interest times the price. Since we are dealing with utilities here, the "rate of interest" is simply λ. The "marginal productivity" is the contribution to H. Thus the equation for private capital is,

$$(\partial H / \partial k_p) + \dot{p}_p = \lambda \, p_p,$$

and a corresponding equation holds for government capital. From (25), we find, after some simplification,

$$(27) \qquad \dot{p}_p = \omega \, p_p - p_g \, f_p \ ,$$

$$(28) \qquad \dot{p}_g = \omega \, p_g - p_g \, f_g \ .$$

These equations, together with (23), (24), and (26), form a complete dynamic system. The solution is then defined if the initial conditions are specified. The initial values of k_p (O) and k_g (O) are given historically; however, those of the auxiliary variables have to be so chosen that the solution converges to a stationary value.

It is not easy to give a simple interpretation of an interdependent system like this. We clearly need for analysis not only the rates of return, f_p and f_g, but also the auxiliary variables and their rates of change. These solutions are computable, however.

Some insight can be found by looking at the stationary values, which, as before, we denote by superscript ∞. The stationarity of the capital stocks, whose motion is defined by (23) and (24), implies,

$$s \, y_d^{\infty} = \gamma \, k_p^{\infty} \ ,$$

$$x^{\infty} y^{\infty} = \gamma \, k_g^{\infty}.$$

Multiply the second equation by s, and add to the first, while recalling the definition of y_d.

$$(29) \qquad s \, f(k_p^{\infty}, k_g^{\infty}) = \gamma \, (k_p^{\infty} + s \, k_g^{\infty}) \ ,$$

a form of the Harrod-Domar relation. The stationarity of the auxiliary variables, whose motion is defined by (27) and (28), implies,

$$(30) \qquad f_p \, (k_p^{\infty}, k_g^{\infty}) = (p_p^{\infty} / p_g^{\infty}) \, \omega \ ,$$

$$(31) \qquad f_g \, (k_p^{\infty}, k_g^{\infty}) = \omega \ .$$

Equations (29) and (31) involve only k_p^{∞} and k_g^{∞}, which are therefore determined. Then the asymptotic ratio of the auxiliary variables is, from

(30) and (31), in the same ratio as the marginal productivities of the two kinds of capital.

Equation (31) is a little surprising; the long-run rate of return on government capital is the social rate of time preference, even though the return on private capital may be quite different. This holds because the benefits from a government investment project increase national income and therefore are partly saved. Hence, indirectly, the returns from government investment include some benefit from private investment projects. It turns out that in balanced growth this benefit exactly offsets the loss of private investment due to the initial act of government investment.[12]

The uncontrollability of the publicly optimal policy and the need to resort to a second-best policy in the above discussion arose from the restriction to a single financing instrument, the income tax. To illustrate the possibility of controllability with more instruments, suppose that the tax rates of consumption can differ from those on saving, but that a balanced budget is still required (no borrowing). We shall understand the hypothesis of a fixed saving ratio to mean that post-tax saving and post-tax consumption are fixed fractions of total personal income. Thus, expenditures on saving are $s Y$, but the government takes a fraction x_s of this so that private saving is reduced to $s(1 - x_s) Y$; similarly, consumption is $(1 - s) (1 - x_c) Y$. Government tax collections and therefore government investment are given by,

$$[s\, x_s + (1 - s)\, x_c]\, Y.$$

Then,

$$(32) \qquad \dot{k}_p = (1 - x_s)\, y - \gamma\, k_p \,,$$

$$(33) \qquad \dot{k}_g = [s\, x_s + (1 - s)\, x_c]\, y - \gamma\, k_g \,,$$

$$(34) \qquad c = (1 - s) \, (1 - x_c)\, y \,.$$

Suppose the government wishes to control the publicly optimal or indeed any other feasible policy. Since,

$$c + i_p + i_g = y,$$

where,

$$\dot{k}_p = i_p - \gamma\, k_p, \; \dot{k}_g = i_g - \gamma\, k_g \,,$$

it is clear that if the government can choose its instruments, the two tax

12. The reader is referred for a more detailed explanation to Arrow (*ibid.*, p. 26).

rates, to satisfy two of the three equations (32-34), the third is automatically satisfied. Given any policy determining consumption and the two kinds of capital as functions of time, it is then only necessary to solve (34) for x_c, the consumption tax, and (32) for x_s, the tax on saving. The consumption tax thus insures that the correct amount of aggregate investment is forthcoming, while the tax on saving allocates it between the two forms of capital formation.[13]

Thus, the rule that the rate of discount for government investment should equal that in the private sector requires not only that the appropriate level of investment be forthcoming, as argued in section 5, but also, in a mixed economy, that the financing be accomplished by the unique appropriate mixture of taxes (or of borrowing and taxes).[14]

7. CONTROLLABILITY WITH PERFECTLY RATIONAL CONSUMERS

The fixed saving ratio assumption is perhaps extreme in emphasizing the short-sightedness of the consumer. The opposite extreme hypothesis is that the consumer chooses his consumption pattern over time to maximize the sum of discounted utilities in full knowledge of all future interest rates and wage levels. We can then ask under what conditions the publicly optimal policy is controllable.

Although more general cases can be analyzed, I confine myself here to the case where there is no divergence between public and private values. It is assumed, that is, that the consumer is seeking to maximize the same criterion function, (5) or (8), as the government.

We will assume here that the government borrows (or lends) and can impose one kind of tax. We also assume that bonds are a perfect substitute for private capital from the viewpoint of the consumer, so that the rate of interest on government bonds equals the marginal productivity of private capital. (Government bonds are assumed to be short-term bonds, so that capital gains may be ignored.)

---

13. Controllability is also achieved if the government can both borrow and impose an income tax; see Arrow, *ibid.*, sec. 6.

14. It may be worth noting that merely counting instruments is not a sufficient criterion for controllability. Two kinds of taxes or borrowing plus an income tax or a consumption tax suffice for controllability; but it can easily be shown that borrowing plus a tax on saving is not sufficient.

I only summarize the results here. The fact that there may be an initial debt is important, because the interest on it must be financed in any case, in addition to subsequent government investment. Actually, if the initial debt has an appropriate initial value, then choosing government investment according to the publicly optimal policy and financing it out of borrowing alone is optimal. An income tax in the ordinary sense cannot be used; it destroys optimality through the well known double taxation of saving. But if the initial debt differs from the critical initial value just described, then an initial capital levy (which has no incentive effects) can be used to change the debt to the appropriate level, after which again financing is done only by borrowing. The initial capital levy might be thought of as a limiting form of the income tax.

The most interesting case is that where the sole tax is the consumption tax. It turns out that the publicly optimal policy can be carried out with a consumption tax whose rate is constant over time: the remainder of the government investment is financed by borrowing. Of course, this remainder might be negative in which case the government retires debt or even lends to the private sector. Incidentally, the constant rate of the consumption tax has a simple interpretation. Define *private wealth* to be the sum of government debt, private capital, and future wages discounted to the present according to the wages and interest rates implicit in the publicly optimal policy (wages equals marginal product of labor). Then the consumption tax is the ratio of private wealth to the total of future consumption discounted to the present. Notice that the consumption tax rate will thus depend, among other things, on the initial level of debt.

8. RISK AND THE RATE OF RETURN[15]

The analysis so far has implicitly assumed that the returns to government investment are riskless. If they are not, then it is contended here that as a general rule the uncertain benefits and costs should be evaluated at their expected value and discounted at the rate of return appropriate to riskless investments. This statement is not intended as a result applicable to all circumstances but as a proposition which follows from certain hypotheses that are approximately fulfilled with some exceptions.

---

15. This section draws on a paper done jointly with Robert C. Lind, of Standard University, forthcoming in the *American Economic Review*.

First suppose that (a) before the government investment in question there is an optimal allocation of risk-bearing, and (b) the random returns on the government investment are statistically independent of those in the economy before the investment takes place. Then it can be shown that the proposed new investment should be introduced if and only if its expected net return is positive. I briefly recapitulate an argument given earlier.[16] Let p_s be the price of a unit conditional claim to one unit of consumption if state of nature s prevails, and let π_s be the probability of state s. If the consumer is, before trade, entitled to $\bar{y}_s$ in state s, then his behavior in choosing actual claims is determined by maximizing,

$$\sum_s \pi_s U(y_s),$$

subject to a budget constraint, $\sum_s p_s y_s = \sum_s p_s \bar{y}_s$, according to the Bernoulli-von Neumann-Morgenstern theory. Then necessarily,

$$(35) \qquad p_s/p_t = (\pi_s/\pi_t) [U'(y_s)/U'(y_t)] .$$

Consider a government investment yielding a return h_s in state s. Then, for a marginal investment, it should be accepted if and only if $\sum_s p_s h_s \geq O$. From (35), this is equivalent to the condition,

$$\sum_s \pi_s U'(y_s) h_s \geq O ,$$

or,

$$E [U'(y_s) h_s] \geq O .$$

But if h_s is distributed independently of national income before investment, then,

$$E [U'(y_s) h_s] = E [U'(y_s)] E(h_s) ,$$

and since certainly,

$$E [U'(y_s)] > O .$$

the condition reduces simply to $E(h_s) \geq O$.

The assumption of statistical independence appears not unreasonable as a first approximation. However that of the optimality of risk-bearing in the private sector is more dubious. But much the same result still holds if the assumption is dropped; for the allocation of risks among all taxpayers implies not only that the risk to any one is negligible but more strongly that the total of all risk premiums tends to zero as the number of individuals grows indefinitely large. If the government

16. See K. J. Arrow, "Discounting and Public Investment Criteria," *op. cit.*, pp. 28-30.

adopts an expected value criterion, while private industry does not, then it may indeed happen that a government investment displaces a private investment of higher expected value; but this is correct in the context, because the government is supplying a valuable complementary activity of risk-bearing which the private sector is not.

I do note however the possibility that the benefits accruing to an individual as a result of government investment may increase his uncertainty, e.g., introduction of irrigation with an uncertain water supply into a predictably dry climate. Then indeed the benefits should be discounted at a rate higher than the riskless; but the preceding analysis shows that it would be still better for the government to offer insurance against failure of the irrigated water and then evaluate the total package of water and insurance at the riskless rate.

Note that no contention has been made that the government uses a riskless rate because it can spread its risks over a great many projects; Hirshleifer[17] is certainly right in asserting that each project should be evaluated separately if the appropriate discount factors are used.

9. SOME LOOSE ENDS

There are some aspects considered in the literature which have not been taken account of here. In effect, I have been assuming that the problem of determining the social discount rate arises from a particular set of imperfections in the market structure, the inappropriability of the products of government investment, the existence of an initial debt which needs financing, and, in section 6, the imperfection of private capital markets as reflected in the fixed saving ratio hypothesis. Implicitly, it has been assumed that the market structure is otherwise perfect. If, however, there are imperfections elsewhere in the market structure, such as monopolistic price distortions, excise taxes, or the corporate income tax, which falls on the fruits of some but not all private investment, then as is well known the analysis becomes far more complicated. Any suggested policy must be evaluated in terms of all sorts of cross-effects.[18]

---

17. J. Hirshleifer, "Investment Decision Under Uncertainty: Applications of the State-Preference Approach," *Quarterly Journal of Economics* **80**: 252-277 at pp. 270-275.

18. See J. Lesourne, *Le calcul économique* (Paris: Dunod, 1964), pp. 33-39.

Another neglected aspect is the relation between government bond rates and return on private capital. In the preceding discussion and indeed in virtually all analysis, the two are assumed equal, whenever government borrowing is considered as a possible means of financing, but this is very far from the case in fact. This raises the possibility that if public investment is financed from bonds, the government is in effect producing a joint product; the investment creates the opportunity to produce bonds, which are preferred to private capital. This suggests the appropriateness of discounting by the government bond rate rather than the average observed rate of return.

DISCUSSION: PROFESSOR ARROW ON THE SOCIAL DISCOUNT RATE

ARNOLD C. HARBERGER

University of Chicago

IN these comments I shall first briefly summarize the approach that Professor Arrow has taken in his stimulating paper. Then in section II I shall express a few thoughts and puzzles that remained in my mind after reading it. Finally, in section III I shall contrast Arrow's approach with one that I have been developing during the past year or so.

I

My summary of Professor Arrow's approach will be concerned mainly with the material presented in sections 4 through 7, which I regard as the analytical core of his paper. In section 4, he assumes output to be a function of private capital, government capital, and labor (defined to include labor-augmenting technical progress at an annual rate of τ per cent). The production function is assumed to be homogeneous of degree one, and the labor force is assumed to grow at π per cent per year. These assumptions are sufficient to determine that the natural, steady-state rate of growth of the economy will be equal to γ ($= \pi + \tau$) per cent per year. He then shows that essentially similar results are obtained when government capital is labor-augmenting.

Arrow next introduces a criterion function for the evaluation of alternative policies. This is the present value of all future utility, where utility at any time is defined as population times the utility associated with the then-prevailing level of per capita consumption. The discount rate used to obtain this present value is ρ, which is described as "a discount factor for utilities (not necessarily for commodities)." The function that converts per capita consumption into utility units is assumed to be homogeneous of degree 1 - σ, with $\sigma > 0$.

In the analysis all variables are recast in growth-normalized form, such that if the economy were in fact enjoying steady and balanced growth at the rate of γ per cent per year, the growth-normalized time paths of output, consumption, and private and government investment would all be horizontal lines. This normalization is the key that takes what might otherwise look to be insoluble problems and converts them into a convenient and manageable form.

In section 5, the publicly optimal policy is derived. Not surprisingly, it is found that optimality requires the marginal net rates of productivity of the two types of capital to be the same, and also to be equal to the consumption rate of interest. Arrow's results imply that the consumption rate of interest, r_c, is in turn equal to ρ, the utility discount rate, when the utility function is homogeneous of degree 1 ($\sigma=0$), but r_c is greater than ρ when there is diminishing marginal utility of consumption. In this latter case, the optimal rate of change of growth-adjusted consumption is proportional to the discrepancy between the current marginal rate of productivity of capital g^1 (K) and its steady-state level, ω.

In section 6, Professor Arrow works out some of the implications of his model, when the private sector always saves a given fraction of its disposable income. Within this context, he first explores the consequences of constraining the government to raise money only via an income tax. He shows that this constraint in general precludes the achievement of the full optimum described in section 5. But he also shows that a second-best solution can be obtained by introducing appropriate shadow prices (P_p and P_g) for private capital and government capital respectively. Arrow then describes the steady-state growth path which emerges when the private sector, investing a fraction S of its disposable income, and the government, investing a fraction x of national income, cause, by this behavior, the respective capital stocks to grow at the natural growth rate, γ. He finds, in equations (30) and (31), that along this path the marginal net rate of productivity of government capital will be equal to the social rate of time preference, whereas the corresponding rate for private-sector capital will be the social rate of time preference times the steady-state value of (P_p/P_g).

Arrow next shows that the constraint imposed by limiting the government to obtain funds only by income taxation is absent when two distinct instruments — taxation of consumption and of saving at different rates — are available to it. That is to say, the appropriate choice of the tax rates on consumption and saving are sufficient to guarantee that the optimum will be achieved.

In section 7, the assumption that consumers save a constant fraction of their income is dropped, and consumers are instead assumed to maximize "the sum of discounted utilities in full knowledge of all future interest rates and wage levels." Arrow shows here that the government can assure that the optimum will be achieved even if it is limited to use only one tax, so long as it can borrow as well. However, the tax in question cannot be an income tax because the double taxation of savings that an income tax entails would induce non-optimal decisions on the part of individuals. Arrow carries out his analysis in terms of a consumption tax; it is likely that only a consumption tax or a head tax would fulfill the requirements of optimality.

II

My direct comments on Professor Arrow's paper take the form of two questions and two observations.

What Is ρ?

The criterion function (5) discounts utility at a rate ρ, which is simply defined as "a discount factor for utilities." An abundant literature in capital theory adopts the same approach; so Professor Arrow is in good company. Yet I have for a long time been bothered by a lingering doubt about the validity of the approach. In a nutshell, the problem is that economic theory tells us that individuals accommodate their behavior to current and expected market prices — including market interest rates. Now the models that generate a natural rate of growth generally also yield up an equilibrium rate of marginal productivity of capital. With a constant savings rate and a Cobb-Douglas production function, the equilibrium marginal productivity of capital is proportional to the natural rate of growth and inversely proportional to the rate of saving. Thus it could well be that, for example, with one rate of technical advance the equilibrium m.p.k. would be 6 per cent, and with another, 9 per cent. It seems to me that the way that individuals discount the future should be different under these alternative cirsumstances, yet Arrow's equation (5) appears to say that it will not differ between the two circumstances.[1]

If I am right in interpreting ρ as a number that is characteristic of the typical utility function and not related or responsive to market phenomena, then I am disturbed by the power that the value of ρ has in

1. This refers to the discounting of future utilities. As far as discounting of future consumption is concerned, Arrow's "consumption rate of interest," r_c, is dependent on the rate of technical advance, but not in the case where the the utility function is homogeneous of degree one. It seems to me that even with a homogeneous function, discounting of consumption should take place at a different rate when the marginal (net) productivity of capital is 6 as against 9 per cent.

determining Arrow's main results. In the optimal situation with a linear homogeneous utility function, the marginal rate of productivity of capital and the consumption rate of interest both have to be equal to ρ. When the utility function exhibits a degree of homogeneity of $(1 - \sigma)$ these rates are still basically determined by ρ but with adjustments that depend on the value of σ, and that are likely to be small relative to ρ if σ is small.[2] It seems, then, that unless my interpretation is wrong Arrow's system produces an optimum in which the basic determinant of the interest rate is the rather nebulous and difficult-to-quantify "utility discount factor," ρ. Moreover, it is hard to see how this really could be the case wherever the equilibrium value of the marginal productivity of capital depends on parameters of the model other than ρ.

Can an Optimum be Achieved when Savings are Taxed at Positive Rates?

In section 7 of the paper, Professor Arrow notes that an income tax cannot be the tax part of an optimal tax-cum-borrowing package, because of "the well known double taxation of saving." Yet in section 6 separate taxes on consumption and saving are sufficient to produce an optimum. I realize that Arrow is assuming in section 6 that people always save a constant fraction of their income, and that he refers to Section 1, where he gives "good reasons for believing that private saving behavior is not a decisive indicator of individual time preference." Yet I again have doubts about the result. In the first place, and without having investigated the issue in detail, it would seem plausible that, just as a Cobb-Douglas utility function leads an individual to spend a given fraction of his income on each of the various goods in his market basket, regardless of changes in income and relative prices, so also there should be some particular form or forms of the utility function, such that utility maximization would lead to a constant savings rate regardless of changes in relative prices, interest rates, etc. If such a form exists, then it is clear that any solution with a positive tax on savings is non-optimal, at least for that case, and assuming utility maximization by consumers. For just as an income tax makes the marginal rate of substitution between present and future consumption differ

---

2. My hunch is that something like 0.2 is a plausible upper limit for σ. A value of $1/2$ for σ implies that the utility of 100 is only $3/7$ greater than the utility of 49, and that of 225 is only 50 per cent greater than that of 100. Such rapidly diminishing marginal utility seems to me to be belied by the way people behave vis-à-vis risk.

from the marginal rate of transformation, so also does any tax on saving in conjunction with a tax on consumption.

It may well be, however, that no utility function exists which can generate a constant savings rate in any and all circumstances. If this is so, the above comment is obviously inapplicable.[3]

A Comment on Shadow Prices for Investible Funds

In the first part of section (b), where a second-best solution is derived for the fixed-saving-ratio, income-tax-only case, shadow prices for private and for government investment emerge from the analysis. This is a characteristic outcome whenever the discount rate differs from the true opportunity cost of capital. I should like merely to add that there is a companion outcome in the form of the so-called reinvestment problem. If discounting is done at the rate or r_1 and if the social yield from additional savings is $r_2 > r_1$, then one must inquire, in a properly done cost-benefit analysis, what will be the effect of the particular project on savings (investment) at each future point in time. When r_2 equals r_1, one can ignore this complication. The two rates are the same for Arrow's optimal cases but not for the sub-optimal one here under discussion. Since the reinvestment problem is, for the real-world cost-benefit analyst, an extremely thorny one, there are perhaps grounds for preferring, among alternative approaches to measuring the discount rate, one that manages to avoid this problem. Such an approach will be outlined in section III below.

On Optimization in General

Professor Arrow's treatment is one in which the government authorities actually, in all cases but one, pursue policies that take the community to a full optimum, and in the one remaining case they take the community

3. Arrow recognizes in footnote 8 that the model of section 6 has at least one implication that is non-optimal for utility-maximizing consumers. He there points out that the optimum can be achieved when the government finances itself only by an income tax and by borrowing. In section 7, where fully rational consumer behavior is postulated, this is shown to be non-optimal. The key issue, in my view, is the existence of a utility function generating a constant savings rate. This issue is not discussed by Arrow. If no such utility function exists, then Arrow's section 6 appears to be on safe ground. On the other hand, if such a function exists, the results of section 6, where the constant savings rate is generated by utility maximization, are inconsistent with those of section 7.

to a constrained optimum.   In section 7, Arrow mentions that "if, however, there are imperfections elsewhere in the market structure, such as monopolistic price distortions, excise taxes, or the corporate income tax . . ., then as is well known the analysis becomes far more complicated." I would add that not only does the analysis become more complicated; its nature also changes.   We may not know the precise path from an existing real-world situation characterized by numerous distortions toward an optimum, but we can be sure that certain events will have to take place somewhere along the way.   Most import tariffs and excise taxes would be eliminated, the corporation income tax and the property tax would disappear, and the personal income tax would be presumably replaced by a consumption tax (even this would not quite reach a genuine allocative optimum, but it would not entail much of a deviation from it).   Much as many of us might like to see the sort of radical overhaul of tax systems that pursuit of an allocative optimum would imply, I am afraid that no one alive today will have the pleasure of that vision.

Once it is recognized that most existing distortions are going to be with us for some time, the task of cost-benefit analysis must to some extent be redefined.   We have to estimate the social opportunity costs of factors and of outputs, in the presence of the current and expected patterns of distortions.   Optimization in the strict sense is not really present — not even the sort of constrained optimization that is associated with the literature on "second best."   Cost-benefit analysis in this real-world context is, in my view, a highly decentralized instrument of governmental decision-making. For a given project, the question is, "Does this project move us up or down on the utility hill?" Between alternative projects the question is "which one takes us farther up the hill?"   At a more subtle level a sort of optimization is possible in the designing of a project, involving the choice of that design which promises to have the highest net present value.   Operating at this mundane level the overall and constrained optima of which Professor Arrow's analysis speaks seem hopelessly far away.   One also wonders how many of the acute insights that one obtains from such a celestial flight of theorizing will have counterparts that will prove to be useful in the jungle of distortions in which we live.

III

In this section I briefly sketch an alternative conceptual framework for measuring the social rate of discount.   In it, the discount rate is obtained by tracing through the effects of additional government borrowing on various classes of investment and saving. The resulting figure for the social rate of discount is a weighted average of the marginal rates of productivity of capital in the various sectors from which investment is displaced, and of the marginal rates of time preference applicable to the various groups (if any) whose saving is stimulated (through higher interest rates) by the additional government borrowing.

We approach the problem indirectly, considering first the social opportunity cost of an input into a public-sector project, the private use of which is subject to a tax; second the social opportunity cost of foreign exchange under both uniform and diverse tariff treatment of various classes of imports; and only then the social opportunity cost of public funds. This indirect approach will reveal that essentially the same methodology is applicable to all three cases, thus reinforcing its credibility when it is applied to the discount rate problem.

The Social Opportunity Cost of an Input

Let S(P) be the total supply of the input in question, and D[P(1+t)] be the total private-sector demand. The net-of-tax price is P, and t is the rate at which the use of the input by the private sector is taxed. Following the established convention of cost-benefit analysis that a competitive demand price reflects the value of the commodity to the purchaser, and a competitive supply price reflects the value of the commodity to the seller, we can say that the social opportunity cost of an additional unit of the commodity taken by the government will be a weighted average of P and P(1+t), the weights depending on the relative impact of added government demand in stimulating additional production of the input on the one hand and in displacing its private-sector use on the other. The weights can be derived from the identity:

(1) $G \equiv S(P) - D[P(1+t)]$,

by differentiating with respect to G, which refers to government demand. This yields:

$$(2) \quad \frac{\partial S}{\partial G} = \frac{\partial S}{\partial P} \frac{\partial P}{\partial G} = \frac{S'}{S' - D'(1+t)} = \frac{\epsilon}{\epsilon - \eta(D/S)}$$

$$-\frac{\partial D}{\partial G} = \frac{-\partial D}{\partial P} \frac{\partial P}{\partial G} = \frac{-D'(1+t)}{S' - D'(1+t)} = \frac{-\eta(D/S)}{\epsilon - \eta(D/S)} ,$$

where ϵ and η (defined as < 0) are the elasticities of supply and demand for the good. The social opportunity cost of the input, P_s, is obtained using these weights.

$$(3) \qquad P_s = \frac{\epsilon P - \eta(D/S) \, P(1+t)}{\epsilon - \eta(D/S)}$$

The Social Opportunity Cost of Foreign Exchange

For this case we assume the country in question to have no influence over the world prices of its exports or its imports. This permits the aggregation of heterogeneous commodities, with the common unit of account being the "dollar's worth" at world market prices. If X represents private-sector exports, M private-sector imports, N net demand on the part of the public sector for foreign exchange, E the exchange rate, and t the uniform *ad valorem* duty on private-sector imports, then (1) is replaced by

$$(4) \qquad N \equiv X(E) - M[E(1+t)] \,,$$

and (3) becomes

$$(5) \qquad E_S = \frac{\epsilon E - \eta \, (M/X) \, E(1+t)}{\epsilon - \eta \, (M/X)} \,,$$

where E_S is the social opportunity cost of foreign exchange and ϵ and η here refer to the elasticities of the private sector's supply of exports and of its demand for imports, respectively.

Assuming now that there are several categories of imports, each struck by a different tariff rate t_i, (4) must be replaced by

$$(4') \qquad N \equiv X(E) - \sum_i M_i[E(1+t_i)],$$

and (5) becomes

$$(5') \qquad E_S = \frac{\epsilon E - \sum_i \eta_i(M_i/X) \, E(1+t_i)}{\epsilon - \sum_i \eta_i(M_i/X)}$$

Here the social opportunity cost of foreign exchange is a weighted average of the exchange rate governing exports, and of the internal values that a dollar's worth of foreign exchange produces when spent on imports in the various categories. The weights are the fractions in which an extra dollar of net government demand for foreign exchange will be reflected in increased exports on the one hand and in reduced imports of the various categories on the other.

The Social Opportunity of Cost of Capital

In most modern economies the effective weight of taxation of income from capital varies substantially among sectors. Let us assume that the rate of return i, defined to be after such taxes as corporation income and property taxes but before personal income tax, is equalized in all lines of investment, through the operation of market forces. The marginal productivity of capital will accordingly be different in the various lines of activity, being equal to $\rho_j = i/(1 - t_j)$, where t_j is the average rate at which such levies as corporation income and property taxes, taken together, strike the income from capital in sector j. At the same time, although savers by assumption all receive the same rate of return, i, before personal income taxes, their after-tax rates of return will differ as among marginal tax rate brackets. Hence we can express the marginal rate of time preference of savers in the kth tax bracket as $r_k = i(1 - t_k)$.

Using S_k to denote private saving by individuals in the kth tax bracket, I_j to denote private investment in the jth sector, and B to denote net government borrowing, we have, as the counterpart of $(4')$,

$$(6) \qquad B \equiv \sum_k S_k[i(1 - t_k)] - \sum_j I_j[i/(1 - t_j)]$$

and as the counterpart of $(5')$,

$$(7) \qquad i_s = \frac{\sum_k \epsilon_k(S_k/S)r_k - \sum_j \eta_j(I_j/S)\rho_j}{\sum_k \epsilon_k(S_k/S) - \sum_j \eta_j(I_j/S)} .$$

Here ϵ_k refers to the elasticity of supply of savings with respect to their rate of yield, by individuals in the kth tax bracket, η_j refers to the elasticity of the investment schedule of the jth sector with respect to the cost of capital, and S denotes total private savings. The savings and investment schedules are defined at the full employment level of income.

In words, (7) says that the social opportunity cost of capital will be a weighted average of the marginal rates of time preference of the various categories of savers, and of the rates of marginal productivity of capital in the various sectors. The weights are proportional to the extents to which the various types of saving increase and the various types of investment decrease when new net borrowing occurs in the capital market. In the model just sketched, which assumes that the net yield i, after other but before personal income taxes, is the same in all sectors, (7) measures not only the social opportunity cost of public borrowing, but also that of any net increment to private borrowing (i.e., an upward shift of any of the I_j schedules). In this case the I_j and S_k schedules should be defined not including the shift, and the shift itself, $\triangle I_j$, replaces B in (6). By the same token, i_s as measured in (7) represents both the social yield of any autonomous increment in private savings (i.e., rightward shift in any of the S_j schedules), and also the potential social yield of any increase in taxes, as well as the social opportunity cost of any increment in government expenditures. The analogy with the foreign exchange market is useful here. What we defined as E_s in subsection III b) above is not only the social opportunity cost of public expenditures of foreign exchange, it is also the social opportunity cost of private expenditures of foreign exchange and at the same time the social opportunity yield of increments of foreign exchange, regardless of whether they are generated in the public or private sector.

Advantages of the i_s Approach

The advantages of this approach, as I see them, are the following:

1. The basic data from which estimates of i_s are generated can in principle be obtained from market observations. In the case treated above, where a single interest rate i rules throughout the capital market, these observations are simply the after-personal-tax rates of return on saving r_k, in each tax bracket, and the before-tax rates of return, ρ_j, on capital in each sector. When a more complicated case is treated, in which there is a whole gamut of interest rates reflecting all kinds of variations in riskiness, in preferences concerning asset types, etc., the basic data needed are the rate of return i_g on government bonds, plus a weighted average of the distortions (taxes in our example, but monopoly profits and external effects in general can also be incorporated) prevailing in the various sectors and affecting the various income brackets.[4] Though there are unquestioned

---

4. Defining $\delta_k = (r_k - i)$, and $\delta_j = (\rho_j - i$, (7) can be re-expressed as

$$(7^1) \quad i_s = i + \frac{\sum\limits_{k} \epsilon_k(S_k/S)\delta_k - \sum\limits_{j} \eta_j(I_j/S)\delta_j}{\sum\limits_{k} \epsilon_k(S_k/S) - \sum\limits_{j} \eta_j(I_j/S)} ;$$

when the assumption of a single interest rate i, is dropped, the equation corresponding to (7^1) contains i_g in place of i. The interpretation of δ_k and δ_j also changes in this case, becoming $(r_k - i_k)$ and $(\rho_j - i_j)$ respectively, i_k being the before-personal-tax yield required to elicit the marginal unit of savings from the kth income bracket, and i_j the expected rate of return, before personal taxes but after other ones, which is required to obtain voluntary financing for the marginal unit of investment in sector j. These modifications are discussed in detail in Section II of "On Measuring the Social Opportunity Cost of Public Funds," to be published in *Proceedings* of the December, 1968 Meeting of the Water Resources Research Committee, Western Agricultural Research Council. The entire approach is also presented there much more fully than is possible here.

practical problems connected with the estimation of these magnitudes, there can be no question that the discount rate i_s is in principle related and responsive to market phenomena. The fundamental questions that we raised above concerning "what is ρ?" have no counterpart here.

2. The procedures used to obtain i_s are fully consistent with the tenets that underlie cost-benefit analysis as such. I take these to be a) competitive supply price measures marginal private opportunity cost, b) competitive demand price measures marginal private benefit, and c) the Hicks-Kaldor principle of potential compensation is accepted. In particular, defining i_s^t as the social opportunity cost of using funds for the period between t - 1 and t, it can be shown that a rate of return of i_s^t, on a project with costs only in t - 1 and benefits only in t, would be just barely sufficient to compensate all parties affected by the government's borrowing the required funds in year t-1 and effectuating the corresponding compensations in year t.[5] The principle thus developed for the case of a one-year project can readily be extended to cover all projects.

This result is a matter of some importance. For, so long as i_s^t reflects at one and the same time the social rate of discount applied to benefits, and the social rate of return obtainable from private savings, the so-called reinvestment problem disappears, since the discounted value of the income stream produced by a given amount of savings is necessarily equal to that amount.

In saying that the reinvestment problem disappears, I do not mean to assert that there can never be circumstances where consideration of it would be important. Rather, I say that so long as one accepts the three basic tenets of cost-benefit analysis set out above, the "natural" measure of the social discount rate is i_s, and that when i_s is used, no reinvestment problem will emerge, nor will any problem of the shadow pricing of investible funds. Put another way, the occasions on which a reinvestment

5. The discounting in cost-benefit analysis should in principle be at a rate which can vary through time. If discounting is done to year 0 (the initiation of a project), this implies that the costs and benefits of year j should be divided by $\prod_{t=1}^{j} (1+i_s^t)$. This also emphasizes the fact that the most important uses of cost-benefit analysis are forward-looking. Past data on observed yields on capital are relevant, but only because they provide us with experience to help us reach judgments concerning their likely trend in the future.

problem is really and unavoidably present are at the same time occasions which call for some deviation from one or more of what I have called the basic tenets of cost-benefit analysis.

3. The approach underlying i_s, and the measure itself, take existing distortions amply into account. They thus seem far more suited to the way cost-benefit problems appear in real-world situations than do approaches which implicitly posit optimization.

One may question, however, whether the i_s measure does not build in too great a degree of rigidity in the pattern of distortions. Is it not, in a sense, too fatalistic about the possibilities of reducing or eliminating distortions? I think that the answer is no. In the first place, the values of i_s^t projected for future years may embody any desired set of changes in the pattern of distortions. The corporation income tax may be projected to decline, the personal tax to rise, etc. No limits are in principle imposed on the analyst — but the ultimate test is the realism of his projections.

There is a second way in which the approach in question can be defended against the charge of excessive rigidity or "fatalism" regarding distortions. For although the analysis builds in distortions, it also throws out strong signals as to the changes in the pattern of distortions that would most improve the economy. For example, suppose that the highest sectoral marginal productivity of capital, ρ_j, is 15 per cent in the corporate sector (as distinct from the housing and unincorporated business sectors) of the economy, and that the lowest marginal rate of time preference, r_k, is 3 per cent, in the highest personal income tax bracket. The social rate of discount, i_s, must necessarily lie between these two extremes. Obviously, whether or not i_s is used, the prospect of obtaining funds at a social cost of 3 per cent, and putting them to use with a social yield of 15 per cent, is very appealing indeed. If we leave tax rates unchanged, we cannot accomplish this, for the market, not the borrower, dictates what investments will be foregone and what savings will be stimulated as a consequence of additional public borrowing. However, if the government reduces somewhat the highest personal tax rate, it will thereby generate a certain increment of saving by the affected group. It can then borrow these incremental savings without affecting the interest rate, and hence without influencing the saving of other income groups. By the same token, lending by the government to the private capital market would without tax rate changes affect investment in all sectors. However, if the government lowers somewhat the corporation income tax, additional investible funds will be demanded by the corporate sector at the same interest rate as before. The government can therefore under such circumstances lend the relevant amount of funds to the corporate sector, financing the additional investment there — without affecting investment in other sectors of the economy.

If policy-makers obey the implicit signals emitted by the approach underlying i_s, they will obviously at each point in time reduce the highest sectoral taxes t_j and the highest bracket personal taxes t_k. The end result of this procedure is the complete elimination of corporate, property, and personal income taxes. What would replace them? In theory, perhaps, the proverbial head tax, with no distorting properties at all. But in practice some combination of a value-added tax of the consumption type and a progressive consumption-expenditure tax of the type advocated by Kaldor would be a more plausible alternative. Such taxes have a certain (probably very mild) distorting effect on the labor-leisure choice, but otherwise they are neutral as among goods and services and as between saving and consumption. Given that they can provide any desired degree of progression in the tax structure, economic theory leads us naturally to prefer a system based on them to the present pattern of personal income, corporate, and property taxes. Thus, when the methodology underlying i_s is used for the purpose of seeking reform, rather than sticking with given or sluggishly changing tax rates, it leads to conclusions that follow directly from economic theory. Whatever degree of fatalism may be implied by an analyst's assuming that the tax structure will not change much or rapidly over time must therefore (assuming he is right) be attributed to the realities of political life — not to the i_s methodology!

GRANT L. REUBER
University of Western Ontario

IN an age of large-scale government expenditures the question of the discount rate is not only important but also unavoidable. Every time a public investment is undertaken some assumption *is* made about the discount rate, whether explicitly or implicitly.

One thing on which almost everyone agrees is that the discount rate is positive. I state this banality because even this weak condition is probably not met by all public investments in some countries, such as Canada, where the most rudimentary cost-benefit calculus is only making its appearance on the public expenditure scene.

This said, there remains the critical question of what positive discount rate should be used to evaluate public expenditures in mixed economies such as Canada and the U.S. While professional disagreements on this question differ in detail, a critical issue, as Professor Arrow suggests, is the question of how much normative significance can be attributed to market rates of interest. In order to clarify this issue it may be useful to approach it at different levels of generality. Starting with the most restricted case first, we can assume that the level and allocation of private investment is completely predetermined and that the option facing the authorities is between public investment and consumption. In this situation one would evaluate the benefits and costs of public investment over time as best one could, derive the internal rate of return on each project and undertake projects in the order of their internal rate of return until the total pool of resources was exhausted. In applying this approach one would encounter, of course, all the difficulties of arriving at reliable estimates of benefits and costs. In addition, there is the question of the cut-off rate of return below which it would be preferable for the government to opt in favour of current consumption and against further public investment. If one assumes that the tax-adjusted rate at which the government borrows provides a rough approximation to the marginal rate of time preference by consumers, one might argue that the cut-off rate of return should be the tax-adjusted rate on government bonds. Some economists, however, would object to choosing the cut-off point on the basis of market rates for a number of reasons, including the following: a) the current generation may have a "weakness of imagination" and be myopic as far as the future is concerned; hence the government should give some weight to the interests of future generations which may not be adequately reflected in market rates; b) citizens may have a different time preference collectively from what they have individually; c) the question is essentially political and consequently should be decided by votes cast in the polling booth rather than in the market place; and d) market rates are neither unique nor necessarily consistent with the observed savings behaviour of consumers. It is this latter point that is emphasized by Professor Arrow.

More realistically one may assume that the total amount of investible resources available for both private and public investment is predetermined and that capital is freely transferable between the private and public sectors. On these assumptions public investment is undertaken at the expense of private investment. Given the level of investible resources, one could think of pooling all private and public projects and, proceeding as before, simply undertaking them in order of their internal rate of return until the total pool of resources is exhausted. In a market-oriented economy, however, private projects are ranked by the private sector, leaving it for the public sector to determine the appropriate cut-off rate for its projects and, at the same time, the division of the given pool of investible resources between public and private projects. In this case one might argue that the appropriate discount rate to use in evaluating public projects is the pre-tax rate of return in the private sector since this is the rate of return at the margin in that sector. Using a lower rate of return would imply that the present value of net benefits derivable from the total pool of investible resources could be increased by transferring resources from the public to the private sector — a proposition that Professor Arrow accepts in his most general case.

This still leaves us with two important questions to be settled. The first is to determine what is the rate of return at the margin in the private sector for use as the discount rate in evaluating public projects. It is to this that Professor Harberger, among others, has given considerable attention.[1] The second question arises from the possibility that even though we know the marginal productivity of capital in the private sector and equate it with the marginal productivity of capital in the public sector, we may find that this rate is higher than the social discount rate, implying that the total level of investment in the community is too low. Professor Arrow wishes to ensure not only the appropriate division of investment between the public and private sectors but also the appropriate rate of capital formation in the aggregate.

Professor Arrow takes a much bigger bite at the cherry than is feasible within the conventional framework by generalizing the problem within

---

1. Harberger's adjustments allow not only for resources to be drawn from the private investment sector but also from increased savings; the weights he uses to derive the discount rate for evaluating public projects reflect the empirical judgment that most of the resources are drawn from changes in the private investment sector rather than from changes in savings.

the context of growth theory and looking at it in terms of deploying available instruments to achieve defined targets. As I understand him, he would like the policy-maker to specify the target rate of growth in consumption adjusted for population growth, technical change and other factors. This target having been specified along with effective constraints in the system, one would then derive the implied social discount rate which would determine that level of private and public investment that is consistent with the defined consumption goal of the community. Where the savings ratio is predetermined and taxes are the only instruments of policy, one would derive the tax rates on consumption and saving. With only one tax rate, implying a second-best solution, the equilibrium discount rate to be used to evaluate public projects is the implied social discount rate which is likely to differ from the rate on private projects. When separate tax rates on consumption and on saving are allowed, thus providing one additional instrument, the three rates are again equated at equilibrium: the consumption tax insures the appropriate level of investment and the savings tax insures the appropriate allocation between the private and public sectors. And when government borrowing is permitted along with taxes, "the rates of return in the private and public sector should be equated at every instant of time but the government through its borrowing and tax policies should aim at deriving the common rate of return towards the natural rate of interest".[2]

Rather than comment in any detail on Professor Arrow's paper, I should like to focus the remainder of my remarks on four points.

First, it is evident that Professor Arrow's paper greatly illuminates the difficult conceptual questions at issue and places the whole discussion of the discount rate in a much broader perspective within the framework of capital and growth theory. Thus, even if it should turn out that the empirical potential of this approach is limited, work along this line is very valuable in improving our understanding of this difficult and controversial issue and in shedding light on the weaknesses and strengths of empirical estimates, however these may be derived. Nevertheless, there is the question whether this approach is operational in the sense of pointing the way to eventually deriving more meaningful estimates of the discount rate than is now feasible, even though estimates based on this approach have so

---

2. K. J. Arrow, "Discounting and Public Investment Criteria," in *Water Resources Development*, ed. A. V. Kneese and S. C. Smith (Baltimore: Johns Hopkins Press, 1966), p. 16 (cited in Arrow's paper).

far not been provided. One can only speculate on the answer to such a question, but one can hardly be optimistic about the empirical potential of the approach given the difficulties of specifying the criterion function and other features of the model. Nor do I believe that this approach is more likely to lead to greater agreement among economists on what the social discount rate is than present methods based on market rates of interest.[3]

Secondly, whatever its long-run potential, as a practical matter of deriving a discount rate for use in current work on project assessment I question whether an approach along the lines suggested by Professor Arrow may not be overly ambitious and whether it might not lead to the pursuit of substantial but largely unattainable gains in public policy at the expense of more modest but largely attainable gains. The main reason I say this is because for the present Professor Arrow's approach may be unrealistic in trying to resolve too many issues simultaneously and in a general equilibrium context. This implies knowing not only a great deal about the structure of the economy but also about the range of constraints applicable to policy. Moreover, in pursuing this approach, I suspect one would find that the problems would snowball in size and complexity as one confronted questions of not only the optimum level of investment but also of the optimum mix of targets and policies, and so forth. This may, of course, be the wave of the future so that, following in Professor Arrow's footsteps, economists in time will be able to resolve a wide range of these questions simultaneously and consistently. For the present, however, given the embryonic state of cost-benefit analysis in most countries and the wide range of considerations that impinge in a very complicated way on the broad question of the total level of savings, I should opt for the simple rule that the rate of return on public projects should equal the marginal rate of return calculated à la Harberger. I think this approach may largely meet one of Professor Arrow's criteria but it would not necessarily meet his second which is concerned with the total level of investment.

Thirdly, there is the question of the reliability of market interest rates as a guide to the marginal rate of return on investment in the private sector. Simply observing that there are a host of imperfections does not by itself

---

3. In his earlier paper Professor Arrow remarked that while some interest rates are "market prices in a reasonably strict sense, others have to be imputed, sometimes by methods of such subtlety that experts find themselves in sharp disagreement" (*ibid.*, p. 14).

lead to the conclusion that market rates, adjusted for such imperfections as one can identify, lead to a worse approximation of the marginal rate of return in the private sector than some direct method of estimation. And indeed there is always the hope that the two approaches may result in more or less the same answer, or at least answers that leave a fairly narrow range of uncertainty. Let me illustrate my point with some very crude empiricism. Assuming a Cobb-Douglas aggregate production function and that labour and capital are paid according to their marginal productivity, one can derive a direct estimate of the marginal productivity of capital if one knows the output/capital ratio and labour's share of national income and if one is prepared to accept that these ratios remain fairly constant over time.[4] Labour's share in Canada in the mid-1950's typically was about 65 per cent of national income and our best estimate of the output/capital ratio is about .32 for 1955.[5] This implies that the marginal productivity of capital is about 11 per cent. Corporate tax rates were about 50 per cent and the average rate on corporate borrowing was probably on the order of about 5 per cent in 1955. This suggests a pre-tax rate of return in the corporate sector of about 10 per cent. One could, of course, make many additional adjustments to allow, for example, for the pre-tax rate of return in the unincorporated business sector, in the housing sector and on personal savings. However, the point of these rough and ready calculations is only to illustrate that these two types of estimates are not wildly different and that both approaches indicate a rate of return that is substantially above the government bond rate.

Finally, almost everyone writing on this subject assumes a closed economy even though every country is either a net international borrower or lender. This means that the supply of domestic saving can be augmented or reduced at a price. Presumably as foreign borrowing increases the price of borrowing increases and as foreign lending increases the return on foreign lending decreases; and vice versa. Also, we know that the elasticity of international capital flows with respect to interest rates is very high

4. $O = aL^{\alpha} K^{1-\alpha}$ where O represents national output, L labour employed, K the stock of capital, and α labour's share of output.
$$\frac{\partial O}{\partial K} = (1 - \alpha) aL^{\alpha} K^{-\alpha} = (1 - \alpha) \frac{O}{K}$$

5. Anthony Scott, "Canada's Reproducible Wealth," in *The Measurement of National Wealth,* Income and Wealth Series VIII, ed. Raymond Goldsmith and Christopher Saunders (London: Bowes and Bowes, 1959), p. 215. This figure is based on a definition of capital that includes structures, equipment, livestock and inventories.

for many countries. I'm not sure how Professor Arrow's analysis works out formally if one adds this dimension. I suspect that optimality might require equating the rate of return in both the private and the public sector with the consumption rate of interest which, in turn, is equated with the rate at which international capital can be borrowed and lent, assuming we are maximizing welfare for one country only and that the *general* level of external interest rates is predetermined. This leads to the further question of what if any adjustments should be made on the interest rates at which a country borrows and lends internationally to arrive at the *marginal* real cost of increased borrowing or reduced lending abroad.

It is evident that the inclusion of the international sector can make a major difference in countries that engage in foreign borrowing or lending. For example, there is some evidence to suggest that during the period from 1952 to 1961 a $100 increase in borrowing by the Canadian government at the margin led to an increase of $75 in Canadian foreign borrowing[6] (abstracting from exchange rate adjustments and their consequences). And while this factor is likely to be less important for a country like the U.S., even here it may be fairly significant at the margin.

Inclusion of this consideration suggests a number of questions that are not normally covered in the cost-benefit literature. For instance, if one found a disparity between the cost of borrowing abroad and the rate of return in the private sector, presumably the government might evaluate its projects at the marginal real cost of foreign borrowing, thereby stimulating domestic capital formation and savings and eventually driving down the rate of return in the private sector to the point where all rates are equated. This is somewhat analagous to Professor Arrow's case with two tax rates. Better still, the government might borrow abroad and provide the funds to both the private and public sectors in accordance with the highest rate of return available in either to the point where the rate in both sectors has been driven down to the marginal real cost of borrowing abroad.

Within the Harberger framework one would wish to include foreign borrowing or lending as one of the areas from which resources are drawn when a project is undertaken. Thus, one would appraise the marginal real cost of foreign funds and average this cost in with the cost of other sources of funds, using appropriate weights to reflect the relative importance of external funds as well as funds drawn from various domestic sectors. These weights would differ depending on whether the project was financed by borrowing or taxing and might also differ depending upon the particular kind of taxes or borrowing employed to finance the project.

6. These figures are derived in a forthcoming volume by Richard E. Caves and Grant L. Reuber, with R. W. Baguley, J. M. Curtis, and R. Lubitz, *Capital Transfers and Economic Policy: Canada, 1951-1962,* chap. 8.

Part II

*Application of Cost-Benefit
Analysis to Manpower
Programs*

BENEFIT-COST ANALYSES OF OCCUPATIONAL TRAINING PROGRAMS: A COMPARISON OF RECENT STUDIES

EINAR HARDIN
Michigan State University

R ETRAINING courses for adult experienced workers have now been arranged by government agencies in the United States for about a decade, and research workers as well as private foundations and government agencies have early seen them as worthy objects of the developing art of benefit-cost analysis. After the long delay charactertstic of field survey work, several serious studies of the strictly economic benefits and costs of retraining have now been completed. Some of these studies are collected in a volume edited by Somers,[1] but others are scattered in journal articles and reports. In this paper I attempt to compare concepts, methods, and findings of these analyses.

Studies Covered by the Comparison

All studies covered by my comparison have their focus on occupationally oriented, institutional training of adult workers, usually but not exclusively unemployed or underemployed. West Virginia retraining courses sponsored by the state government or by the Area Redevelopment Administration (ARA) have been studied in a major project under the general direction of Somers, and reports containing results about economic benefits and costs have been published by Gibbard and Somers,[2] Cain and Stroms-

---

1. Gerald G. Somers, ed., *Retraining the Unemployed* (Madison: University of Wisconsin Press, 1968).

2. Harold A. Gibbard and Gerald G. Somers, "Government Retraining of the Unemployed in West Virginia," in *Retraining the Unemployed, ibid.*, chap. 2, pp. 17-124.

dorfer,[3] and Stromsdorfer.[4] Solie has published a report on ARA retraining in Tennessee[5] as part of the Somers project. Borus has analyzed state-sponsored and ARA retraining in Connecticut.[6] Page and Gooding have studied state-sponsored retraining in Massachusetts.[7] Hardin and Borus have evaluated ARA and Manpower Development and Training Act (MDTA) retraining in Michigan.[8] Finally, Main in cooperation with the National Opinion Research Corporation has made a nationwide study of MDTA retraining.[9] My analysis will give special attention to those studies which result in complete benefit-cost ratios and will slight the analyses which deal largely with other important economic aspects of the retraining process.[10]

3. Glen G. Cain and Ernst W. Stromsdorfer, "An Economic Evaluation of Government Retraining Programs in West Virginia," in *Retraining the Unemployed, ibid.,* chap. 9, pp. 299-335.

4. Ernst W. Stromsdorfer, "Determinants of Economic Success in Retraining the Unemployed," *Journal of Human Resources* 3 (Spring 1968): 139-158.

5. Richard J. Solie, "Employment Effects of Retraining the Unemployed," *Industrial and Labor Relations Review* 21 (January 1968): 210-225.

———, "An Evaluation of the Effects of Retraining in Tennessee," in *Retraining the Unemployed, op. cit.,* chap. 6, pp. 193-211.

6. Michael E. Borus, "A Benefit-Cost Analysis of the Economic Effectiveness of Retraining the Unemployed," *Yale Economic Essays* 4 (Fall 1964): 371-429.

———, *The Economic Effectiveness of Retraining the Unemployed,* Federal Reserve Bank, Research Report No. 35 (Boston, 1966).

———, "The Effects of Retraining the Unemployed in Connecticut," in *Retraining the Unemployed, op. cit.,* chap. 3, pp. 125-148.

———, "Time Trends in the Benefits from Retraining in Connecticut," *Proceedings of the Twentieth Annual Winter Meeting* (Madison: Industrial Relations Research Association, 1968), pp. 36-46.

7. E. C. Gooding, *The Massachusetts Retraining Program, Statistical Supplement* (Boston: Federal Reserve Bank, 1962).

David A. Page, "Retraining under the Manpower Development Act: A Cost-Benefit Analysis," in *Public Policy,* vol. 13, ed. John D. Montgomery and Arthur Smithies (Cambridge: Graduate School of Public Administration, Harvard University, 1964), pp. 257-276.

"Retraining the Unemployed: Part III, Retraining — A Good Investment," *New England Business Review,* April 1963, pp. 1-4.

8. Einar Hardin and Michael E. Borus, "An Economic Evaluation of the Retraining Program in Michigan: Methodological Problems of Research," *Proceedings of the 1966 Social Statistics Section Meetings* (Washington: American Statistical Association, 1966), pp. 133-137.

———, *Economic Benefits and Costs of Retraining Courses in Michigan,* Final Report, Contract MDTA 9-63 (Washington: Department of Labor, forthcoming).

9. Earl D. Main, "A Nationwide Evaluation of M.D.T.A. Institutional Job Training," *Journal of Human Resources* 3 (Spring 1968): 159-170.

10. Being one of the authors of research on retraining, yet including my own work in the reports to be reviewed, I may be guilty of biases in assessment. However, I am hopeful, and indeed, confident, that discussants and conference members will eagerly and perceptively point out these and other errors of my ways.

CONCEPTS AND METHODS

Benefit-cost analysis of occupational training may in principle be undertaken from at least three points of view: society as a whole, the individual trainee, and the government as an organization. I shall consider in turn the concepts used in relation to each of these points of view, starting with that of society.

Concepts of Social Economic Benefits and Costs

Page defines the economic benefits for society as the sum of the growth in trainee earnings and the decline in trainee transfer payments which occur after the course and are attributable to it. The economic costs of society consist of the sum of the rental of private instructional facilities, the operating costs of instruction in public facilities, and the excess of subsistence allowances received by trainees over the unemployment benefits they will receive during the class, if they do not enroll. Travel costs and the cost of capital in public instructional facilities are believed to be zero, and the administrative costs are assumed to be zero because data are lacking.

Cain and Stromsdorfer define the benefits as the increase in trainee earnings resulting from training. The costs of training consist of the sum of trainee earnings forgone during the class, the direct instructional costs, and the increase in transfer payments to trainees during the class. Overhead and fixed costs are disregarded. In the closely related study by *Stromsdorfer,* the same concepts of benefits and costs are employed.

Borus defines the benefits as the aggregate increase in earnings in society, including an allowance for multiplier effects, which results from training. The costs of training consist of the transportation expenses of the trainees and the output lost by society in other activities because instructional and administrative resources are transferred into training. (Forgone trainee earnings are not included among social costs, since it is assumed that society loses no output from having persons in training. No multiplier adjustment is applied to the total costs or the cost components.)

Hardin and Borus define the benefits from training as the increase in trainee earnings occurring after the course and in result of it. The costs of training consist of the earnings forgone and expenses incurred by trainees during the course, the instructional costs, and the administrative costs. A common idea in these concepts appears to be that a person's earnings measure his contribution to production and that the impact of training upon national product can, therefore, be inferred from the impact of training upon earnings. However, the concepts used by Page and by Cain and Stromsdorfer go beyond this idea, since they take account of social payments being made to individual trainees and non-trainees instead of employers. These payments do not distort the relationship between earnings and contribution to production, and allowance for them must be justified on the premise that society is indifferent between an additional dollar of output and a dollar less of social payments, a premise for which the authors offer no supporting evidence.

The implied connection between earnings and output is loosened by at least two factors. First, according to the marginal productivity theory, the appropriate concept of wages is that of employee compensation, including fringe benefits, and employee compensation necessarily exceeds direct earnings. Furthermore, even employee compensation fails to reflect adequately any external economic effects which may exist. Thus, even if training enables society to save on resources used in offsetting adverse effects of unemployment and low earnings on physical and mental health of the family, on deliquency, and on social organization, this saving of resources cannot be expected to emerge as an increase in employee compensation attributable to training. All the studies under review disregard these two factors.

Second, the connection between production and trainee earnings is loosened even more, if one chooses, as does Borus, to take account of so-called vacuum and displacement effects and to allow for multiplier effects. In his Connecticut study, Borus distinguishes between the total gain of society and the gain registered by the trainees. He believes that some trainees who obtain training-related employment fill vacancies which will otherwise remain unfilled, and that jobs which trainees hold before the course or will hold during the course if they do not enroll are easily filled by the unemployed. In consequence, society should not count any forgone earnings of trainees during the course, but it must count as gains the entire earnings which trainees obtain after the course in training-related employment. Finally, those trainees who do not hold training-related employment are assumed not to give rise to any gains from the point of view of society, since they merely hold jobs that persons not trained will otherwise hold instead of being unemployed. In brief, and using terminology discussed elsewhere, one may say that Borus assumes that placement of trainees in training-related jobs causes a pure vacuum effect and that all other effects observable in comparisons of trainees and non-trainees are pure displacement effects. The Hardin and Borus study of Michigan and the other studies, in contrast, disregard vacuum, displacement, and multiplier effects.

The difference in concepts may be traced, at least in part, to an ambiguity in defining the impact of training upon national product: do we wish to measure the impact on actual production or on productive capacity? If the actual-output orientation is chosen, one must consider such things as vacuum and displacement effects, allow for multiplier effects of all exogenous increases in spending, whether on the cost side or the benefit side, and in general trace out the entire expansion or contraction process. Borus' concepts seem to aim in this direction without allowing for the full consequences.

If the productive-capacity orientation is chosen, different concepts follow. No allowance should be made for multiplier effects, and the full amount of earnings forgone by trainees during the course, reflecting the temporary reduction in productive capacity associated with putting people into training, should be included among the social costs of training, even if one believes that the jobs forgone by trainees are easily filled by the unemployed.

Whether the economic benefits, under the capacity interpretation, are represented by the impact of training upon trainee earnings depends on the relationship between earnings and marginal value product. When serious manpower shortages exist, there is no necessary equalization of earnings with marginal value product, and the impact of training upon trainee earnings understates the impact of training on national product. Thus, the Hardin and Borus concepts as well as those used by several other authors may be interpreted as having a productive-capacity orientation without necessarily allowing fully for the capacity effects of training.

Society probably places a greater value on an actual increase in output than on an option to increase output by the same amount. The actual-output interpretation should perhaps be preferred, therefore, to the productive-capacity interpretation. However, the former interpretation raises two major practical problems. First, it is very difficult, in the present stage of our knowledge, to estimate the magnitude, or even determine the existence of, any direct displacement and vacuum effects, and the indirect effects on the economy are even more diffuse. In my opinion, the task of estimation currently requires the analyst to make very subjective and arbitrary assumptions. Second, when the state of economic activity changes, the relative importance of displacement and vacuum effects is likely to shift, and the assumptions of the analyst become obsolete. Therefore, if the actual-output interpretation is chosen, the analyst should make a clear distinction in his reporting between hard information and soft assumptions and generally make it as easy as possible for users of the analysis to apply the assumptions which seem warranted to them in the framework of a particular decision situation.

Concepts of Private Economic Benefits and Costs

Analyses from the point of view of the individual trainee have been presented by Cain and Stromsdorfer, Borus, and Hardin and Borus. Several other authors have published analyses of the impact of training upon component variables. Thus, Gibbard and Somers, Stromsdorfer, and Main have estimated the impact of training on employment and earnings, and Solie has estimated the impact of training upon employment and unemployment. (In addition, several authors have analyzed the relationship between training and labor force status.)

Cain and *Stromsdorfer* define the private benefits as the effect of training on the after-tax earnings of trainees, plus the earnings imputed for the time the trainees are voluntarily out of the labor force, less the reduction in transfer payments to the trainees. The private cost of training appears to be defined analogously.

Borus defines the benefits as the gain in after-tax earnings, less the reduction in social payments.[11] The cost of training consists of the loss in after-tax earnings (if any), minus the increase in social payments during the class, plus trainee expenses.

Hardin and *Borus* define benefits and costs in terms of changes in disposable income as a result of training. Disposable income is calculated as gross earnings, less federal income taxes and employee contributions to

---

11. These social payments include "unemployment compensation, special veterans benefits, food stamps, aid to dependent children, and relief" (Borus, "A Benefit-Cost Analysis . . .," *op. cit.,* p. 385).

social security, plus transfer payments (unemployment benefits, welfare payments, and trainee allowances), and less trainee expenses for training.

The difference in treatment of effects on voluntary leisure is clearly one of objectives. Apparently, Cain and Stromsdorfer attempt to estimate the impact of training upon the "welfare" of the trainee, while Hardin and Borus focus on the effects upon disposable income.

If training enables a person to earn additional income so that he can afford to be out of the labor force for a longer period of time, this is a gain which is not reflected in the change in disposable income. In estimating this gain, however, one should perhaps also consider the possible effects of retraining upon the length of the workweek. Furthermore, the valuation of voluntary leisure raises empirical, if not conceptual problems, which suggests that the effect of training on voluntary leisure should be shown separately from the impact on disposable income.

Concepts of Government Economic Benefits and Costs

Analyses from the point of view of the government have been presented by Borus and by Hardin and Borus. (Estimates of some components of benefits and costs have been prepared by various authors, including Gibbard and Somers, Page, and Cain and Stromsdorfer.)

Borus defines the benefits as the sum of the increase in aggregate tax collections and decline in social payments occurring after training and as a result of it. Consistently with the actual-output principle and with the assumption of vacuum and displacement effects, he applies the marginal tax rate to the earnings gain including the vacuum effect and adjusted for the multiplier effect. To this he adds the decline in social payments for the trainees. However, consistency requires that account also be taken of the reduction in social payments for those persons who, according to the vacuum hypothesis, move from unemployment into the jobs which the trainees leave when filling the vacuum.

Hardin and Borus define the benefits and costs in terms of the impact on the funds of the government. The benefits consist of the increase in government tax collections (federal income tax, employer and employee contributions to social security, and state sales tax) from trainees and the reduction in the sum of unemployment benefits and welfare payments to trainees in consequence of training. The costs consist of the government outlays on instruction, the government administrative cost, the reduction in government tax collections from trainees during the class, and the net increase in transfer payments (training allowances, unemployment benefits, and welfare payments) to trainees during the class. These definitions are formally consistent with the capacity orientation used in measuring the output effects of training, an orientation which in the context of government effects is intuitively less meaningful than an actual-effects orientation. However, they are also consistent with a transfer-of-funds orientation: they lead to estimates of the net transfer of funds between the trainees and the government which are caused by training. Thus, they may be seen as an aspect of redistribution between trainees and the rest of society.

Control Groups

Many estimates of components of the effects of training are based on comparisons between "experimental groups" of persons who are trained and "control groups" of persons who are not trained. The authors follow different approaches in defining the two groups.

Page and *Gooding* compare persons who enroll in a set of training courses with persons who file regular claims for unemployment compensation in the years when the courses are conducted and who reportedly are similar to the first group in demographic characteristics.

The studies based on the West Virginia project cover persons who: (1) complete a training course, (2) enroll but leave the course before its end, (3) qualify for enrollment and are invited but do not enroll, (4) are reviewed for possible enrollment but are not called, and (5) are so-called non-applicants. The last group is selected from the persons in the "active" and "inactive" job application files of the state employment service in the counties where the courses are conducted, and it is confined to individuals who are unemployed when the courses are organized and who are not applicants for retraining.

Gibbard and Somers calculate the impact of training mainly from comparisons between the first group, which we may call graduates, and the last group, the non-applicants, and *Cain and Stromsdorfer* rely exclusively on comparisons between these two groups. In his own article, *Stromsdorfer* presents two analyses, one based on the full five-category classification and one based on a comparison of graduates and non-applicants.

The Tennessee study by *Solie,* covers essentially the same categories of persons as the West Virginia study, and the effects of training are calculated from comparisons between graduates and non-applicants.

Main includes in his trainee group all persons who enroll in training and uses a "snowball process" to identify for each trainee a control-group person who is unemployed about the time the course starts and who is a friend, neighbor, or relative of the trainee.

Borus defines six categories of persons in his study of Connecticut retraining. These consist of workers who: (1) utilize retraining, (2) complete but do not utilize retraining, (3) withdraw from retraining for employment reasons, (4) withdraw from retraining without employment, (5) refuse retraining for employment reasons, and (6) refuse retraining without employment. Because of the assumption of a pure vacuum effect, he uses no control group comparisons to calculate the impact of training upon output and taxable earnings; instead, he takes the annual earnings per person in category (1), "workers who utilized training," and adjusts this amount ($4,359) for the probability of a trainee landing in such an occupation and staying in it. In making the estimate of the private benefits from training, he compares the "workers who utilized retraining" primarily with those who complete training without utilizing it but also with those who drop out without having employment or who refuse training without having employment.[12]

Hardin and Borus count as trainees all persons who enroll in selected training courses, whether or not they graduate, and they include in their control groups all persons who seek to enroll in the same set of courses and who qualify for enrollment in them but who for a variety of reasons do not enroll in training at all. The training effects are calculated from comparisons between enrollees and non-enrollees.

This variability in the use of comparison groups affects the comparability of the estimates of training effects which are offered by the various studies. It does not arise merely from differences in the treatment of vacuum and displacement effects, for Borus finds that the private economic benefits, before adjusting for the probability of use of training, range from $424 to $1,176 per calendar year depending on which of his three control groups one utilizes. Therefore, it is urgent to learn how various control

12. An adjustment is also made in the private benefits for the probability of a trainee using his skills in each of a series of years after the course.

groups meet the requirement of comparability and, subsequently, to agree upon common standards of control groups in future studies. In the hope of furthering a discussion of this matter I offer some comments on criteria for the choice of comparison groups.

First, difficult data problems arise, if one decides to regard as the experimental group those trainees who satisfy the twin conditions of (1) landing a job because of having taken the retraining course and (2) using the skills from the course on that job, conditions specified by Borus. Whose report is to be used to determine whether these conditions are met, what must be the amount of influence or extent of use required to classify a person in this category, and what influence do work experience and attitudes toward training play in the answers given to interview questions on this point? Similar problems arise in attempts to classify persons according to reasons for dropping out of the course or for not enrolling in it.

Second, the treatment which is given in the training program consists in arranging courses and in putting persons into these courses and exposing them to training. Thus, in principle, the experimental group should consist of those who become enrolled in training, including both dropouts and graduates. Comparisons between graduates and non-trainees distort the estimates of the earnings benefits from training and the loss of earnings during the course, unless the dropouts neither gain, nor lose from enrolling in a course. Actually, it is virtually certain that some dropouts lose earnings, while they are still in the course, and it is possible that many dropouts learn some new skills while enrolled or become demoralized by their classroom failures, with effects on their subsequent earnings.

Third, courses for different occupations draw on different subgroups of the population. Therefore, since the control groups should consist of persons who are as similar as possible to the trainees in terms of personal characteristics existing before the start of training, it seems desirable to use control groups composed of persons who are available and qualified for training for the same occupation as the trainee but who do not enroll. The use of a random sample of the members in the active and inactive files of the Public Employment Service in areas where courses are arranged tends to match the labor market settings of trainees and control groups, but it does not match the personal characteristics of the two groups. A heavy and perhaps impossible burden is then placed on the use of statistical analysis to hold constant a variety of personal characteristics,

Fourth, the use of qualified applicant non-enrollees as control groups also raises problems. In particular, some applicants may withdraw their applications or fail to report, because they find employment. If the period of observation after training is short or if the employment these persons obtain is lasting, comparisons of trainees with a control group of applicants who do not enroll may yield distorted results. Statistical control may help reduce these distortions, but we do not know that it will entirely eliminate them. However, a qualified applicant may become a non-enrollee for several reasons which may be random relative to his labor market opportunities, his ability to learn from training, and his motivation to work. In this regard, defending the kinds of control groups used in the Hardin and Borus study of Michigan, I derive comfort from the erratic judgment by the local employment service screening the applicants, failure of notices of enrollment to reach the applicants, temporary illness preventing enrollment in the course, and haphazard ineligibility for training allowances.

Estimating the Differential Effects of Training

The relation between economic benefits and costs is not necessarily the same for all kinds of courses, occupations, and labor markets, nor is it necessarily the same for all kinds of trainees. Estimates of the economic benefits and costs may be particularly valuable, if they are allowed to vary with course, occupation, labor market, and personal characteristics.

Page, Solie, and *Main* present only overall estimates. *Gibbard and Somers* calculate earnings after the end of training, classified according to age, education, and sex of trainees, but do not calculate benefit-cost ratios. *Cain and Stromsdorfer* as well as *Stromsdorfer* present separate benefit-cost estimates for men and women, and the former study also shows earnings and transfer payment effects according to sex, age, and education. When regression equations are used, these authors include the training status variables only as main effects, leaving out the interaction terms which alone can enable them to estimate differential effects in a single equation.[13]

Borus reports benefit-cost ratios for different categories of persons. However, in his underlying regression analysis, there is no allowance for

---

13. Stromsdorfer and Main present some analyses based on trainees alone and use course characteristics as independent variables. Since no comparisons are made with non-trainees, the variability attributed to course characteristics may represent differences in prior earnings among persons who enroll in courses of different kinds and cannot safely be interpreted as effects of training.

differential effects on earnings, and the variations in benefit-cost ratios result primarily from varying assumptions concerning the probability of a person utilizing his training.

Hardin and Borus seek to determine whether and how much the effects of training vary with course, occupation, labor market, and trainee characteristics. The differences in effects of training are derived from regression equations in which training status enters not only as a main effect but also in interaction with various other factors. Benefit-cost results are presented according to length of training, type of occupation, and personal characteristics of trainees.

Observation Period and Time Trends

Information about the experiences of trainees and non-trainees for a period of time after the end of the course is clearly required. This period should be defined alike for trainees and non-trainees belonging to a single course, a condition violated in Main's study, and it should be long enough to permit permanent effects to become visible.

Gibbard and Somers use an after-training period of 6, 12, or 18 months, depending on the analysis. *Cain and Stromsdorfer* base their analysis on data for an 18 month period, a fixed calendar quarter, and the whole after-training period for which data are available, ranging from 18 to 27 months. *Borus* bases his analysis of the earnings effects of Connecticut retraining upon four fixed calendar quarters. *Hardin and Borus* define the after-training period as the 365 days following the end of the class.

In principle, these follow-up periods are too brief, since it is theoretically possible that the effects of training either vanish soon afterwards or grow over the years. Some evidence on this matter is presented by Borus, who has followed up his Connecticut study by obtaining social security data on earnings for the years 1962-66. From his analysis[14] he concludes, "This indicates that the benefits from retraining are not only of a short term nature, but continue to accrue for at least five years after the end of the courses. . . . The average earnings gain from training increased at an annual rate of approximately six per cent during the five years following the training course."

14. Michael E. Borus, "Time Trends in the Benefits from Retraining in Connecticut," *op. cit.*

Statistical Methods and Data

The studies need also be reviewed with respect to the sampling of courses and persons, the quality of the data used, and the methods of statistical analysis employed.

Sampling Methods. Main's sample of MDTA trainees is obtained by probability sampling from each of 49 N.O.R.C. sampling areas, while his "partially matched" sample of non-trainees selected according to the "snowball technique" may be regarded as a quota sample. The West Virginia and Tennessee projects first select a sample of courses on a judgment basis with heterogeneity desired, and all graduates in the selected courses are eligible for interviewing. The non-applicants are drawn by taking every tenth job application (excluding ineligible applicants) from the files of the Employment Service. Borus selects the Connecticut courses on a judgment basis and attempts to interview all persons who are eligible to enroll in these courses. Hardin and Borus first select a sample of 49 training classes on a judgment basis designed to ensure the inclusion of a wide range of course, labor market, and personal characteristics. All persons enrolling in the selected courses and all persons identified as qualified and interested but not actually enrolled are eligible to be interviewed in most of the field work; under the pressure of the high cost and time of interviewing, however, the authors later shift to the principle of drawing a random sample of the enrollees (without regard to course completion) and a random sample of non-trainees from each of the classes remaining to be interviewed. The Page-Gooding study is based on the mailing of questionnaires to all enrollees in courses conducted during a given period of time and to a sample of unemployment claimants reportedly similar in personal characteristics to the enrollees.

It is evident that the sampling methods in these studies of retraining, with the possible exception of the Main study, are not beyond reproach. The principle of random sampling is used only in parts of the project and, except for Main, is not used in the key task of selecting the courses. Serious thought should be given in the future to the use of simple or stratified random sampling of courses or trainees, even though improved sampling will probably raise the cost of data collection.

Response Rates. Locating the persons who have been identified as trainees and non-trainees is one of the most difficult tasks of the survey work, since addresses available in source documents are frequently obsolete. Lack of success in this task accounts for most of the discrepancy between intended and actual sample size, refusals to be interviewed being relatively infrequent. An overall loss rate of 21 per cent is reported by Main and a 20 per cent rate by Hardin and Borus. Further reductions in sample size occur when the informaton obtained is defective or when the interview results indicate the person is misclassified on the source documents and is not eligible for inclusion.

While the rate of non-response and the degree of unusable information can always distort the results, the risk of distortion does not, in general, seem more serious in these studies than in most acceptable surveys. However, it should be noted that the Page-Gooding calculations of the earnings effects of training are based on data for 78 trainees and for 104 non-trainees, although 585 questionnaires appear to have been returned by the trainees and an approximately equal number of the non-trainees, and although the results are interpreted as applicable to 907 trainees. One may legitimately wonder how much and in which direction this loss rate has affected the averages crucial to the Page analysis.

Data Quality. One of the major tasks of the interview work is to obtain continuous data covering a period of years and useful in calculating the total earnings, unemployment benefits, etc., for defined periods before, during, and after the class. This task is much more difficult than that of ascertaining the respondent's personal characteristics and his status as of the time of the survey. A detailed schedule which systematically maps the respondent's circumstances over the entire period is used in most of these studies. The resulting information requires a great deal of editing, such as checking for completeness, consistency, and plausibility. The studies by Main and Gooding-Page have tried to bypass this task by asking a few rudimentary questions as a basis for the analysis. Thus, in the Massachusetts mail questionnaire, the respondent is asked to state his weekly wage at the time of the interview and his number of weeks of work since the course, and the analyst estimates the respondent's total earnings for the year as the product of the two answers, adjusted to an annual basis. However, inspection of the work histories of trainees and non-trainees in the Michigan sample indicates a great amount of change in employment, hours of work, and rates of pay. Thus, earnings averages estimated from rudimentary, point-of-time questions are likely to have only a loose relationship to the true averages for the full period, and they may be almost useless in elaborate statistical analyses in which the individual person is the unit of observation.

Some studies are based, at least in part, on earnings and transfer payment data collected from government agencies. Thus, Borus has used state files of reports on quarterly earnings from covered workers, and Hardin and Borus have used state government records on unemployment benefits, welfare payments, and training allowances. Nevertheless, direct interviews or mail questionnaire surveys have remained necessary, since many required data have not been available in any other way.

Statistical Analysis. Two basic approaches are available for measurement of the effects of training: cross-tabulations in which training status (enrollee-non-enrollee, etc.) is a basis of classification and multivariate regression analysis in which training status is one of the independent variables. The studies under review vary widely in the relative use made of these two approaches. At one end, Cain and Stromsdorfer rely exclusively on cross-tabulations in their joint study and remark that "the lack of refinement in the methods used in this paper is not serious." At the other end, Hardin and Borus use multiple regression analysis for all estimates except the administrative costs, and their equations allow for differential effects of training by containing terms for interaction with training status.

Cross-tabulation and multivariate regression analysis have their own advantages. The former is conceptually simple, requires little calculation, does not presuppose a particular mathematical form of the relationship, and may be preferable, when there are enough observations to permit the analyst to hold constant whatever needs to be held constant. Multivariate regression analysis is more economical with observations in case of continuous independent variables and may be the only feasible approach in detailed studies of differential effects of training, unless very large numbers of observations are available.

The two methods have some problems in common, although the problems are more obvious in the regression approach. First, they share the problem of unequal disturbance variance. Second, when two or more dependent variables are analyzed, they share the problem of interdependence in the causation of the dependent variables. Third, they share the problem of limitations on the dependent variable. More attention should perhaps be given to the ensuing statistical difficulties than has been done so far.

FINDINGS

Five of the studies reviewed in this paper contain comparisons between benefits and costs. I shall summarize and attempt to reconcile these benefit-cost results and disregard the findings on various components of benefits or costs.

Social Economic Benefits and Costs

Cain and Stromsdorfer calculate that training causes an earnings gain of graduates over non-applicants by $1,008 for the average man, $192 for the average woman, and $736 per average graduate in the first year after the the class and somewhat lower figures in the second year after training. The social costs per trainee are estimated to be $918 for a man, $527 for a woman, and $787 for the average graduate. Given their assumptions of service life until retirement or until an extrapolation of the change from the first to the second year reduces the measured gain to zero, they report net expected capital values which correspond to benefit-cost ratios of 10.5, 2.7, and 9.3, respectively, at a 10 per cent discount rate.

Using essentially the same data but a different method of analysis, *Stromsdorfer* calculates annual economic benefits of $828 for men and $336 for women and assumes these to remain constant for their entire service life. Accepting the cost estimates of Cain and Stromsdorfer, he calculates rates of return of 90 per cent for men and 64 per cent for women but presents no benefit-cost ratios. However, his results appear to imply benefit-cost ratios of 17 for men and 11 for women, when a discount rate of 4 per cent is used, and ratios of about 13 for men and 9 for women, when a 6 per cent discount rate is applied.

Page presents results which imply a benefit-cost ratio of about 6.2 for training of 907 persons in Massachusetts, given a 10 per cent discount rate and a 35 year service life.

Borus calculates benefit-cost ratios for Connecticut training ranging from 73.3 to 137.3 depending on assumptions concerning the use of skills learned in the course. A 5 per cent discount rate and a 10 year service life, adjusted for out-migration from the training-related occupation, are assumed.

Hardin and Borus calculate a benefit-cost ratio of 1.2 for Michigan training, assuming a 10 year service life and a 10 per cent discount rate. Training in courses for 60-200 hours per enrollee has a benefit-cost ratio of 17.3, while training courses for 201-1,920 hours has zero or negative ratios, resulting from an absence of earnings gains from training in combination with a high cost of training. A ratio of 1.5 is obtained when the full sample is reweighted in accordance with the estimated composition of Michigan training according to course duration.

Attempted Reconciliation. I have tried to put the results of these studies on a comparable basis by making three assumptions: (1) the annual benefits in the first year after training remain unchanged for a total of

TABLE 1

Economic Benefits and Costs for Society
Attempted Reconciliation of Results[a]

Author and Group	Annual Benefits per Trainee	Initial Cost per Trainee	Annual Benefits in % of Cost	Benefits / Costs
Cain and Stromsdorfer				
Men	$1,008	$ 918	108.8	6.7
Women	192	527	36.4	2.2
Both Sexes	736	787	93.5	5.7
Stromsdorfer				
Men	828	918	90.2	5.5
Women	336	527	63.8	3.9
Hardin and Borus				
60-200 hours	976	346	282.1	17.3
201-1,920 hours	-57	1,665	-3.4	(-0.2)
All Course Lengths	251	1,272	19.7	1.2
Reweighted[b]	316	1,289	24.5	1.5
Borus				
Alternative I	335	(346)	(96.8)	(5.9)
Alternative II	818	(346)	(236.4)	(14.5)
Page	446	698	63.9	3.9

a Based on a discount rate of 10 per cent and a 10 year service life.
b Weights based on the estimated distribution of Michigan trainees according to course length (60-200, 201-600, 601-1,200, and 1,201-1,920 hours).

10 years and then become zero; (2) the appropriate social discount rate is 10 per cent; and (3) the estimate of social gains is based on the difference in earnings between trainees and non-trainees, disregarding vacuum, displacement, and mutiplier effects.

Two alternative sets of assumptions are used in my attempt to make the Borus results comparable with the other studies. In alternative I, it is assumed that trainees who "utilize their training" gain $500 from taking training, trainees who do not utilize their training gain nothing, and the probability of a trainee using his training is 0.67. The annual benefits to society per trainee will then be $335. In alternative II, it is assumed that an enrollee has a 0.67 chance of using his training, only graduates use their training, the dropout rate is 10 per cent, and the earnings data in Borus' Table 2 relating to dropouts and non-trainees are applicable to all dropouts and non-trainees. The social cost of training is probably higher than the $218 reported by Borus under the displacement effect assumption and is here assumed to equal the Hardin and Borus figure of $346 for short classes.

The results of this reconciliation are summarized in Table 1. It appears that the training programs in West Virginia, Michigan, Connecticut, and Massachusetts are all reasonable investments for society. In no state is there any indication that the nation would be better off discontinuing the program and investing its resources elsewhere at 10 per cent, such as in tangible capital in manufacturing.

The low average profitability of Michigan training may be a result, at least in part, of the relatively long duration of Michigan courses. Thus, only 30 per cent of the 503 trainees are in classes scheduled for 60-200 hours, and the average class length, weighted by the number of persons associated with each class, is about 18 weeks. In contrast, the Connecticut training classes last 4 to 8 weeks, with an average of 6.2 weeks. The West Virginia classes have an average length of 3.2 months for men and 2.2 months for women but the number of classroom hours per enrollee per week is apparently often small, so that the total classroom hours per enrollee may be closer to the Connecticut than the Michigan average. The courses covered by Page average 34 weeks, substantially more than the Michigan classes, but show a higher benefit-cost ratio. This apparent contradiction may be real, but the inclusion of social payments and the low response rate are warnings to interpret Page's findings cautiously.

The Hardin and Borus conclusion concerning the relative efficacy of short and long courses has vast policy significance. It suggests that a drastic shift in the direction of shorter courses than arranged in the past will greatly increase the social economic yield on investment in retraining. A reassessment of other bodies of data to ascertain whether there is supporting evidence for such an inverse relationship between training gains and course duration may make an important contribution to policy formulation.

Private Economic Benefits and Costs

Cain and Stromsdorfer calculate the net present value of training to be $3,325 for men, $76 for women, and $1,638 for both sexes combined, given a 10 per cent discount rate, and net present values of $3,985, $80, and $1,990, respectively, when the discount rate is 5 per cent. The private cost is estimated to be $233 for men, $30 for women, and $165 per average graduate. These results imply benefit-cost ratios of 15.3, 3.5, and 10.9, respectively, given a 10 per cent discount rate, and ratios of 18.1, 3.7, and 13.1 for a discount rate of 5 per cent.

Borus reports present values of future benefits from $535 to $1,031 depending on the assumptions concerning the discount rate (5 or 15 per cent) and the rate of out-migration from the training-related occupation. The private cost per trainee is not estimated as a single figure, but a range of possibilities is given, from a bonus (negative cost) of $30 to a positive cost of "$166 or more."

Hardin and Borus calculate the annual benefits for their entire sample as $174 per trainee and the cost as $180 per trainee, which represents a benefit-cost ratio of 5.9, given a 10 per cent discount rate and a 10 year service life. Like the social benefits, the private benefits decline rapidly with increased class length and are positive only among trainees in short classes. The average annual benefit for trainees in classes of 60-200 hours is $743, and the cost is negative, -$56, because of large transfer payments to trainees. Given a 10 per cent discount rate and a 10 year service life, there is a net capital value of $4,623 obtained by enrolling in a class for 60-200 hours. In contrast, net losses of capital are incurred by enrolling in classes for 201-1,920 hours.

The $67 monthly gain in net earnings plus imputed value of voluntary non-participation in the labor force, which *Cain and Stromsdorfer* present for men, and the corresponding $9 monthly gain for women imply a private benefit-cost ratio of 21.2 for men and 22.1 for women, given a 10 per cent discount rate and a 10 year service life.

Thus, enrollment in a training class appears to be financially attractive for the average trainee. In particular, however, enrollment in short classes is attractive and does not seem to require any capital investment beyond the reach of potential trainees.

Economic Benefits and Costs for the Government

Systematic attempts to calculate the effect of training on the government have been made only by Borus for Connecticut and by Hardin and Borus for Michigan. As mentioned earlier, these studies use different concepts.

Borus calculates a wide range of benefit-cost ratios corresponding to different sets of assumptions. Given the actual sample of trainees and the actual training allowance rules of the retraining program, he finds benefit-cost ratios in the order of 25.3 and 35.8, depending on assumptions concerning out-migration from the training-related occupation.

In contrast, *Hardin and Borus* calculate that the government is able to collect an average of only $88 per trainee per year after training but incurs an outlay of $1,115 per trainee. Thus, the annual gains being slightly lower than 8 per cent of the initial outlay, the government is not able to recoup its investment of funds from the trainees, unless the discount rate is substantially less than 8 per cent. In fact, given a service life of 10 years, the internal rate of return is negative. Re-weighting of the sample in accordance with probable Michigan course length changes the results very little.

Since tax collections and welfare payments vary with earnings, the inverse relationship of benefits to course duration also appears to be present in government benefits. A trainee in a class for 60-200 hours returns to the government an annual amount averaging $275 after training, and the government spends only an average of $404 on him. If the service life is 10 years, the benefit-cost ratio for the government is about 4.2, given a 10 per cent discount rate, and about 5.5 given a 4 per cent discount rate. In contrast, the average benefit per trainee is small or even negative in longer classes, while the initial outlay is positive and large. Hence, a transfer of retraining efforts from medium and long classes to short classes will, according to the Hardin and Borus analysis, improve the government's recovery of funds from the trainees.

CONCLUSIONS

What conclusions can be drawn from this review of research on the economic benefits and costs of retraining courses? I offer the following dozen:

Methods

(1) Progress has been made in estimating the economic consequences of an important manpower program from the point of view of society as a whole, that of the participant trainee, and perhaps that of the government as an organization.

(2) Further progress in measuring the social economic benefits and costs requires, among other things, a clearer definition of the social effects, especially the choice between the productive-capacity and the actual-output interpretations, and, if the latter interpretation is chosen, an improved method of assessing vacuum and displacement effects; a decision whether to focus on effects on goods and services or to include also a consideration of transfer payments in valuing the social effects; estimation of output effects from employee compensation instead of earnings; and progress in identifying and measuring any external effects of training. Similarly, a choice need be made between definition of private benefits and costs in terms of disposable income or other criteria, possibly including the value of increased or reduced leisure, and a clarification of what is to be meant by economic effects on the government.

(3) More emphasis should be placed on estimating the variations in the benefit-cost relationship associated with forms and degrees of training and other conditioning variables.

(4) The follow-up period should be lengthened.

(5) Methods of strict random sampling should be substituted for the judgment sampling characteristic of most published work.

(6) The research should be designed, so far as possible, to include the principle of randomization, and the choice between ex-applicants and random samples of the active or inactive unemployed as control groups need be studied.

(7) More efforts should be made to conduct evaluation studies in geographic areas where adequate government data are available to the analyst, so that the cost of the evaluation may be reduced and the results may become available while still relevant to policy problems.

(8) The use of non-linear estimation methods and simultaneous equations approaches for estimating the impact of training should be explored.

Results

(9) Whether or not the government ever recovers the funds it spends on retraining remains an open question, especially in long courses.

(10) There is, in general, an adequate economic incentive for individuals to enroll when training is of short duration.

(11) Differences in concepts and methods limit the comparability of published estimates of the social economic benefits and costs of retraining courses. Despite these variations, however, it appears that retraining is a socially profitable undertaking. At the very least, it does not appear inferior, in terms of output contribution, to investment of the resources of society in tangible capital in manufacturing.

(12) Length of training appears to exert a strong influence on the profitability of training. In the only study addressing itself to the role of the amount of training, it is found that short classes have very high profitability, while classes of intermediate and long duration have negative profitability. This finding suggests the desirability, from a purely economic point of view, of a sharply decreased stress in government policy upon long training.

EVALUATING MANPOWER PROGRAMS FOR THE DISADVANTAGED

GLEN G. CAIN and ROBINSON G. HOLLISTER*

The University of Wisconsin

MANPOWER programs used to consist almost entirely of vocational training and various but limited types of assistance for the worker in searching for jobs within local labor markets. But with the recent emphasis on problems of poverty and the disadvantaged worker, manpower programs have come to involve remedial and general education, to intermesh with community action programs providing a variety of welfare services, and, on a trial basis, to assist in migration between labor markets. They are part of a broader class of programs which, for lack of a better term, we might call social action programs. Our paper will include many references to this broader class, and in particular to anti-poverty programs. In so doing, we hope to provide a more general and more relevant perspective of the topic of evaluation methodology.

We hold the opinion, apparently widely shared, that existing evaluations of social action programs (and we are including our own) have fallen short of meeting the standards possible within the disciplines of the social sciences. The reasons for these shortcomings are easy to identify. The programs typically involve investments in human beings, a relatively new area of empirical research in economics. They are aimed at such social and political goals as equality and election victories, as well as economic objectives concerning, say, income and employment. They often attempt to deliver services on a large enough scale to make a noticeable impact upon the community. And at the same time, they are expected to

* We are grateful to the following persons, who have increased our understanding of the ideas in this paper or have commented directly on an earlier draft (or have done both): David Bradford, Frank Cassels, John Evans, Woodrow Ginsberg, Thomas Glennan, Robert Levine, Guy Orcutt, Gerald Somers, Ernst Stromsdorfer, Harold Watts, Arnold Weber, Burton Weisbrod, and Walter Williams.

provide a quasi-experimental basis for determining what programs ought to be implemented and how they ought to be run.

It is not surprising then, that evaluations of social action programs have often not been attempted and, when attempted, have not been successful. Despite this background, we believe that existing data and methods permit evaluations which, while not satisfying the methodological purists, can at least provide the rules of evidence for judging the degree to which programs have succeeded or failed. Specifically, the theme we will develop is that evaluations should be set up to provide the ingredients of an experimental situation: a model suitable for statistical testing, wide range in the values of the variables representing the program inputs, and the judicious use of control groups.

This paper reflects several backgrounds in which we have had some experience — the tradition of benefit-cost analyses from economics, the approach of quasi-experimental research from other social sciences; and the perspective of one initiating and using evaluation studies from a governmental agency. Each of these points of view has its own literature which we have by no means covered, but to which we are indebted.[1]

TYPES OF EVALUATION

There are two broad types of evaluation. The first, which we call "process evaluation," is mainly administrative monitoring. Any program must be monitored (or evaluated) regarding the integrity of its financial transactions and accounting system. There is also an obvious need to check on other managerial functions, including whether or not accurate records are being kept. A component of process evaluations is progress

---

1 As examples of the benefit-cost literature, see Robert Dorfman, ed., *Measuring Benefits of Government Investments* (Washington: Brookings Institution, 1965), and A. R. Prest and R. Turvey, "Cost-Benefit Analysis: A Survey," *Economic Journal* 75 (December 1965): 683-735. As examples of the evaluation research literature, see Edward A. Suchman, *Evaluation Research* (New York: Russell Sage Foundation, 1967), Donald T. Campbell and Julian C. Stanley, *Experimental and Quasi-Experimental Designs for Research* (Chicago: Rand-McNally, 1966), G. H. Orcutt and A. G. Orcutt, "Incentive and Disincentive Experimentation for Income Maintenance Policy Purposes," *American Economic Review* 58 (September 1968): 754-772, and Harold Watts, "Graduated Work Incentives: Progress toward an Experiment in Negative Taxation," Discussion Papers Series (Madison: Institute for Research on Poverty, University of Wisconsin, 1968). For examples of the point of view of officials of governmental agencies, see William Gorham, "Notes of a Practitioner," and Elizabeth Drew, "HEW Grapples with PPBS," in *The Public Interest* 8 (Summer 1967).

reports aimed at determining the need for possible administrative changes in the operation of the program. In sum "process evaluation" addresses the question: Given the existence of the program, is it being run honestly and administered efficiently?

A second type of evaluation, and the one with which we are concerned, may be called "outcome evaluation," more familiarly known as "cost-benefit analysis." Although both the inputs and outcomes of the program require measurements, the toughest problem is deciding on and measuring the outcomes. With this type of evaluation the whole concept of the program is brought into question, and it is certainly possible that a project might be judged to be a success or a failure irrespective of how well it was being administered.

A useful categorization of cost-benefit evaluations draws a distinction between *a priori* analyses and *ex post* analyses. An example of *a priori* analysis is the cost-effectiveness studies of weapons systems conducted by the Defense Department, which have analyzed war situations where there were no "real outcomes" and, thus, no *ex post* results with which to test the evaluation models. Similarly, most evaluations of water resource projects are confined to alternative proposals where the benefits and costs are estimated prior to the actual undertaking of the projects.[2] Only in the area of "social action" programs such as poverty, labor training, and to some extent housing, have substantial attempts been made to evaluate programs, not just in terms of before-the-fact estimates of probable outcomes or in terms of simulated hypothetical outcomes, but also on the basis of data actually gathered during or after the operation of the program.

A priori cost-benefit analyses of social action programs can, of course, be useful in program planning and feasibility studies, but the real demand and challenge lies in *ex post* evaluations. This more stringent demand made of social action programs may say something about the degree of skepticism and lack of sympathy Congress (or "society") has concerning

---

2 There does seem to be a developing literature in which the *a priori* benefit-cost estimates are compared with the *ex post* results for water projects. See Maynard Hufschmidt, "'Systematic Errors' in Cost Estimation in Public Investment," to appear in the Universities-National Bureau of Economic Research Conference volume, *The Economics of Public Output*. It may be that similar follow-up studies are being undertaken for defense projects — one can at least say that Congressional committees are determined to carry out their own follow-up evaluations on projects such as the TFX.

these programs, but this posture appears to be one of the facts of political life.

Two additional differences between human investment programs and physical investment programs deserve mention — although whether these differences are real or merely apparent is a debatable point. One is the complexity of behavioral relations which the social action programs try to change. Is it correct to say that these relations are more difficult to analyze and predict than the technological relations which appear in defense and water resource analysis? Perhaps, but if the analysis of the latter really requires data on propensities of aggressive behavior or on values of recreational activities, respectively, then we may question whether these are easier to analyze than, say, employment behavior. A second difference is the shorter history and subsequent dearth of analytic studies of social action programs, a fact clearly related to the weaknesses of our theory and empirical knowledge of the behavioral relationships affected by the policies.

An awareness of these rather basic differences between the evaluations (or benefit-cost analyses) which have been carried out allegedly with some speed and success in other areas and the evaluations which have been looked for and generally not been forthcoming in the social action area is important in understanding the relatively "poor performance" of evaluators in the latter area. We can then be better prepared to recognize that the methodology for evaluation of social action programs will have to be developed in new ways to cope with their special difficulties.

PROBLEMS OF THE DESIGN OF THE EVALUATION

Specification of the Objectives

In the methodology of program evaluation which has been constructed one of the principal tenets is that the first step in the analysis must be to specify the objectives of the program. Unfortunately, agreement on this principle has not facilitated its implementation, the problem being that few programs have a clearly defined single objective or even one dominant objective.

It becomes necessary to assign weights to the different objectives and to guard against both double-counting and under-counting. Arguments arise concerning "ultimate" objectives and "intermediate" objectives, and

there will usually be a struggle to agree upon some measurable intermediate objectives which can serve as proxies for (practically speaking)
unmeasurable ultimate objectives. Economists, who deal theoretically with
the concepts of "welfare" and "utility," while their empirical work involves incomes and prices, should not find it difficult to appreciate the
legitimacy of non-measurable entities.

We suggest, however, that in general the measures of program outputs,
which may be proxies for ultimate objectives, should be measures of behavior and of tangible changes, such as income change, employment gain, and
educational attainment. Lower priority should be given to the less tangible
measures of self-images, community images, and opinion polls of peoples'
attitudes toward the programs. The defense of this position rests mainly
on the practical grounds of choosing outcomes which may be more accurately measured, both immediately and in terms of measures of outcomes,
and choosing those which are more stable as predictors of a longer run or
permanent assessment. We would argue that the relatively hard measures
of cognitive educational gain are a more reliable and valid measure of the
benefits of a Head Start program than are surveys of parents' or teachers'
attitudes about the program. The latter should not be ignored, only given
less weight. We suggest that, over the long run, *but not necessarily in the
short run,* attitudes will closely correlate with the more tangible performance indicators. So, why not aim right from the beginning at measuring
the program's substance rather than its public relations effects?

Although some measurable objectives are necessary for all but the
crudest, journalistic type of evaluation, not all such objectives provide an
obvious or easy translation into dollars to permit the desired benefit-cost
calculation. In our judgment and experience, however, the problem of
assigning dollar values is a step we seldom reach because we are unable
to measure in the first instance the more direct or specific program outcome. Our failures in this respect are numerous — witness Head Start,
health programs, and many of the manpower programs in which we
simply do not know what difference the program has made. It is absolu-
tely necessary that we first concentrate on assessing the change in educational attainment, in health, in employment and earnings or in whatever the
program objective is. If this is done, we as economists may then offer
some guides regarding the dollar worth of these changes, but even if the

policy maker decides on his own system of pricing, we will have constrained the possibilities for mistaken judgments.

Indeed, the problems of specifying objectives will not disappear even if there is agreement on a translation of program outcomes to dollar values. Consider a program which provides for a simple transfer of money to the participant, who let us assume, is poor. Obviously, the objective of improving the economic status of the participant is unambiguously attained, but are we satisfied with this objective? It is instructive to begin any discussion of the objectives of social action programs aimed at the poor or disadvantaged person with a simple income-transfer program, because all the arguments about self-help, non-economic goals, and community-wide goals can be explicitly aired. Economists in particular are forced to face these issues and will be better prepared for them when they arise, sometimes in disguised forms, in analysing more complicated programs of assistance. At the same time, when non-economists are directly confronted with the example of a simple income-transfer program, they will be better able to understand and accept the extent to which such a transfer program is the implicit criterion of a benefit-cost ratio of one, as used in benefit-cost analysis.

Specifying program objectives is an important step, but there is a risk that the attempt to reach unanimous agreement on the whole hierarchy of intermediate and ultimate objectives will become a road-block to the undertaking of program evaluations. There have been numerous cases in which months, and even years, have been taken up in arguments over what the program objectives "really are" or how multiple objectives are to be "weighted" to add up to some overall goal measure. In the meantime, programs have stumbled on with no evaluation or new programs have been forestalled because no *a priori* evaluation was undertaken to assess the feasibility of the program. Wily bureaucrats have been able to prevent evaluation of their programs for many months by refusing to "sign off" on a defined set of objectives. (The legislative history of a program, like the Scriptures, provides a boundless source of Pharisaical counter- interpretations as to intended objectives.)

In the same vein, it must be recognized that there are some important social action programs for which it is necessary to observe what a program is doing and, in the process of observation, identify what the objectives are. Some programs leave considerable operational discretion to the local level, so that the program as actually implemented may differ considerably from area to area. In others, the legislative or administrative mandate may reflect a compromised mixture of several loosely related program proposals. An obvious example is the Community Action Program of OEO. What is necessary here is something which might be called a "search-evaluation." The first stages of the evaluation must be to find out the actual nature of the program in various areas. Of course, some sort of theory is required defining which objectives are relevant, but the search process may modify our theory. An iterative procedure is called for in which the process of evaluation goes on simultaneously with a "search" for the objectives of various elements of the program. The attempt to follow the usual dogma of evaluation, starting with the definition of a single objective — or a hierarchy of objectives — for the program, are bound to fail.

It may be helpful, in sum, to suggest that the structure of the dogma of evaluation developed in defense and water resources was largely a deductive structure, whereas the structure suggested for "search evaluation" situations is essentially, in its initial phases, inductive in nature. Analysts familiar with the first type are reluctant to accept the latter. In certain situations, however, the choice is between a "search evaluation" or no evaluation.

The Use of Control Groups

Given the objective of the program, the question, "What difference did the program make?", should be taken literally; we want to know the difference between the behavior with the program and the behavior if there had been no program. To answer it, some form of control group is essential. If we want to know what difference the program makes, we must ask: differences relative to what? And the basis for comparison must be some base group that performs the methodological function of a control group. Let us consider some alternatives.

The Before-and-After Study. In the before-and-after study, the assumption is that each subject is his own control (or the aggregate is its own control) and that the behavior of the group before the program is a measure of performance that would have occurred if there had been no program. However it is well known that there are many situations in which this assumption is not tenable. We might briefly cite some examples found in manpower programs.

Sometimes the "before situation" is at a point in time when the participants are at a particularly low state — lower, that is, than is normal for the group. The very fact of being eligible for participation in a poverty program may, for example, reflect transitory conditions. Under such conditions we should expect a "natural" regression toward their mean level of performance if we measure their status in an "after situation," even if there were no program in the intervening period. Using zero earnings as the permanent measure of earnings of an unemployed person is an example of attributing normality to a transitory status. Another similar situation is when young people are involved, and the "natural" tendency over the passage of time would be expected to be improvement in their wages and employment situation.

There may be some structural change in the personal situations of the participants before and after the program, which has nothing to do with the program but would vitiate any simple before-and-after comparison. We should not, for example, look upon the relatively high earnings record of coal miners or packinghouse workers as characteristic of their "before situation" if, in fact, they have been permanently displaced from their jobs.

As a final example of a situation in which the before-and-after comparison is invalid, there is the frequent occurrence of significant environmental changes, particularly in labor market environments, which are characterized by seasonal and cyclical fluctuations. Is it the program or the changed environment which has brought about the change in behavior?

All of the above examples of invalidated evaluations could have been at least partially corrected if the control groups had been other similar persons who were in similar situations in the pre-training period.

Control Groups Which are not Program Participants: Small Group Studies Versus Large Group Studies. The particular strength of the small scale study is that it greatly facilitates the desideratum of random assignments to "treatment groups" and "control groups" or, at least, a closely supervised matching of treatment and control groups. Its particular shortcoming is that it is likely to lack representativeness — both in terms of the characteristics of the program participants and in terms of the character of the program. There is first the problem of a "hot house environment" of the small group study. (See discussion of "replicability" below.) Second, a wide range of values of the program inputs (i.e., in terms of levels of a given treatment or in terms of qualitatively different types of treatments) is less likely to be available in a small group study. (See the discussion on "statistical considerations" below.) The small group study may not be able to detect differential effects on different types of participants (e.g., by age, sex, color, residence, etc.), either because the variety of participant types are not available or because their numbers are too small. Finally, it is both a strength and a weakness of the small scale study that it is usually confined to a single geographic location. Thus, although "extraneous" noise from different environments is eliminated, we may learn little or nothing about how the program would operate in different environments.

The large scale study, which involves gathering data over a wide range of environments, customarily achieves "control" over the characteristics of participants and non-participants and over programs and environmental characteristics by statistical methods, rather than by randomization or careful matching, individual by individual. These studies have the capability of correcting each of the shortcomings attributed to the small scale studies in the preceding paragraph. But because they are almost impossible to operate with randomization, the large scale studies run afoul of the familiar problem in which the selectivity of the participants may be associated with some unmeasured variable(s) which makes it impossible to determine the net effect of the treatment. Since this shortcoming is so serious in the minds of many analysts, particularly statisticians, and because the small scale studies have a longer history of usage and acceptability in sociology and psychology, it may be worthwhile to defend at greater length the large scale studies, which are more common to economists.

Randomization is seldom attempted for reasons having to do with the attitudes of the administrators of a program, local pressures from the client population, or various logistic problems. Indeed, all these reasons may serve to botch an *attempted* randomization procedure. Furthermore, we can say with greater certitude that the ideal "double-blind experiment with placebos" is almost impossible to achieve. If we are to do something other than abandon evaluation efforts in the face of these obstacles to randomization, we will have to turn to the large scale study and the statistical design issues that go along with it.

The fact that the programs vary across cities or among administrators may be turned to our advantage by viewing these as "natural experiments"[3] which may permit an extrapolation of the results of the treatment to the "zero" or "no-treatment" level. This latter device may be particularly useful if the analyst can work with the administrator in advance to design the program variability in ways which minimize the confounding of results with environmental influences. Furthermore, the ethical problems raised by deliberately excluding some persons from the presumed beneficial treatments are to some extent avoided by assignments to differing treatments (although, here again, randomization is the ideal way to make these assignments).

It is difficult, at this stage, to provide more than superficial observations regarding the choice between small and large scale studies. It would seem that for those evaluations that have a design concept which is radically different from existing designs or where there is a quite narrow hypothesis which requires detailed examination, a small group study would be preferable. Conversely, when the concept underlying a program is quite broad and where large amounts of resources are to be allocated, the large group approach is probably more relevant — a point argued in greater detail in our discussion of the "replicability criterion."

The Replicability Criterion

A source of friction between administrators of programs and those doing evaluation research (usually academicians) is the failure to agree upon the level of decision-making for which the results of the evaluation are to be used. This failure, which is all the more serious because the issue is often not explicitly addressed, leads to disputes regarding two related issues — the scope of the evaluation study and the selection of variables to be studied. To deal with these disputes, we suggest applying the "replicability criterion." We apply this name to the criterion because of the large number of cases in which evaluations of concepts have been made on the basis of projects which are not likely to be replicable on a large scale or which focus on characteristics of the project which are not within the ability of decision-makers to control. To take an extreme example, it has sometimes been stated that the success of a compensatory education program depended upon the "warmth and enthusiasm" of the teachers.

---

3 We are indebted to Thomas K. Glennan, RAND Corporation, for his ideas on this point.

In a context of a nationwide program, no administrator has control over the level of "warmth and enthusiasm" of teachers.

It is sometimes argued by administrators that evaluations which are based upon samples drawn from any centers of a program are not legitimate tests of the program concept since they do not adequately take into account the differences in the details of individual projects or of differentiated populations. These attitudes frequently lead the administrators or other champions of the program to select, either *ex ante* or *ex post*, particular "pet" projects for evaluations that "really count." In the extreme, this approach consists of looking at the successful programs (based on observations of ongoing or even completed programs) and then claiming that these are really the ones that should be the basis for the evaluation of the program as a whole. *If* these successful programs have worked with representative participants in representative surroundings and *if* the techniques used — including the quality of the administrative and operational personnel — can be replicated on a nationwide basis, *then* it makes sense to say that the evaluation of the particular program can stand for an evaluation of the overall program. But we can seldom assume these conditional statements. After all, each of the individual programs, a few political plums notwithstanding, was set up because someone thought it was worthwhile. Of course, some will flop because of poor teachers or because one or more operations were fouled up — but it is in the nature of the beast that some incompetent administrative and operational foul-ups will occur. It is a strength of summary, overall measures of performance that they will include the "accidental" foul-ups with the "accidental" successes, the few bad administrators and teachers as well as the few charismatic leaders. As a case in point, consider the success (according to prevailing opinion) of Reverend Sullivan's Operation Industrial Council in Philadelphia with the (as yet) absence of any evidence that the OIC type of manpower program has been successfully transferred elsewhere.[4]

Small scale studies of pre-selected particular programs are most useful either for assessing radically different program ideas or for providing the administrator with information relevant to decisions of program content *within* the confines of his overall program. These are important uses, but the decisions at a broader level which concern the allocation of resources

---

4 Briefly, the OIC concept combines elements of training, job development (often aided by pressure tactics against employers), and a psychological up-lifting of the participants which is conducted with an ideology of militancy and participatory democracy.

among programs of widely differing concept call for a different type of evaluation with a focus on different variables.

It may be helpful to cite an example of the way in which the replicability criterion should have been applied. A few years ago, a broad scale evaluation of the Work Experience Program[5] was carried out. (The evaluation was of necessity based upon very fragmentary data, but we are here concerned with the issues it raised rather than with its own merits.) The evaluation indicated that on the average the unemployment rates among the completers of the program were just as high as those with similar characteristics who had not been in the program. On the basis of this evaluation, it was argued that the concept of the program was faulty, and that some rather major shifts in the design and in the allocation of resources to the program were advocated.[6] Other analysts objected to this rather drastic conclusion and argued that the "proper" evaluative procedure was to examine individual projects within the program, pick out those projects which had higher "success rates," and then attempt to determine which characteristics of these projects were related to those "success rates."[7]

The argument as to which approach is proper depends on the particular decision framework to which the results of the evaluation were to be applied. To the administrators of the program, it is really the project by project type of analysis which is relevant to the decision variables which they control. The broader type of evaluation would be of interest but their primary concern is to adjust the mix of program elements to obtain the best results within the given broad concept of the program. Even for program administrators, however, there will be elements and personnel peculiar to a given area or project that will not be replicable in other areas and other projects.

For decision-makers at levels higher than the program administrator the broader type of evaluation will provide the sort of information rele-

5 The Work Experience program consisted of public employment of welfare recipients and other adult poor under Title V of the Economic Opportunity Act. Only minimal training was offered, but it was hoped that work-for-pay would, by itself, provide a springboard to self-sustaining employment in the private market.

6 U.S. Congress, House Committee on Ways and Means, *Community Work and Training Program*, 90th Congress, 1st Sess., House Document No. 96 (Washington: U.S. Government Printing Office, 1967).

7 Worth Bateman, "Assessing Program Effectiveness," *Welfare in Review* 6 (January-February 1968).

vant to their decision frame. Their task is to allocate resources among programs based upon different broad concepts. Negative findings from the broader evaluation argue against increasing the allocation to the program, although a conservative response is to hold the line on the program while awaiting the more detailed project-by-project evaluation to determine whether there is something salvagable in the concept embodied in the program. There will always be alternative programs serving the same population however, and the decision-maker is justified in shifting resources toward those programs which hold out the promise of better results.

The basic point is that project-by-project evaluations are bound to turn up some "successful" project somewhere, but unless there is good evidence that that "success" can be broadly replicated and that the administrative controls are adequate to insure such replication, then the individual project success is irrelevant. Resources must be allocated in light of evidence that concepts are not only "successful" on *a priori* grounds or in particular small scale contexts but that they are in fact "successful" in large scale implementation.

The Theoretical Framework — Some Statistical Considerations

The main function of a theoretical framework in cost-benefit evaluations is to provide a statistical model suitable for testing. A discussion of the economic content of the statistical model is taken up in the next section; here we focus on more general questions of the statistical design of the evaluation. Generally, it makes little or no difference whether the statistical method is analysis of variance, regression analysis, or simply working with cell values in tables, but we will adopt the terminology of the regression model for the purposes of this discussion. The objective of the social action program is the dependent variable in this model, and the various variables that describe or represent the program (or program inputs) are the particular set of independent variables which are of most interest to us, and which will sometimes be referred to as "treatment variables."

Usually our theory (which includes the body of substantive findings from previous studies) can tell us *something* about what variability can be expected in the behavior described by the dependent variable, and this information is necessary for determining the appropriate sample size. On the same issue, the theory can tell us what independent variables may be included as statistical controls for the purpose of reducing the unexplained or residual variation in the dependent variable. Clearly, the smaller the residual variation is, the smaller is the sample size needed to attain a given level of precision (or statistical significance) in our results. (Another way of making this point is to say that the smaller the residual variation the greater is the statistical significance we achieve for a given sample size.)

As an example of these considerations, assume that the objective of the program is to improve the wage earnings of a group of low-wage workers. Our dependent variable is some measure of earnings over a period of at least one year after those who were in the training program had left it. We can say at the outset that on the basis of the existing studies of income variability, we should be prepared for large variation in the earnings of our subjects — standard deviations in the hundreds of dollars would be typical. Moreover, these same studies combined with other *a priori* information can indicate what independent variables (like the worker's age, education, etc.) will account for some of this variation and thereby produce a smaller residual variation. We might add that the existing studies of determinants of earnings indicate that we should expect a relatively large residual variation to remain. Thus, we might still have to contend with unexplained variability (or standard errors of estimates) in the hundreds of dollars per subject.

How serious is a large residual variation in terms of preventing the detection of an effect on some training program? This depends on how large an effect we expect the training program to bring about, or, in more technical terms, the size of the partial regression coefficients representing the programs. Here again, our existing theory can narrow the range of our ignorance. Thus, we might be able to combine our information on the amount of variability in the dependent variable, earnings, with educated guesses about the earnings effect of a training program to permit us to decide how large a sample will be required to achieve some selected confidence interval on our estimates.[8] Suppose that we have, for example,

---

8 One range for a confidence interval of special interest is almost always that which includes zero for its lower limit (thinking now of a social action program that has some positive effect), so that the investigator is able to test the null hypothesis that the program makes "no difference." This is conventional, and so is the practice of measuring the quantitative magnitude of the effect when the null hypothesis is rejected. We should not overlook, however, the information about the range of quantitative effects of variables even when their confidence intervals include zero and when, therefore, the null hypothesis of "no effect" is accepted. Clearly, we would want to know that the interval was, say, -$5 to $455 rather than -$455 and $5. Furthermore, there are any number of situations when we should be interested in weighing the seriousness of negative effects with the benefits from, possibly, very large positive effects. Put in other terms zero is bracketed by -$5 to +$5 as well as by -$500 to +$500, and there may be situations in which it is important to distinguish between the two cases.

relevant studies of the effects of investments in education or training suggesting that rates of return of 5 to 25 per cent might be expected. Thus, on an investment of $1,000, the annual earnings of a worker might be raised by $50 to $250.[9] Obviously, for the given level of significance, a larger sample will be required and/or more statistical controls will be necessary to detect changes of this order of magnitude than if the program were expected to increase earnings of the participant by $1,000.

Indeed, it is precisely programs which have large and dramatic effects which can be evaluated with a loose design and an almost journalistic level of evaluation, but we would contend that almost all social action programs, and particularly those in the field of manpower training and education, are unlikely to bring about spectacular changes.[10] Regarding the *results* of a program, the analogy between a Salk vaccine for polio and a social action treatment for poverty does not hold. The irony is that regarding the *means* of evaluation, in many ways the test of the Salk vaccine provides an excellent model for the social scientist to study.

Up to now we have discussed the role of theory in providing information on expected variability in the dependent variable representing the goals of the program and on the expected effect of various independent variables — effects of treatment variables representing the program and of control variables which help reduce the residual variation in the dependent variable. Note that the failure to attain statistical significance of the effect of the treatment variable because of either a large unexplained variation in the dependent variable or small effects of treatment variables, can be overcome with sufficiently large sample sizes. But in our opinion, the most serious defect in evaluation studies are biases in the measures of effects of the treatment variables and this error is unlikely to be removed by enlarging the sample size.

One source of bias is inaccurate measures of the treatment variable, but a more pervasive and more serious problem is the presence of variables, not included in the statistical model, which are correlated with both the de-

---

9 In the absence of an *ex post* evaluation, such *a priori* analysis would be useful in assessing the general feasibility of the project.

10 We may well have in mind attempting a number of different programs that are radically innovative and for which our *a priori* notions predict either spectacular success or complete failure. A program to cure narcotics addiction might be such a program. Given the costliness of properly designed evaluation schemes, we might justify pushing ahead with the programs without waiting on formal evaluation procedures in the hope that even "casual observation" will render a valid verdict of the program.

pendent variable and the treatment variable. Had the assignment to a program been made on a random basis, the laws of probability would have assured a low correlation (zero in the limit of a large enough sample size) between participation in the program and these omitted variables. In the absence of randomization, we must fall back on statistical controls. At this point our theory and *a priori* information are crucially important. The requirements are obvious: to identify the variables whose omisson leads to biases in the measured effects of the treatment variables and to include them in the model. These variables may be objectively measurable, such as age or education or previous work experience. Or they may be such difficult-to-measure characteristics as ambition, motivation, or an "appealing personality."[11]

As we know too well, however, our theories are woefully weak in providing us with the correct list of variables for explaining such dependent variables as income change, employment experience, health status, or educational attainment, and we often do not have measures of those we do know about. The latter problem frequently arises because of the unfortunate practice of inviting the evaluator in *after* the program has been run and data have been collected.

Even in the best of situations regarding the availability of objective measures of important variables, if we do not have random assignments we must still admit the possibility that *self-selectivity* or the *selectivity procedures* of the program administrators has introduced a systematic difference between the participants and the non-participants. We do not claim, as the purists would, that non-random procedures invalidate all evaluations, although there are cases when they undoubtedly have, but there are immense advantages in randomization and we can do a great deal more to achieve this procedure if we can only convince each other of its im-

---

11 An important point to be remembered is that, for any given amount of resources available for an evaluation study, there is a trade-off between an allocation of these resources for increased sample size and allocation for improved quality of measurement, which might take the form of an expanded set of variables, improved measures of variables, or reduced attrition from the sample. Too often we have witnessed a single-minded attachment to larger sample sizes, probably stemming from the analyst's fear that he will end up with "too few observations in the cells" of some only vaguely imagined cross-tabulation. This fear should be balanced by an awareness both of the rapidity with which marginal gains in precision of estimates decline with increases in "medium size" samples and of the extent to which a theoretically justified multiple regression model can overcome some of the limitations which cross-tabulation analysis impose on a given-sized sample.

portance. It is clear that those responsible for the tests of the Salk vaccine were convinced.

Another important advantage of randomization should be mentioned. We have noted that variables which are correlated with both the treatment variable and the dependent variable must be included in the model to measure treatment effects without bias. However, since our information about the effect of the treatment variable necessarily depends on variability in treatments, and since the only variation we can observe within the framework of the statistical model is the residual variation in treatments — that is, variation which remains after the entire set of independent variables is included, greater efficiency is obtained when the treatment variable is uncorrelated with the other independent variables. In the opposite extreme, if the treatment variables were perfectly correlated with some other variable or combination of variables, we would be unable to distinguish between which of the two sets of factors caused a change. It follows that even in the absence of randomization, designing the programs to be studied with as wide a range in levels and types of "treatments" as possible will serve to maximize the information we can extract from an *ex post* analysis.

There are reasons in addition to those of statistical efficiency for planning for a wide range of values in the treatment or programmatic variables. One is that social action programs have a tendency to change, rather frequently and radically, during the course of their operation. Evaluations designed to test a single type of program are rendered meaningless because the program-type perishes. But if the design covers a wider variety of programs, then a built-in hedge against the effects of change is attained. Indeed, there is an even more fundamental reason why a wide range of inputs and program types should be planned for, and it is simply this: we seldom know enough about what will work in a social action program to justify putting our eggs in the single basket of one type of program. This evaluation model for a single type of project, sometimes described as the analogue of the "pilot plant," is not the appropriate model for social action programs given our current state of knowledge.[12]

The Theoretical Framework — Some Economic Considerations

For operational purposes we will assume that the evaluation of each social action program, can at least in principle, be cast in the statistical

---

12 See the vigorous defense of the experimental method in social action programs in: Guy H. Orcutt and Alice G. Orcutt, *op. cit.*

model discussed in the previous section, complete with variables representing an objective of the program, treatment variables representing the program inputs, control variables, and control groups.[13] However, the substantive theoretical content of these models — the particular selection of variables and their functional form — must come from one or more of the traditional disciplines such as educational psychology (e.g., for Head Start), demography (e.g., for a family planning program), medical science (e.g., for a neighborhood health center), economics (e.g., for a manpower training program), and so on.

Sooner or later economics must enter all evaluations, since "costing out" the programs and the setting of implicit or explicit dollar measures of the worth of a program are essential steps in a complete evaluation. And this is true even though the most difficult part of the evaluation may lie in determining what the specific program effects are in terms of educational achievement, health, or some other non-monetary benefit.

In making the required cost-benefit analysis, the part of economic theory that applies is the investment theory of public finance economics, with its infusion of welfare economics. The function of investment theory is to make commensurable inputs and outcomes of a social action program which are spaced over time. Welfare economics analyzes the distinctions between financial costs and real resource costs, between direct effects of a program and externalities, and between efficiency criteria and equity (or distributional) criteria.

We will say very little about the distributional or equity question of *who pays* and *who receives,* even though we strongly feel that accurate data on the distribution of benefits and costs is essential to an evaluation of social action programs. However, the task of conducting a "conventional" benefit-cost analysis (wherein the criterion is allocative efficiency) is sufficiently complex that we believe it preferable to separate the distributional questions.

1. *Program Inputs.* In the investment theory model costs are at-

---

13 This assumption will strike some readers as too positivistic, too restrictive to "things measurable," and too oblivious to the unmeasurable and subjective variables. Let us say in defense of this assumption only that it is a "working assumption" that permits us to discuss an important region of evaluation which covers the measurable portion, that it is desirable to expand this region and, therefore to narrow the area left for subjective judgments, and that, in any case, the objective portion is necessary to an improved overall judgment that spans both measurable and unmeasurable inputs and outputs of a program.

tached to all inputs of a program and a single number emerges which measures the present value of the resources used. Although the purpose of this procedure is to reduce the potentially infinite variety of program mixes to a common dollar denominator, we (economists especially) should not lose sight of the particular quantitative and qualitative mix of inputs, which, after all, defines a program and which provides the information necessary to determine the ingredients of a program success or failure. On the other hand program administrators should recognize that the notion that "every program or particular project is different" can be pushed to the point of stifling all evaluations. Evaluations must be relative and comparative.

Most of the technical problems faced by the analysts on the input side are those of traditional cost accounting. We will confine our remarks to the two familiar and somewhat controversial problems of opportunity costs and transfer payments, which arise in nearly every manpower program. Both of these problems are most effectively dealt with if one starts by asking: What is the decision context for which these input measures are defined?

The most general decision context — and the one to which economists most naturally refer — is that of the productivity of alternative resource utilizations in society or the nation *as a whole*. In this case, one wishes to measure the cost of inputs in terms of the net reduction in value of alternative socially productive activities which is caused by the use of the inputs in this particular activity. Now, the value of most inputs in terms of their alternative use will be more or less clearly indicated by their market price, but there are some inputs for which this will not be true. The most troublesome cases often concern the time of people. A well known example is the value of the time spent by students in school: since those over 14 or so could be in the job market, the social product (or national income) is less; therefore, an estimate is needed of what their earnings would be had they not been in school. (Such an estimate should reflect whatever amount of unemployment would be considered "normal.")

Sometimes the prices of inputs (market prices or prices fixed by the government) do not adequately reflect their marginal social productivity, and "corrected" or "shadow prices" are necessary. For example, the ostensible prices of leisure or of the housework of a wife are zero and obviously below their real price. By contrast a governmental fixed price of some surplus commodity is too high.

For manpower programs the best evaluation design would provide a control group to measure the opportunity costs of the time spent by the trainees in the program. Or, in measuring the value of the time of teen-agers participating in a summer Upward Bound program, at least the question of market earnings foregone would be answered with a minimum of conjecture if control groups were available.

The definition and treatment of transfer payments also depend on the decision context of the analysis. From the national perspective, money outlays from the budget of one program that are offset by reduced outlays elsewhere in society do not decrease the value of the social product. When these outlays are in the form of cash payments or consumption goods, they are called transfer payments. An example is the provision of room and board for Job Corps trainees. Since it must be assumed that someone (their parents, themselves or some welfare agency) would be meeting the costs of their room and board if they were not in the program, the provision of these services by the program reflects no *net* reduction in the value of alternative socially productive activities. Whoever was paying these costs before will be relieved of that burden and will spend the money thus saved on other goods and services. If there has been an actual *increase* in the value of food consumed by the trainee or in the quality of this housing, the net increase can be counted as a program input — a cost, but in general, it would be equal to the net increase in the value of food and housing consumed — a benefit.[14] To summarize, if these input costs are simply being *transferred* from one individual or agency to another individual or agency they either represent no real cost of resources of this program or they are a cost which is immediately offset by the benefit it yields to the recipient — remembering that the decision context is the general one which includes all members of society, with no one member receiving any different weight in the calculation of benefits.

In a narrower decision context, the accounting basis may shift; some input costs counted in the broader context are not counted in the narrower one and vice versa. One example of a narrow decision context — a favorite of people in government, but repugnant to most econo-

---

14 When the program produces an increase in consumption of goods and services, the treatment of these transfer payments can become more complicated if we do not assume that the goods and service have a value to the recipients equal to their cost. See A. A. Alchian and W. R. Allen, *University Economics*, 2nd ed. (Belmont, California: Wadsworth, 1967), pp. 135-140 for an extended discussion.

mists — is the vaguely defined "public budget." Alternatively, the decision context might be considered that of the "taxpayers' viewpoint" if the program participants and their families are excluded from the group considered as taxpayers. In this context the only costs that are to be counted are those that come from the public budget. Some of the examples we discussed above are now reversed. Presumably, most of the opportunity costs of a student's time spent in school is of no interest to the taxpayer since it is a "cost" which is not directly imposed upon the public budget. (A qualification is that the taxpayer should be interested in the taxes that the student would pay if he were working.) By contrast the payments for the cost of room and board to a Job Corpsman, which was considered a transfer payment above, would now be considered an input cost from the "taxpayer's viewpoint." The fact that the trainee or his family is relieved of this burden would be of no interest since it would not be reflected in the public budget. However, if the costs of room and board had been met previously by a public welfare agency, then from the "taxpayer's viewpoint," the costs would not be charged to the Job Corps program.

It is not uncommon to see several decision contests used in one analysis, and used inconsistently. For example, the post-training earnings improvement from participation in a Job Corps program are considered benefits. We all recognize, of course, that the earnings will be used mostly for consumption by the Job Corps graduate. But in the same study, his consumption during training (room, meals, and spending allowance), is not viewed as conferring benefits to the Corpsman.[15] Or is it that the benefits should not count because, while in training, he is not considered a member of "our society"? We leave this puzzle to those who prefer these restricted decision contexts. There are other such examples and still other and more narrow decision contexts, such as that of a local government or of one project by itself. But it is probably clear that our preference is for the national or total societal perspective.

2. *Program Outcomes.* The problems of measurement on the outcome side of the evaluation problem are tougher to handle, and *ex post* evaluations of social action programs face particular problems because these outcomes are likely to involve behavioral relationships which are not

---

15 For just one of many examples of this type of treatment of transfer payments see, "The Feasibility of Benefit-Cost Analysis in the War on Poverty: A Test Application to Manpower Programs," prepared for the General Accounting Office Resource Management Corporation, UR-054, December 13, 1968.

well understood. It is particularly difficult to predict long run or permanent behavioral changes from the short run indicators revealed by the ongoing or just completed program.

The outcomes we wish to measure from many social action programs occur months or years after the participants have completed the program. We can use proxy measures, which can themselves be measured during and soon after the program, but follow-up studies are clearly preferred and may in many cases be essential. A good deal depends on the confidence we have in the power of our theories to link the proxies or short-run effects (e.g., test scores, health treatments, employment experience in the short-run, etc.) with the longer run goals (longer run educational attainment, longevity, incomes, or all of these and perhaps other "softer" measures of "well-being"). It is a role for "basic research" in the social sciences to provide this type of theoretical-empirical information to evaluations, but we can also hope that the more thorough evaluation studies will contribute to our stock of "basic research" findings.

The problems of measuring longer run effects of a program and of conducting follow-up studies make up a long list, and most are familiar to administrators and analysts of social action programs. Some of these arose in our discussion of control groups where we noted the critical importance of identifying characteristics of respondents which would be related to the effects of the program and which may distinguish from the non-participants acting as a comparison group.

The problems of inadequate measures of variables and those of errors in the data are pervasive, particularly since the participants in the programs are often disadvantaged groups. Employment histories are checkered, making it difficult to determine the respondent's normal income, normal occupation and other variables. Years of schooling completed may be a poor measure of education attainment, police records may be an important source of employment difficulties, and so on. All of the above are examples of the problems encountered in determining relevant data.

Measures of the status of a participant before entering the program usually come from the data gathered as part of the program intake procedure. A problem arises when potential enrollees are aware of criteria for program admittance, for they may report inaccurate data in order to meet these criteria. Merely by sampling the data, the amount of inaccuracies can be approximately determined and appropriate correction factors can be devised.

The major obstacle to follow-up measures is the difficulty in locating people, particularly those from disadvantaged populations who may be less responsive and who may have irregular patterns of living. The biases due to non-responsive may be severe, since those participants who are easiest to locate are likely to be the most "successful," both because of their apparent stability and because those who have "failed" may well be less responsive to requests to reveal their current status. One way around the costly problem of tracking down respondents for earnings data is to use Social Security records for participants and control groups. The rights of confidentiality may be preserved by aggregating the data.

Another problem in measuring outcomes, which also tends to be more talked about despairingly, than coped with positively, is the category of external or third-party effects of the program. As a typical illustration consider a youth training program, which not only increases the earnings of the youths but also reduces the incidence of crime among these groups, which benefits the community through less damage and lower costs of prevention and rehabilitation programs. Another source of third-party effects is those accruing to the participant's family members, including those yet to be born. It is an open question, however, whether the problem for concern is the lack of measurement of these external effects, or the tendency by administrators and others (particularly friends of the programs) to exaggerate their likely importance and to count those effects as external or secondary benefits which, while benefiting some people do so at the expense of others.[16]

Concerning training and education programs, in particular, two types of effects that have received scant investigation are "negative effects" and

16 For a notable exception to the absence of attempted measurement of the type of third-party effects discussed above see Thomas I. Ribich, *Education and Poverty* (Washington: The Brookings Institution, 1968). Ribich's study also gives us some evidence of the likelihood of relatively small quantitative magnitudes of these effects. A rather free-wheeling listing of third-party effects runs the risk of double counting benefits. For example, although other family members benefit from the better education and earnings of the head of the household, we should not forget that had the investment expenditure been made elsewhere, even if in the form of an across-the-board tax cut, *other* family heads would have had larger incomes, at least, with resulting benefits to *their* families. In his examination of cost-benefit analysis of water resource developments Roland N. McKean gives an extended discussion of the pitfalls of double-counting. See his *Efficiency in Government Through Systems Analysis* (New York: John Wiley and Sons, 1958), especially chap. 9.

those which affect the structure of communities. A discussion, though little measurement, of such effects has appeared in studies and accounts of public housing, urban renewal, and road building programs.[17] The following list of three potential negative effects of manpower programs can serve as examples.

(a) Programs placing the hard-core poor into jobs have had, according to some reports, disruptive effects in the plant — both because of the behavior of the trainee-participants (e.g., disciplinary problems and high rates of absenteeism) and because of the special treatment which the participants received.

(b) Programs which augment the supply of workers in a particular occupation will have the effect of exerting downward pressure on the wages of existing workers in that occupation. It is worth noting that the workers earning high wages are likely to belong to unions which will block these programs in their field (e.g., the building trades), but that low wage workers (like hospital workers) have little or no power to protect their economic interests.

(c) Programs which engender high hopes among some applicants or entrants may lead to a further alienation and hostility for some of those who are rejected or otherwise refused admission or for those who enter and fail. Admission policies are, in fact, just one example of administrative discretionary behavior that can have considerable separate influence on the positive and negative effects of programs — a point brought out in debates about the relative merits of self-help programs, transfer payment programs, and welfare and relief programs.[18]

Community effects of social action programs can be viewed as a special type of external effect, since the changes in the community structure or in various community institutions are assumed to be important because of the benefits or costs they ultimately provide for third-party individuals

---

17 An exceptionally good discussion of negative external effects, including disruption to the community structure, is contained in Anthony Downs, "Uncompensated Non-Construction Costs Which Urban Highways and Urban Renewal Impose on Residential Households" which will appear in a Universities-National Bureau of Economic Research Conference volume entitled, *Economics of Public Output.* The literature on urban renewal and public housing is extensive and too well known to require listing here.

18 For an excellent discussion of many of these issues see Joel F. Handler, "Controlling Official Behavior in Welfare Administration," *The Law of the Poor,* ed. J. tenBroek (Chicago: Chandler, 1966). (Also published in *The California Law Review* 54 (1966): 479.)

in the community. Thus, we are not proposing that the "community" be viewed as an "entity" separate from the individuals who comprise it. However, a separate focus on measures of community institutional changes appears necessary since the present state of our theories of community organization permit us little scope for anything except qualitative linkages between institutional changes and their effects on individuals in the community. We can, for example, consider better communication between the neighborhood populace and the police, school officials, or the employment service as "good things," either in their own right (as expressions of the democratic ethic), or because we believe that such changes will have tangible effects in safety, school achievement, or better jobs.

Evaluations of social action programs may well have to deal with the problems of measuring variables that represent community effects even when such effects are not significant outcomes of a program. This need will arise when we have reason to believe that community institutions or aspects of the community structure are important independent or "control" variables that affect the program's objective. We have relatively well developed measures of some variables of the community structure, such as the components of a transportation system, but we are far less able to measure, for example, the degree of trust and rapport between the local branch of the State Employment Service and the poverty population in the community.

One major barrier to an adequate accounting of "community effects" is the scarcity of data pertaining to the community structure, although here we might argue, at the risk of revealing our prejudices or ignorance, that there is an overriding primary need for better theories of community structure and behavior. Without theory it is hard to know what facts or data we should be collecting.

The discussion of program outcomes again raises the problem of how to weigh and combine multiple objectives. Assuming that the separate objectives have been validly measured, the analyst might present the decision-makers with an array of multiple "effectiveness" measures and let them apply their own weights, explicitly or implicitly, to arrive at an overall assessment, or he can use his own expertise and judgment to reduce the disparate outcomes to reasonably commensurable terms. The latter approach may be rationalized on the grounds that *some* such weighting scheme is inevitable and that an explicit method is better than a subjective one. For at least one aspect of commensurability — that of comparing goods and services that are identical except regarding *time* — the investment theory of economics provides a highly systematized method. Since this concerns the discount rate applicable to governmental investment programs and it is treated elsewhere in this conference, we are happy to by-pass this issue.

Organizational Problems

Timing and the Ability to Hold to Design. The effectiveness of evaluations of social action programs is highly dependent on the manner in which a number of organizational and administrative problems are handled. Although a thorough review of these problems is properly consigned to the literature of public administration, we feel it is important to discuss a few obstacles that can block even the best intentioned evaluator armed with the most sophisticated statistical and economic design.

In the beginning stages of planning and evaluation there are some important questions about the timing of the evaluation. As social action programs are often innovative, it is not surprising that there is often a great clamor for an evaluation almost immediately after the program is begun. This is unrealistic since it takes some time for any program to settle down into "normal" operations, and program administrators are well aware of their tendency to progress along some kind of learning curve toward their maximum performance. In response to these points, it is sometimes argued that a "fair" evaluation of a program concept can only be undertaken a couple of years after a program has begun.

However, when the program to be evaluated is large scale and widespread, the organizational problems of setting up the evaluation can almost equal those of setting up a major project in the program. This means that the evaluative mechanism will need to be developed concurrently with the program organization. A failure to generate adequate information for analysis has been largely responsible for the paucity of meaningful evaluations of social action programs.

A related problem is that of insuring that programs hold to the initial design concept long enough to allow an evaluation to be completed. It is not uncommon to hear administrators complain that the evaluation they receive is well done but irrelevant, since the data used were taken from a period before certain fundamental changes were made in the program. The problem for the evaluator, then, is to complete his evaluation somewhere in the period between the "settling down" of the initial organization and the beginning of fundamental shifts in the program process. (To some analysts this optimum period has begun to appear to be of about a week's duration.) If program evaluation is to become an effective element in decision-making it is important that there be an increased awareness both of the time it takes to set up and carry out an adequate evaluation and of the necessity of holding a program to a given design concept a sufficient length of time to allow such an evaluation process to be completed. Assuming that the design of the evaluation provided for a wide range of variability in treatment variables, it is not likely to be irrelevant.

Internal Data Systems. The modernization of the management of public programs has led to an increasing interest in the internal data systems (sometimes called information systems) of programs. These systems are designed to facilitate the management of programs, including those functions we have characterized as "process evaluations" in section two, but they can also be a great help for benefit-cost evaluations. There are several reasons, however, why an evaluator should not rely totally on an internal data system.

Administrators, especially at local levels, tend to place a low priority on data collection and analysis, and the result is that systems operators are seldom able to deliver on schedule the range of data which they originally promise. We have to recognize, also, that project operators sometimes have incentives to provide biased or simply manufactured data. Finally, internal data systems are notoriously inflexible, since the systems are usually designed with a limited set of users in mind. The result is that the analyst finds it impossible to obtain disaggregations of these data or reaggregations by different sets of classifications. The importance of conserving micro-data has still not been generally appreciated.

For all of these reasons, the analyst is well-advised to supplement the internal data system with other information sources, perhaps by sampling from the system and perhaps through an outside source, such as the Social Security system. This procedure has the further advantage of liberating the internal data system from the burden of collecting for every participant all sorts of information vaguely believed to be necessary for "eventual" benefit-cost analyses but where the decisions about the selection of variables are made by others than those who are planning the evaluation. For the purposes of the analyst, an internal data system which permits stratification and sampling may be all that is required.[19]

INTENTIONAL EXPERIMENTS: A SUGGESTED STRATEGY

Underlying the growing interest in evaluations of social action programs is the enlightened idea that the scientific method can be applied to program experience to establish and measure particular cause and effect relationships which are amenable to change through the agents of public policy. However, traditional methods in science, whether the laboratory experimentation of the physical scientists, the testing of pilot models by engineers, or field testing of drugs by medical scientists, are seldom models that can be directly copied, helpful though they are as standards of rigor.

In particular, evaluation designs patterned after the testing of pilot models, corresponding to "demonstration projects" in the field of social action programs, have been inadequate for both theoretical and operational reasons. The present state of our theories of social behavior does not justify settling on a unique plan of action, and we cannot, almost by definition, learn much about alternative courses of action from a single pilot project. It is somewhat paradoxical that on the operational level the pilot model has failed to give us much information because the design has frequently been impossible to control and has spun off in different directions.

The combination of, first, loose administration of and rapid changes in the operation of individual projects, and second, a large scale program with many heterogeneous projects (different administrations, different environments, different clientele, etc.), has led to the interesting view that this heterogeneity creates what are, in effect, "natural experiments" for an evaluation design. For economists, who are used to thinking of the measurement of consumers' responses to changes in the price of wheat or investors' responses to changes in the interest rate, the idea of "natural experiments" has a certain appeal. Certainly much of this paper has dealt with the problems and methods of coping with evaluations which attempt to take advantage of "natural experiments" within a program. But what

19 It has often proved surprisingly difficult to convince program managers that for the purposes of evaluation small samples of data are perfectly adequate and that, in some cases, data gathered on the entire "universe" of the program are cumbersome or costly to manipulate, are notoriously error-laden, and generally add little additional useful information.

should be clear from this discussion — and others before us have reached the same conclusion — is that a greatly improved evaluation could be obtained if social action programs were initiated in *intentional* experiments.

When one talks of "experiments" in the social sciences what inevitably comes to mind is a small scale, carefully controlled study, such as those traditionally employed in psychology. Thus, when one suggests that social action programs be initiated in intentional experiments, people imagine a process which would involve a series of small test projects, a period of delay while those projects are completed and evaluated, and perhaps more retesting before any major program is mounted. This very definitely is *not* what we mean when we suggest social action programs as intentional experimentation. We would stress the word *action* to highlight the difference between what we suggest and the traditional small scale experimentation.

Social action programs are undertaken because there is a clearly perceived social problem that requires some form of amelioration. In general, (with the exception perhaps of the area of medicinal drugs where a counter tradition has been carefully or painfully built up), we are not willing to postpone large scale attempts at amelioration of such problems until all the steps of a careful testing of hypotheses, development of pilot projects, etc. have been carried out. The practice, particularly in recent years, has been to proceed to action on a large scale with whichever seems — on reasonable, but essentially superificial, grounds — the best design at hand. We would suggest that large scale ameliorative social action and intentional experimentation are not incompatible; that experimental designs can be built into a large scale social action program.

If a commitment is made to a more frankly experimental social action program by decision-makers and administrators then many of the objectives we have advocated can be addressed directly at the planning stage. If we begin a large national program with a frank awareness that we do not know which program concept is more likely to be most efficacious, then several program models could be selected for implementation in several areas, with enough variability in the key elements which make up the concepts to allow good measures of the differential responses to those elements. If social action programs are approached with an "intentionally experimental" point of view, then the analytical powers of our statistical models of evaluation can be greatly enhanced by attempts to insure that "confounding" effects are minimized — i.e., that program treatment variables are uncorrelated with participant characteristics and particular types of environments.

A less technical, but equally important, gain from this approach to social action programs is the understanding on the part of administrators, decision-makers, and legislators that if we are to learn anything from experience it is necessary to hold the design of the program (that is the designed project differentials in treatment variables) constant for a long enough period of time to allow for the "settling down" of the program and the collection and analysis of the data. *A commitment to hold to design for a long enough period so that we could learn from experience is a central element in the experimental approach to social action.*

The idea that social action programs should be experimental is simple, but we cannot be sanguine about the speed with which the full implications of this simple idea will be accepted by decision-makers and the public as a whole. The view that programs can be large-scale *action* programs and still be designed as intentional experiments has not been easy to get across, even to those trained in experimental methods in the social sciences, with its tradition of small-scale research.

The emphasis on *ex post* evaluation is evidence of the fact that at some level legislators understand that social action programs are "testing" concepts. But it will require more explicit acceptance of the idea that some aspects of programs "tested" in action will fail before the full advantages of the intentionally experimental aproach can be realized. It takes restraint to mount a program with a built-in experimental design and wait for it to mature before deciding on a single program concept, but we emphasize that restraint does not mean small-scale or limited action.

It is not unfair, we think, to charactetrize the approach to social action programs that has been taken in the past as one of serial experimentation through program failure. A program is built around a single concept, eventually it is realized that it does not work, so the program is scrapped (or allowed to fade away) and a new program and concept is tried. Certainly serial experimentation through failure is the hard way to learn. An intentionally experimental approach would allow us to learn faster by trying alternative concepts *simultaneously* and would make it more likely that we could determine not only *that* a particular concept failed, but also *why* it failed.

THE ACCEPTABILITY OF EVALUATION RESULTS

It does little violence to the facts to state that few decisions about social action programs have been made on the basis of the types of evaluations we have been discussing thus far in this paper. A major reason for this, we feel, is an inadequate taste for rigor (or an overweening penchant for visceral judgments) by administrators and legislators and excessive taste for the purely scientific standards by academics. It often seems that the scholars conspire with the legislators to beat down any attempt to bring to bear more orderly evidence about the effectiveness of alternative programs. It is not at all difficult to find experts who will testify that virtually any evaluation study is not adequately "scientific" to provide a sound basis for making program decisions. There is a reasonable and appropriate fear on the part of academics that sophisticated techniques of analysis will be used as deceptive wrapping around an essentially political kernel to mislead administrators or the public. This fear, however, often leads to the setting of standards of "proof" which cannot, at present, given the state of the art of social sciences, or perhaps never, given the inherent nature of social action programs, be satisfied. The result generally is that the evaluation is discredited, the information it provides ignored, and the decision-maker and legislator can resume the exercise of their visceral talents.

A first step toward creating a more favorable atmosphere for evaluation studies is to recognize that they will not be final arbiters of the worth of a program. A positive but more modest role for evaluation research was recently stated by Kenneth Arrow in a discussion of the relative virtues of the traditional processes of public decision-making (characterized as an adversary process) and the recently developed procedure of the Programming, Planning, Budgeting System (characterized as a rationalistic or "synoptic process").[20] Arrow advocated an approach in between forensics and synoptics.[21] He illustrated his argument by making an analogy with the court system, suggesting that what was happening through the introduction of the more rationalistic processes was the creation of a body of "rules of evidence." The use of systematic evaluation (along with the other elements of the PPBS) represents an attempt to raise the standards

---

20 For a more complete discussion of this terminology, see Henry Rowen, "Recent Developments in the Measurement of Public Outputs," to be published in a Universities-National Bureau of Economic Research Conference volume, *The Economics of Public Output.*

21 Remarks by Kenneth Arrow during the NBER conference cited in the previous footnote.

of what is admissible as evidence in a decision process that is inherently likely to remain adversary in nature. Higher standards of evaluation will lessen the role of "hearsay" testimony in the decision process, but they are not meant to provide a hard and fast decision rule in and of themselves. The public decision-making process is still a long way from the point at which the evidence from a hard evaluation is the primary or even the significant factor in the totality of factors which determine major decisions about programs. Therefore, the fear of many academics that poorly understood evaluations will exercise an inordinate influence on public decisions is, to say the least, extremely premature. But if standards for the acceptance of evaluation results are viewed in terms of the "rules of evidence" analogy, we can begin to move toward the judicious mix of rigor and pragmatism that is so badly needed in evaluation analysis.

The predominant view of the role of "serious," independent evaluations[22] (particularly in the eyes of harried administrators), seems to be that of a trial (to continue the analogy) aimed at finding a program guilty of failure. In a sense this paranoid view of evaluation is correct. The statistical procedures used usually start with a null hypothesis of "no effect," and the burden of the analysis is to provide evidence that is sufficiently strong to overturn the null hypothesis. As we have pointed out, however, problems of data, organization, and methods conspire to make clear-cut positive findings in evaluations difficult to demonstrate.

The atmosphere for evaluations would be much healthier if the underlying stance were shifted from this old world juridical rule. Let the program be assumed innocent of failure until proven guilty through clear-cut negative findings. In more precise terms, we should try to avoid commiting what are called in statistical theory Type II errors. Thus, an evaluation that does not permit rejection of the null hypothesis (of a zero effect of the program), at customary levels of statistical significance, may be consistent with a finding that a very large positive effect may be just as likely as a zero or negative effect.[23] "Rules of evidence" which emphasize

22 We mean here to exclude the quick and casual sort of evaluations, mainly "in-house" evaluations, that more often than not are meant to provide a gloss of technical justification for a program.

23 Harold Watts has stressed this point in conversations with the authors. See Glen G. Cain and Harold W. Watts, "The Controversy about the Coleman Report: Comment," *Journal of Human Resources* 3 (Summer 1968): 389-392; also Harold W. Watts and David L. Horner, "The Educational Benefits of Head Start: A Quantitative Analysis," Discussion Paper Series (Madison: The Institute for Research on Poverty, University of Wisconsin).

the avoidance of Type II errors are equivalent to an attitude which we have characterized as "innocent until proven guilty." (We must frankly admit that, like court rules of evidence, this basic stance may provide incentives to the program administrators to provide data which are sufficient only for arriving at a "no conclusion" evaluative outcome.)

As a final conciliatory comment; when we talk about evaluation studies leading to verdicts of "success" or "failure," it should be recognized that we are greatly simplifying and abbreviating the typical results. Most social action programs are so complex in the variety of inputs and the multiplicity of objectives, that simple over-all judgments are not likely to lead to quick decisions to dump programs. In combination with more detailed studies, the purpose of the evidence provided by the analysts will instead usually be to suggest modifications in the program — to shift the composition of inputs, perhaps to re-emphasize some objectives and de-emphasize others — and to suggest marginal additions or subtractions in the total scale of the program. It is worth emphasizing these modest objectives because the trust and cooperation of program administrators are indispensable to an evaluation of the program.

DISCUSSION: OCCUPATIONAL TRAINING PROGRAMS AND MANPOWER PROGRAMS FOR THE DISADVANTAGED

ERNST W. STROMSDORFER
Pennsylvania State University

I WOULD like to first direct my attention to the Cain-Hollister paper.

There is very little if anything I find to differ with in their analysis. They have covered most of the major issues involved in the economic analysis of government investments and have done so very well. There are certain areas, however, where I would like to expand on their comments. Most of these deal with the issue of cost measurements. It is a cliche that benefits are more difficult to deal with in theoretical and empirical terms than are costs. I think that Professor Judy's emphasis that costs are benefits foregone and vice versa should eliminate this simplistic orientation to cost and benefit measurement. There are areas in cost analysis which are quite difficult to deal with in both practical and theoretical terms. More is involved in these areas than just straightforward cost accounting. For instance, major problems of measurement exist in the treatment of capital costs and in handling joint costs — two problem areas which, for lack of space, the present authors did not discuss. I would like to outline some of the issues involved.

Capital Costs

Social and private capital costs are fundamentally no different in nature than all other social and private alternative or opportunity costs. However, they pose measurement problems because they usually have an economic life longer than that of the treatment being given to any population of subjects using the capital stock. This creates a joint cost problem, since, over time, more than one cohort makes use of the capital stock in question. Second, this capital stock is hard to value in market terms if it exists prior to the inception of a given manpower or education program.

Problems of Valuation[1]

Four possible treatments for valuing this capital exist. First, one can argue that once the capital stock exists, especially the physical plant and

---

[1] These comments are drawn, in part, from Teh-wei Hu, *et al., A Cost-Effectiveness Study of Vocational Education* (University Park: Institute for Research on Human Resources, Pennsylvania State University, March 1969), chap. V.

buildings, it becomes specific to the educational process and thus has no alternative use. In this case, social capital costs would be zero in the short run, since no opportunity cost is involved in their use. This is a tenuous assumption, though, for it is easy to discover some alternative use for such capital. Thus, the value of most existing capital is not zero, but since it is not a perfect substitute for most competing uses, the market value of this capital in its potential competing uses does not exactly reflect the opportunity cost of using the capital.

Second, historical costs can be used as measures of capital costs, but these historical costs are essentially irrelevant since they have no necessary bearing on the present opportunity costs involved in using the capital stock in question. Current economic value could be less than, equal to, or greater than historical cost.

Third, the use of replacement costs is a possibility in the attempt to measure capital costs. However, it will often cost more to replace a building than the building is currently worth in economic terms. The use of replacement costs would likely over-value the capital resource, assuming no compensating technological change in construction technique.

Fourth, an estimate of current assessed valuation could be used to arrive at a measure of the capital costs. However, the valuation standard used becomes critical. In actual practice, the valuation standard often amounts to a combination of historical costs adjusted by a price index of replacement cost so that this measure is no better than the replacement cost measure.

In short, it is not obvious what resulting price among these four measurements should be attached to the capital inputs. None of the above is precisely correct.

The Capital Recovery Factor

Even if the true economic value of the capital resources in use has been measured, the problem still remains as to the measurement of the rate at which the given capital stock is used up over the course of the investment process when more than one cohort of subjects employs the capital stock. Two courses of action have been suggested for use. One is to attempt to measure an imputed rent to the capital stock by making analogies with respect to what amount of rent (i.e., return on the capital investment) the capital item would yield if it were being employed in its next best alternative use. But such a technique is subject to a great deal of arbitrariness and uncertainty.

In order to get a measure of the rental opportunity cost it is necessary to go to the market place and attempt to identify capital resources which represent alternatives to the resources employed. This will allow one to determine the value of foregone alternatives. But, again, any imputed rent based on market observations will most likely overstate the value of the committed capital, since it is unlikely that the capital on which the rent imputation is based will be a perfect substitute for the educational capital in question. Thus, a great deal of judgment is involved in adjusting the observed market prices so that they more closely reflect the true opportunity costs.[2]

An alternative technique for estimating the rate of capital use lies in employing the "capital recovery factor." The application of this technique automatically accounts for rent.

The major problem with the capital recovery factor is that it only states the level annual return (rent) needed to recoup the principal and social opportunity cost, that is, interest, given the life of the capital in question. The actual amount of capital used up in any given year could be the same, more, or less than this amount.

In conclusion, however, it must be noted that physical capital costs are usually low relative to all other opportunity costs. Thus, the relative error or bias which can result from the use of an inappropriate measurement technique may often not be large.

The Joint Cost Problem

The problem of joint costs occurs within two contexts. First, the problem exists at a given point in time when a specific expenditure or facility is used to produce two or more distinct outputs. Second, the problem occurs over time, when a facility is consumed during the investment process by successive cohorts of subjects representing either the same or a different type of output.

---

2 For a general discussion of the problem in imputing opportunity costs to resources employed in the public sector see Roland N. McKean, "The Use of Shadow Prices," in *Problems in Public Expenditure Analysis,* ed. Samuel B. Chase, Jr., Studies of Government Finence, (Washington: The Brookings Institution, 1968).

There are two points of view with respect to the problem of proration. The first advises against prorating. The second argues that proration is possible. The first point of view is supported by such persons as Hitch and McKean and Enthoven.[3]

They argue that the occurrence of joint costs does not affect the determination of marginal costs. And, since efficient investment decisions between two or more alternative projects are made on the basis of marginal costs, the presence of joint costs presents no basic problems to cost-benefit analysis. Not only is such allocation of necessity arbitrary in nature, but it is unnecessary, given the emphasis on marginal costs. When joint costs occur and involve two or more programs or outputs, the total cost of the set of programs or outputs can be measured. Then, the combined total discounted benefits of the set of programs or outputs should equal or exceed their combined total discounted costs. But total *average* costs to each of the two programs simply cannot be measured accurately in any economic sense. This is no real loss though, since, to repeat, investment decisions between two or more programs are correctly made only on the basis of marginal and not average costs. And, to re-emphasize, marginal costs can be measured even in the presence of joint costs.

Consider the following: a vocational school exists wherein all students being trained in the variety of separate occupational skills also attend as a group a set of common courses designed to provide each of them a basic education. The question is, how does one allocate the common costs of the general curriculum among the various skill specialties? The above argument is that the correct allocation of these common costs, is, simply, zero.

This is so because, within the limits of the feasible range of output in the school, the use of the common facilities by the students taking machinist training, for instance, does not reduce the ability of the other students in the school to use the same common facilities. Within very broad limits joint inputs are similar to what is known in economic analysis as a public good. Just as the benefits from a public good are pervasive and need not be rationed or allocated on an individual basis among consumers (since one person's consumption does not diminish the consumption of

3 See Alain G. Enthoven, "Appendix: The Simple Mathematics of Maximization," in *The Economics of Defense in the Nuclear Age,* ed. Charles J. Hitch and Roland N. McKean (Cambridge: Harvard University Press, 1965), pp. 380-385.

that same good by other consumers) so, too, a joint input need not be allocated among the outputs stemming from it.

The argument for proration has been advanced recently by R. L. Weil, and, in this conference, by Professor Judy.[4]

Given a joint input, X, such as the battery of general education courses above which are given to the students majoring in the different skills offered in a vocational school, the argument for proration goes as follows: estimate the total demand and the marginal demand for each of the occupational skills in question. The marginal revenues to each of the skills in question are then used to allocate the joint costs. The sum of the marginal revenues for the skills in question must equal the price of the joint input. Thus, the cost of the joint input is allocated to each skill according to its share of marginal revenue. The allocation of costs in this example will depend to a large extent on the conditions of demand for each of the occupational skills in question.[5] Thus, for an identical production technique occurring in two markets with different demands for the outputs in question, different allocations of joint costs could occur.

The major problem with implementing this technique is that it is extremely difficult to estimate demand curves for goods and services and it is even more difficult to identify specific points on these curves. Thus, the operational practicality of the technique is questionable, given the current state of the art.

Costs and Benefits to Government Units

Both the Cain-Hollister and the Hardin papers discuss the problems of estimating costs and benefits to governmental or other political or social units. I am in agreement with their general position that such an approach is conceptually invalid. I would argue against performing this type of analysis at all. This would then properly focus attention in this area of manpower analysis on social and private costs and benefits. The mare's nest of confusion outlined on pages 138 and 139 of the Cain-Hollister paper could then be avoided.

If a social investment program pays off so that the discounted increase in value added covers all social costs, then, it is easy enough to make it

---

4 See, R. L. Weil, Jr., "Allocating Joint Costs," *American Economic Review* 58 (December 1968): 1342-1345. Also Richard W. Judy, "Costs: Theoretical and Methodological Issues" (A paper presented at this conference).

5 Weil, *op. cit.*

pay off for any given governmental unit. If the current tax rate isn't high enough to cover the tax outlay, the lawmakers concerned with their deficit can raise the tax rate and capture all of the increase in value added, if necessary. If the persons being so taxed do not notice that the added benefits from the social program they participated in are being taxed away, the lawmakers are "home free." If the persons do notice the effect of the tax and refuse to participate in the program because private benefits do not cover private costs, then the lawmaker's won't have to bother with the tax outlay in the first place. Bureaucrats who would operate in this fashion would be the wiliest bureaucrats of all.

Negative Cost-Benefit Ratios

I would like to turn my attention to the Hardin paper. Professor Hardin reports both zero and *negative* cost-benefit ratios for MDTA classes of medium and long duration. A zero cost-benefit ratio is not theoretically unreasonable. This implies that there were zero benefits to the retraining —that the retraining had no effect. And, a negative net present value is not unreasonable, either. The present value of benefits could be zero while the present value of costs was positive. However, a negative cost-benefit ratio implies that the MDTA program actually reduced the subject's marginal productivity. This is difficult to rationalize. If a person is trained for the wrong job, he simply will not get a job in the area he is trained for. This job training will not increase his marginal product but it should leave the level of skills and knowledge he had when he went into the course unaffected. The situation is analogous to the textbook example of inscribing the Lord's Prayer on the point of a pin. Although positive costs are incurred in this exercise, if no one wants to buy the pin, the value of the pin is zero, not negative, unless disposal costs exist. In the case of the retrained worker, he enters the labor market, can get no job which employs his newly acquired skill, and so, he must revert back to his next best alternative.

In defense of the negative cost-benefit ratio, Dr. Hardin pointed out that recurrent failure in the efforts by a trainee to learn a skill could seriously reduce his morale and adversely affect his performance so that his marginal product could actually decrease as a result of retraining. This, of course, is true. Professor Burton Weisbrod also pointed out that, relative to a person not undergoing retraining, a trainee's past skills could deteriorate during the training situation so that his marginal product could diminish as a result of the training process. Of course, it is the passage of time and the concomitant loss of job experience which is bringing about the deterioration.

This depreciation is a result of foregoing on-the-job experience and is an opportunity cost of taking part in the retraining. The question becomes, at this point, whether to call this depreciation a positive cost or a negative benefit. Which course of action one takes is essentially arbitrary. If, for instance, all other specified benefits (negative costs) are zero and depreciation is positive and defined as a negative benefit (positive cost), then the result will be a negative cost-benefit ratio. However, if one chooses to define this depreciation as a cost (negative benefit) and, if, for instance, all other benefits (negative costs) are zero, then the cost-benefit ratio will be zero.[6]

The question then becomes an empirical one as to how large is the loss. How quickly do human skills depreciate? Technological obsolescence can wipe them out quickly. And, like other forms of capital they can depreciate through simple lack of use. But, barring technological change, what is the marginal loss per unit of time, say, one month, of human skills? Within the span of the typical MDTA course we would argue that it is possibly real, though negligible.

Finally, there is one last possibility which may account for the negative cost-benefit ratio. We assume that a worker undergoing retraining has a utility function the value of which he is attempting to maximize. His wage rate is one of the elements in his utility function. If the weights he attaches to the wage rate are different from those implicitly or explicitly assumed by the analysts, it could be possible to measure a negative benefit to retraining. This amounts to saying that the control group is not a correct one.

We come back then, to an attempt to account for the negative cost-benefit ratios found by Hardin and Borus. I think that the source of the negative cost-benefit ratios still lies in either a mis-specified regression model, an inappropriate control group, or both. However, since the results are still not published, this statement cannot be tested.

---

6 Thanks are due to Professor Weisbrod for his ideas on these points. A further elaboration of these points is that a person could be taught counter-productive behavior which could lower his marginal productivity.

I now would like to turn my attention to two final points, the multiplier effect attributed to retraining by Borus and his use of the vacuum and displacement effects.

The Multiplier Effect

As Thomas I. Ribich points out, the multiplier effect is not unique to investments in manpower programs.[7] The choice is not between having retraining programs and doing nothing at all, as Ribich indicates. Thus, alternative uses for the funds exist which will also have a multiplier effect. Only if one could assume that there is some net increase in the multiplier impact which is peculiar to manpower investments could you ascribe this unique increment in the multiplier effect to the manpower investment.

Vacuum and Displacement Effects

Finally, it is difficult to accept an analysis which assumes no opportunity costs during training or which ascribes as benefits the entire wage bill after retraining.

In the first case, you are arguing that the trainees had no other economic alternatives before them. In the extreme case, this implies that their marginal revenue product is zero. Likewise, by counting the entire wage bill after training, you assume that the trainees marginal revenue product was zero at the time he entered the course. This kind of assumption, to my mind, is simply untenable.

Again, as Ribich points out, there is reason to assume, based on the very data Borus employed, that workers *did* forego earnings while in training, since members of the control group used had positive earnings. Likewise, members of the control group also found jobs in areas the trainee group was retrained in.[8]

Thus, one reason for a person's marginal revenue product to be zero, zero probability of employment, did not exist. Likewise, this very reason that his trainee group, assuming his control group was appropriate, did not suffer zero probability of employment, makes it incorrect to ascribe as a benefit the entire post-training wage bill. Borus assumed an extreme type of structural unemployment in his study, when, in fact, the unemployment was a mixture of cyclical and frictional or structural unemployment.

7 Thomas I. Ribich, *Education and Poverty* (Washington: The Brookings Institution, 1968), p. 41. See, also Burton A. Weisbrod, "Conceptual Issues in Evaluating Training Programs," *Monthly Labor Review* 89 (October 1966): 1093.

8 Ribich, *op. cit.*, pp. 42-45.

DAVID O. SEWELL
Queen's University

AS a practitioner in the field of benefit-cost analyses of manpower training programs, I found the paper by Cain and Hollister to be a superb "how-to-do-it" text. I am of the opinion that the homilies in their paper would make suitable required reading for researchers submitting grant proposals for future benefit-cost analyses of "social action" programs. Better still perhaps, their strictures should be required reading for administrators of planned future social action programs. At any rate, I would like to take some of the principles outlined by Cain and Hollister and apply them to the material covered by Hardin.

Hardin's survey covers most of the available benefit-cost analyses of training programs sponsored by the U.S. Department of Labor under the Manpower Development and Training Act, the Area Redevelopment Act and earlier training programs operating under state equivalents of this federal legislation. I thought it was a pity that Hardin did not extend his survey to include benefit-cost analyses of training programs sponsored by other federal agencies. At the moment, there are at least twenty-nine such federally supported training programs operating simultaneously. Obviously, a demand exists for some cross-pollenization of benefit-cost findings from this multiplicity of programs.

Nevertheless, I feel Hardin has to be congratulated on the thorough digging job he has done on the assumptions embodied in past analyses of the MDTA-type programs. I wonder, however, to what extent the findings of the published studies surveyed by Hardin are applicable to today's MDTA program. The training schemes examined in these analyses for the most part took place in the early 1960's, when MDTA was either being conceived or was in its infancy. Since that time, there have been substantial changes in the objectives of MDTA, with particular emphasis developing on training "disadvantaged" members of the labor force.[1]

---

1 The official objective, originally announced in 1966, was that from 1966 on at least 65 per cent of all MDTA enrollees were to be drawn from the "disadvantaged" population. This goal has now apparently been achieved. The term "disadvantaged" trainees comprises principally youths, nonwhite workers, persons with low academic achievement, the long-term unemployed, the rural poor, and older workers. See U.S., Department of Labor, *Manpower Report of the President, 1969* (Washington: Government Printing Office, 1969), pp. 79 and 90. It should also be noted that changes in the emphasis of MDTA may limit the relevance of past analyses of MDTA-type training programs for another reason not mentioned above. As a proportion of total enrollees in MDTA, on-the-job trainees have increased from 6 per cent in fiscal 1963 to 47 per cent in fiscal 1968 (*Manpower Report of the President, 1969*, p. 76). However, the studies surveyed by Hardin consist *exclusively* of analyses of institutional MDTA-type training programs. Indeed, only one exploratory study comparing institutional and on-the-job training is known to the writer, and this research is not cited by Hardin. See Planning Research Corporation, *Cost-Effectiveness Analysis of On-the-Job and Institutional Training Courses*, P.R.C. D-1297 (Washington: Planning Research Corporation, 1967).

To quote Cain and Hollister (for a purpose which they certainly did not intend), are the studies surveyed by Hardin thus "well done but irrelevant since the data used were taken from a period before fundamental changes were made in the program"?

I believe that there is one rather glaring anomaly which limits the extent to which results from many of the analyses surveyed by Hardin are "replicable" in today's MDTA program. The major source of bias involved in evaluations of social action programs, again according to Cain and Hollister, is "the presence of variables, not included in the statistical model, which are correlated with both the dependent variable and the treatment variable". Restricting my comments to the published analyses surveyed by Hardin, I think it is correct to state that only the study by Borus does not rely heavily for its results on comparisons between trainees and so-called "non-applicants" for training. There are rather significant differences between the members of the trainee groups and the non-applicant control groups in all of the other studies. The fact that needs to be stressed is that not all of the people who applied to take part in these training schemes were successful in gaining admission. Entry to these courses was usually based on attaining a high enough score on the General Aptitude Test Battery and passing other formal and informal criteria. The attrition rate in this process could be quite severe — rejects comprised 64% of all applicants in one course studied.[2] The significance of the selection tests, of course, is that the individuals who were least able or least amenable to training were thereby culled out of the training process. To use a simile frequently encountered in discussion of MDTA, the trainees represented the "cream" of the human material available for training.

On these grounds alone, I would argue that experience in these training schemes would be of minor interest in a new MDTA program reoriented to deal more specifically with a clientele considered handicapped in the labor market. The trainees in the programs analysed might have been expected to have risen out of a temporary situation of having low incomes without the aid of training subsidized by the government. The selection criteria,

2 Michael E. Borus, *The Economic Effectiveness of Retraining the Unemployed,* Research Report to the Federal Reserve Bank of Boston, No. 35 (Boston: The Federal Reserve Bank of Boston, 1966), p. 55.

on the other hand, excluded precisely those who might have been expected to be poor in a permanent income sense.[3]

However, let us revert to the point raised by Cain and Hollister, concerning the pitfalls in interpreting results from analyses in which variables are not included in the statistical model, although they are correlated with the treatment variable and the dependent variable. The non-applicants used as control groups in nearly all of the benefit-cost analyses surveyed by Hardin were not chosen on the basis that, like the trainees, they passed the various selection tests. The peril involved in interpreting the results from these studies should thus be obvious. One would expect that the inclusion of independent variables such as education in the regression equations of these analyses would neutralize some but not necessarily all of the effects of the selection criteria on the dependent variables. The possibility remains that ability and intelligence are positively correlated with the treatment variable and consequently that computed benefits from training *include* the returns to ability and intelligence.

The second point I wish to make has considerably more important implications for the calculation of the returns to society from training programs in general, and for the social benefit-cost ratios in the analyses surveyed by Hardin in particular. The point concerned relates to the allocative effects of training programs, or the question of whether such programs raise aggregate output by more than the costs of training. The topic has already been broached at this Conference in the papers of Hardin and Weisbrod. Because of its importance, it is worth recapitulating on the assumptions made concerning the allocative effects of training in the analyses surveyed by Hardin.

The various studies of training programs in West Virginia, together with Page's study of training programs in Massachusetts, assumed that training

---

3 In this connection, I have a modest proposal to make to the U.S. Department of Labor — if that agency desires to increase further the proportion of disadvantaged trainees in MDTA training programs. My suggestion would be to retain the General Aptitude Test Battery as a selection mechanism for training programs, but to put the information provided by these tests to a rather different use than that provided for in the present procedure. Assume there are ten applicants for a particular training program and because of budgetary or other constraints, only five training slots are available. The GATB tests should be run, and the applicants ranked according to their performance on the tests. The applicants who have the most need for the training will now have been identified: the applications of the five persons who performed the most satisfactorily on the GATB tests should accordingly be discarded.

raised aggregate output by the extent to which trainee earnings exceeded the sum that trainees could have earned had they not been trained. This treatment parallels the procedure adopted in most investigations of the returns to investment in human capital.

A significant departure from this procedure occurs in the study by Borus, where training is viewed as increasing aggregate output by the entire earnings of trainees who proceeded to "use" their training in subsequent employment. The reasoning of Borus is based on two assumptions: that the jobs filled by trainees were in "skill-shortage" occupations, and would not otherwise have been filled, and that the trainees were either previously unemployed or had jobs in which they could easily be replaced by unskilled workers.

The hypotheses concerning the allocative effects of training employed in the studies mentioned above cannot be regarded as polar. Hardin and Borus have asserted elsewhere that the allocative effects of training could be greater than the entire income of trainees, if filling a skill-shortage job creates complementary demands for labor and hence raises the income of other workers. The process whereby other members of the labor force may be "sucked" into jobs vacated by the trainees or complementary to those newly occupied by the trainees have been given the title of "vacuum effects".

On the other hand, there is the possibility that training might not result in any net additions to aggregate output and in fact might involve allocative losses to society because of the opportunity cost of resources involved in training. Such "displacement" effects could occur where "trained" workers simply obtain jobs that could have been filled by unskilled workers. Borus is the only analyst who acts on the belief that training has such effects: in constructing his social benefit-cost ratios, he assumes that if trainees did not proceed to use their training in subsequent employment, then training did not add to aggregate output. The possibility that training could have had displacement effects is, however, also canvassed in the West Virginia studies and the study by Page.

I believe that the question of allocative effects is the most important issue involved in benefit-cost analyses of training programs. I note that Hardin advocates discarding the principle of measuring the impact of training on aggregate output, on the grounds that measurement of vacuum and displacement effects involves "entering a never-never land of arbitrary and unjustifiable assumptions". I do not think we need to be this pessimistic: clues to the allocative effects in the training programs surveyed by Hardin are available. In particular, it is my contention that determination of vacuum and displacement effects in these training programs requires a closer analysis of the effects of training on the components of earnings than has hitherto been assumed.

We can break down earnings, considered on a weekly basis, into two major components — the wage rate per hour of work and the number of hours worked per week. I shall subsequently refer to any effect of training on earnings per hour as a "wage effect" and any effect of training on hours worked per week as an "employment effect".

I find it rather enigmatic that this approach of observing the effects of training on both the wage and employment components of earnings has not been adopted in any of the studies surveyed by Hardin. The oversight is, I think especially remarkable in those studies where the effects of training on both total earnings and total employment were considered separately. It is understandable that many of the authors, in addition to studying the effect of training on total earnings, were also interested in distinguishing separately the effects of training on employment. After all, increased employment is a specific goal of MDTA and ARA. However, there are also valid theoretical and empirical reasons why we should pay particular attention to the wage effects of training.

Although most empirical investigations of the returns to investment in human capital have equated a worker's productivity with his annual earnings, it is debatable whether this is the best index of productivity. An elegant argument for the superiority of hourly earnings in this respect has been put forward by Morgan and David:

> Annual money earnings indicate not only productivity but also reflect the unwanted unemployment of the less educated, and the desired extra leisure that can be afforded by those with more education. We should not attribute to education differences which result from the failure to preserve full employment, nor should we undervalue extra education because some of its benefit is taken in longer vacations or shorter hours. Hence, hourly earnings provide a better measure of the value of education than annual earnings.[4]

---

4 James Morgan and Martin David, "Education and Income," *The Quarterly Journal of Economics* 77 (August 1963): 423.

In line with this argument, it should be noted, Morgan and David proceeded to calculate the rate of return to education on the basis of what annual earnings levels would be if members of the labor force worked for the same number of hours per year at *prevailing* hourly wage levels.

Instances of the wage rate being preferred to annual earnings as a measure of productivity can be found in fields even more closely related to manpower training programs than general education. Taussig, in his study of vocational training in New York City high schools, not only required an increase in the hourly wage rate as proof that training increased productivity, but also required an increase in the wage rate as proof that training reduced aggregate unemployment. This last point is of particular relevance to the question of whether MDTA-type training has vacuum or displacement effects. Like Hardin, Taussig rejects the "case-by-case" approach of determining the relevance of training to subsequent employment. As both authors note, asking trainees whether they "use" their training, or relying on the observations of independent observers to determine whether trainees "use" their training frequently results in contradictory or unrealiable information, posing severe problems of interpretation. After reviewing all the evidence he could find, Taussig decided that the only satisfactory method of ascertaining that vocational trainees were obtaining jobs requiring higher productivity — and were not simply taking jobs away from other entrants to the labor force — was by determining whether the vocational trainees received higher hourly wage rates when they entered employment.[5]

It should be noted that Taussig and Morgan and David merely claim that productivity is *best* measured by hourly wage rates, and not that skill levels will necessarily be reflected *only* in hourly wage rates. One of the attractions of jobs requiring higher skill levels may be that such jobs are less subject to unemployment.[6] It follows that skill-training may indeed have genuine employment effects.

However, there are other reasons why it would be wise to discount employment effects revealed in the analyses surveyed by Hardin. Special

5 Michael K. Taussig, "An Economic Analysis of Vocational Education in the New York City High Schools," Supplement to the *Journal of Human Resources* 3 (1968): 74.

6 Although as Taussig notes, ". . . ideally the whole lifetime stream of monetary and non-monetary factors should be taken into account. But in the absence of evidence to the contrary, there is no reason to expect systematic biases in comparisons of wage rates in entry jobs." *Vocational Education in N.Y. City High Schools*, p. 74.

efforts were made to obtain employment for trainees in these MDTA-type programs: efforts which were not duplicated in the case of the non-applicants for training who comprised the control groups in most of these studies. Under these circumstances, as Weisbrod has already observed at this Conference, one has to decide whether any observed employment benefits to the trainees arose from the training or from the job-placement activities of the authorities conducting training.

Moreover, given that special efforts were made to find jobs for trainees, one would expect a marked impact on the findings of the analyses surveyed by Hardin, for two reasons. In the first place, the "observation periods" after the end of the training courses in which data were collected on the experience of trainees and non-trainees were characteristically brief in these analyses. The further removed in time the observation periods were from the completion of the training programs, of course, the less important would be the special efforts made to find employment for trainees when they completed training. Secondly, most of the observation periods in these analyses occurred in the early 1960's, when aggregate unemployment levels were far higher than those existing today. In the slack labor markets of these observation periods, one would expect that greater job-placement efforts on behalf of trainees would have led to marked differences in the earnings levels of trainees and the non-trainee control groups.

The conclusion that emerges from the above analysis is that in deciding whether the studies surveyed by Hardin demonstrated that training led to real increases in aggregate output, less reliance should be placed on proof that this training was associated with positive employment effects and more reliance on proof that this training had positive wage effects.

While it was stated above that none of the published studies cited by Hardin investigated both the wage and employment effects of training, sufficient information is available in these analyses to allow us to reach some conclusions concerning the relative strengths of these effects. That the employment effects are important can be seen in *all* of these studies. But none of the analyses demonstrates unambiguously that these MDTA-type training schemes produced wage effects. On the contrary, the available evidence seems to indicate that the benefits to training were exclusively due to employment effects. Thus Borus notes specifically that the $500 annual improvement in the incomes of workers who used their training (his "treatment" group) was primarily due to a five week reduction in their annual unemployment, and that the hourly wage rates of the workers in his three control groups were approximately the same as those of workers who proceeded to use their training.[7] Main is also forthright on this issue, concluding that "the MDTA program does increase employment, even if it does not lead to better paying jobs".[8] Taking Stromsdorfer's analysis as representative of the studies in the West Virginia project, one can interpret his regression coefficients to indicate that, net of the effect of other variables, the earned income of non-trainees was 30 per cent lower than that of trainees in the after-training period, due to the fact that non-trainees were employed 31 per cent less of the time.[9] In other words, the entire income gain to training in the West Virginia training schemes was due to an employment effect. Page is rather less helpful in providing information on this point than the other authors I have mentioned, but I think it is a fair deduction from the data he presents, on the gains in earned income to trainees and the accompanying decline in transfer payments to trainees, that here again the superior employment record of trainees contributed substantially to their superior earnings experience.[10]

The data cited above lead one to some pessimistic conclusions concerning the allocative effects from the training programs in the studies surveyed by Hardin. In particular, the debate on whether vacuum effects accompanied these training programs acquires an air of surrealism. It will be recalled that the vacuum effect hypothesis rests on the assumptions that trainees take up skilled jobs which would otherwise not be filled, and leave unskilled jobs in which they can easily be replaced. If the trainees in these programs were prepared for skill-shortage jobs, it is exceedingly strange that there were no discernible wage effects

7 Michael E. Borus, "A Benefit-Cost Analysis of the Economic Effectiveness of Retraining the Unemployed," *Yale Economic Essays* 4 (Fall 1964): 381 and 422.

8 Earl D. Main, "A Nationwide Evaluation of MDTA Institutional Job Training," *Journal of Human Resources* 3 (Spring 1968): 159.

9 Stromsdorfer suggested in earlier drafts of his published study that the performance of trainees could be compared to that of non-trainees in relative terms by dividing the training regression coefficients by the intercept term in his regression equations. This suggestion has been used in reaching the conclusions noted in the text. For the data, see Ernst W. Stromsdorfer, "Determinants of Economic Success in Retraining the Unemployed: The West Virginia Experience," *Journal of Human Resources* 3 (Spring 1968): 150.

10 See David A. Page, "Retraining under the Manpower Development Act: A Cost Benefit Analysis," *Public Policy* 13 (1964): 262.

arising from the instruction.[11] Indeed, the absence of any proven wage effects raises the possibility that the employment effects in these training programs did not represent genuine allocative gains to society, but instead were simply pecuniary or displacement effects achieved at the expense of non-participants in the training programs. The latter possibility cannot be lightly dismissed, in view of the special efforts made to find jobs for trainees and the slack labor markets prevailing in the observation periods of most of the published analyses.

Even the more charitable assumption that the employment gains to trainees revealed by these analyses were genuine and not at the expense of non-trainees raises difficulties, in the absence of a wage effect attributable to training. Viewed in this light, the training appears to have been nothing but a substitute for a policy of increasing employment by increasing aggregate demand. Indeed, there exists the very real possibility that the gains to training in these programs might have been wiped out by the uninterrupted economic upswing which has occurred in the years since the observation periods of these analyses. This prolonged increase in aggregate demand, by making it easier for non-trainees to obtain jobs, could have nullified most of the employment effects which constituted the gains to training in these studies of MDTA-type programs.

Support can be found elsewhere for the above adverse conclusions concerning the allocative effects in the analyses surveyed by Hardin. The sample members in the West Virginia training programs studied by Somers and his colleagues were subsequently reinterviewed in 1966, four or five years after the completion of training. The reinterviews provided data for a much longer observation period than that available in the original benefit-cost analyses of the West Virginia project. In analyzing the employment data emerging from this follow-up study, Somers and McKechnie have addressed themselves specifically to the problem of whether the employment effects of training persisted over longer periods. The conclusion reached was one that might be suspected on the basis of our analysis; namely that "there appears to be some indication that the advantages gained by re-

11 It is worth noting that Ribich has marshalled much additional evidence attacking the assumptions that trainees in some of these programs left unskilled jobs to take up training for skilled jobs. See Thomas I. Ribich, *Education and Poverty* (Washington: The Brookings Institution, 1968), pp. 44-45.

training may begin to wash out after years of general employment expansion".[12]

To summarize, published benefit-cost studies of MDTA-type training programs have been examined in this comment and three rather negative conclusions have emerged from the analysis. In the first place, it is doubtful whether the results from past studies have much relevance to the current MDTA program. Secondly, it is entirely possible that the "returns" to training claimed to have been revealed in these studies include the returns to ability, intelligence and the job-placement activities of the authorities conducting training. Finally, while trainees undoubtedly benefitted from participation in many of the training courses studied, such benefits may have been achieved at the expense of non-participants in these programs and it is entirely questionable whether any benefits from the training accrued to society in the form of increases in aggregate output. Whether current benefit-cost analyses of MDTA-type training programs for the disadvantaged will remedy the defects of past analyses and demonstrate that such training is a worthwhile investment to society on efficiency grounds remains to be seen.

12 Gerald G. Somers and Graeme H. McKechnie, "Vocational Retraining Programs for the Unemployed," *Proceedings of the Twentieth Annual Winter Meeting: The Development and Use of Manpower* (Madison: Industrial Relations Research Association, 1967), p. 34.

It should be noted that Borus has also completed a follow-up study of respondents in his original analysis, and came to the conclusion that the benefits to training grew over time. I am not inclined to accept this conclusion, in view of the fact that when Borus made no distinctions among non-trainees according to their reasons for not taking training, the result was that training was not associated with significant effects on income. See Michael E. Borus, "Time Trends in the Benefits from Retraining in Connecticut," *Proceedings of the Twentieth Annual Winter Meeting: The Development and Use of Manpower,* op. cit., pp. 41-43.

MANPOWER PROGRAMS IN THE WAR ON POVERTY

ROBERT A. LEVINE

Urban Institute

I SHOULD like to discuss three areas: first of all I am going to talk about cost-benefit analysis — in order to relate my discussion to the subject matter of the Conference; secondly, I am going to talk about various aspects of manpower; and thirdly, the basic subject of my discussion will be the future direction of some of the anti-poverty programs.

Let me emphasize one point at the outset: both in talking about cost-benefit analysis as such, and in talking about programs in general, I will be conducting my discussion on a level of aggregation somewhat different from that of the Conference proceedings up to this point. I want to talk about "chunks of programs" — about the level of aggregation at which decisions are made. We have to select a course of action from a set of programs, each one of which is quite heterogeneous internally but which has to be treated as a homogeneous "chunk": for example, a program called "Job Corps", a program called "Community Action" and so on. Decisions have to be made on budgetary and other overall policy matters about and between programs like this. In both the cost-benefit and some of the other sections of this address, I want to talk about some of the basic decisions and make some recommendations.

I will start on cost-benefit analysis by expressing some skepticism about the use of cost-benefit analysis as a major policy instrument at this stage. From the proceedings of the Conference to this point it is obvious that I am not alone in this. What I am dubious about is not the cost-benefit method of thinking. I think that the program-budgeting thrust in the last four years has made a big difference to policy evaluation. The idea of conceiving of costs and benefits, and of alternatives in terms of opportunity costs, however, is essentially a style: it is quite a different sort of thing from the cost-benefit analysis we are discussing at this Conference.

In addition to the many reservations made about cost-benefit analysis so far, let me add two or three further qualifications which lead me to believe that cost-benefit analysis, at this stage, is a very partial and small tool in decision-making in manpower programs, and is of even less account in other types of programs.

The first qualification is that, in talking about cost-benefit analysis of manpower programs, and particularly in manpower programs for youth, where a lot of effort has been concentrated, we are talking about a benefit measured by lifetime earnings, but we are estimating these benefits from the first month or so of post-program experience. It is like tracking a missile when it is a few inches off the pad. I am not sure if missilery is that efficient in finding targets when the missile gets off the ground, but cost-benefit and Federal data systems are certainly not that accurate as yet. The prediction of what will happen on the benefit side based on the first month or even the first year, has such a wide range of variability that it seems to me to be a serious limitation on the use of any technique for evaluation concurrent with or near in time to the program being evaluated. In Glen Cain's "Benefit Cost Estimates for Job Corps",[1] which I will refer to again, he tried to substitute educational gain as a predictor of future earnings. In some ways this is more reliable than future earnings, but we do not really know very much about the relationship of educational gains to future earnings. The absence of reliable methods for early prediction of program results constitutes, in my opinion, a severe limitation.

A second severe practical limitation is the control group question. I do not think that we can ever really randomize in Federal programs. The ethos against simply handing out placebos in this kind of program is just too strong. If we cannot randomize, we must find somehow, *ex post,* a control group. Despite substantial efforts in this direction, our doubts about the kinds of control groups we used are so severe that we are still not sure of the meaning of our results. The typical kind of control group used is the "no-show" — the person who signed up for an appointment but did not show up. While he may look demographically in every

1 Glen Cain, "Benefit Cost Estimates For Job Corps," Discussion Paper (Madison: The Institute for Research on Poverty, University of Wisconsin, September 1967).

way like the person who did show up, and who went through the program or part of the program, the question remains, why did he not show up? The answer to this question may place the "no-show" in a sample of an entirely different population from those who turned up. This is a useful area for research, but the doubt that this problem throws on the meaning of the analysis is so strong that we cannot be in any way definite about our conclusions.

The third qualification is that of assessing the comparability of the various studies. This was one of the main areas of discussion in this morning's session. I think that I am willing to state point blank that studies done separately are not comparable. In addition to all the differences which Professor Hardin tried to standardize for, there are subtler differences such as different interviewers, different time periods, different locations, and all sorts of other differences. This means that, while it may be possible to launch a single study now and compare a number of programs on the same basis, the *ex post* comparison of seperate studies, in particular the comparison of numerical results, is meaningless.

I have taken a very skeptical position, but let me describe some of the history of cost-benefit analysis of the Job Corps to illustrate my position. The Job Corps should be fairly easy to evaluate: unlike some other youth programs it is fairly well defined. A lot of money is spent on the program and there is a fairly intensive follow-up study for program purposes which means that reasonable data should be available. Despite these favourable factors, evaluation of the Job Corps turned out to be very difficult and ambiguous. In fact the early Job Corps program attempted to get data to validate itself: the Job Corps perfected the technique of defending oneself when in trouble by throwing out numbers in mass. The data which became available for the Job Corps study in 1967 included detailed information on enrollee characteristic, and follow-up data on post-Job Corps experience. This enabled the Office of Economic Opportunity to make the first attempt at cost-benefit analysis.

In 1967 Glen Cain did a study based on the educational gains in the Job Corps and on initial placement in the Job Corps.[2] Both these techniques indicated benefit-cost ratios which were conservatively estimated at 1.2:1. In general the range of benefit-cost ratios seems to have been

2 *Ibid.*

greater than unity in both the educational gain and placement data. As a control group for the placement portion, Cain used "no-shows", and for the educational gain portion he used cohort data. The "no-shows" were those who signed up for the Job Corps but did not show up for enrollment. Sample data on the "no-shows" as well as on those who completed Job Corps has been gathered systematically and periodically by the Louis Harris polling organization. The difficulty, however, was that the Harris data on both the Job Corpsmen and the "no-shows" were biased by the problem of locating a large portion of both groups for surveying. It is difficult to know how to allow for the bias introduced by collecting data only for the sample of Corpsmen and "no-shows" which could be located. In addition, there is the difficulty I mentioned earlier of using "no-shows" as a control group.

The Cain study made a number of methodological breakthroughs, and, as a cost-benefit analysis, I think it was about the best I have encountered on the Job Corps or on other programs. It did not make some of the obvious mistakes of some other analyses. As a definitive study of the Job Corps, however, I think the data problems began to throw it into question. Subsequent to this study Job Corps did a study of its own and found that, by using the same data somewhat differently, they came up with benefit-cost ratios in the order of 5:1. The obvious next step was a sensitivity analysis: this was done and led to the conclusion that by reasonable variation of assumptions — assumptions about the use of the "no-shows", and various unemployment rates etc. — one could arrive at a benefit-cost ratio anywhere from between 2:1 and 5:1. This is not far from the original Cain range.

The Resources Management Corporation, using roughly the same data, then did another study for the General Accounting Office, and arrived at a benefit-cost ratio of .3:1. A further study which did not go as far as estimating a benefit-cost ratio was also done by GAO for itself. This study also used "no-shows" as the control group, and it showed that those who had been through the Job Corps had virtually the same wage and unemployment rates as the "no-show" control group. The "no-show" control group, however, started out with higher wage rates and thus gained less, so that, depending on whether one looked at the subsequent wage rate or the differential gain, the result could be favourable or unfavourable to the Job Corps. If a "before and after" comparison was made for both groups, the Job Corps program appeared to be quite effective. For reasons which are obscure to me, the GAO chose to interpret this as demonstrating that Job Corps has no effect since both groups ended up in the same position. In my opinion, it is equally legitimate to treat the relative wage gain as a measure of benefit. The main lesson to be learned from this confusion, however, is that there is no unambiguous answer, and that one can come out with almost any answer one wants.

I think that all the studies were undertaken with objectivity in mind. I know that when Cain started we told him to do it as objectively as possible and that if it turned out wrongly we would suppress it! But I think that this is not typical of where we stand on cost-benefit analysis; there is no discoverable objective "truth".

I know of another study done for the Labor Department on some of its programs in which the benefit-cost ratio could have turned out to be negative, given the method used. As was pointed out in discussions this morning, it is difficult to conceive of a manpower program actually *lowering* productivity, but the Labor Department study subtracted certain government savings and benefits from the denominator instead of adding them to the numerator: in this way, if the number subtracted were larger than the number it was subtracted from, the benefit-cost ratio could have become negative by way of infinity.

All of these problems are in the realm of a developing science — the artistic end of the range of developing sciences. Nevertheless benefit-cost ratios do have an important but limited use for political dialogue. They are useful as one factor in the examination of programs. For example, comparisons among Job Corps camps, where the data are reasonably consistent, can usefully be made by means of benefit-cost ratios. And incidentally, when this is done the ordering of benefit-cost among Job Corps camps comes out rather differently from the one used by the current administration in deciding which camps to eliminate, which helps to demonstrate both the utilization and limitation of cost-benefit analysis.

Let me move now from benefit-cost analysis as such to some broader statements about manpower programs — it will have become apparent that the statements I am about to make are in no way scientific. The Job Corps, even before its current illness, was not in the mainstream of manpower programs either in terms of size or central thrust. Let me discuss the mainstream programs both in the present and prospectively, programs both in the area of training and in job creation. These programs are essentially for adults, although to define an adult as over 18 years of age is to include much of the current clientele of youth training programs.

There are a few points which I should make clear at the outset — points which will be relevant to my remarks on anti-poverty programs and anti-poverty strategy. The first comment is on the role of manpower programs in an anti-poverty strategy. I disagree with Pat Moynihan that jobs and income maintenance programs substitute for other programs in an anti-poverty strategy. It seems to me that jobs are part of an overall strategy which necessarily includes income maintenance, education programs, health programs, and programs like Community Action. In talking about manpower programs, therefore, I will be talking about *part of* an anti-poverty program.

The second disagreement I wish to clarify is with the National Manpower Policy Task Force which recently argued that manpower programs were an alternative to income maintenance programs. The Task Force argued that for a category of people described as "able-bodied" or "employable" the objective should be to get them into the labor market.[3] The difficulty with this concept is that nobody can define in advance who is able-bodied and who is employable. This problem is similar to the problem of the "no-shows" in the analysis of the Job Corps. We can take individuals who look exactly the same, both physically and demographically: one individual is going to complete a training program and be employable, and another is not going to complete the program and will not be employable. We do not know in advance who or how many will fail to respond. Thus, in trying to set out program categories in advance for the employable undeserving of income maintenance and for the unemployable (deserving), we are trying to do the impossible, and in rather a harsh way.

Income maintenance programs of the negative income tax type can be built to provide incentives to work, to get into manpower programs. The income guarantee of any feasible income maintenance program will be too low to attract many people away from manpower programs. Income

---

3 National Manpower Policy Task Force, *The Nation's Manpower Programs* (Washington, January 7, 1969), pp. 14-15.

guarantees for a family of four might be around the $1,500 level; when we talk of training, on the other hand, we are talking about training to fit someone for a private job which might start at around $2 - $3 per hour, $4,000 - $6,000 per annum. I do not think, therefore, that there is likely to be any drawing off of people who "ought to be" in manpower programs, by the kind of income maintenance programs being talked about now. In this sense income maintenance programs and manpower programs are not substitutes: in my opinion, they are complementary.

Let me make it clear that, in the policy sense, I put income maintenance chronologically first at this stage in an anti-poverty strategy. The data we have shows that the portion of poverty caused by male unemployment and low-paying jobs has decreased much faster than the "non-employable" portion of the poor. From 1964 to 1967 the poor in families headed by males went down from 18.6 million to 14.2 million. In the same time period, poor families not headed by males went down from 14.4 million to 14.1 million, a reduction which is virtually below the "noise level". This is part of the trend from 1959 to 1967: in these years, male headed family poor was cut in half — from 24.5 million to 12.2 million; the other poor fell from 14.2 million to 13.6 million. It seems to have been on the capable poor that the anti-poverty programs have had their biggest impact. On the basis of the Puritan Ethic — usually we think of someone else's Puritan Ethic, not ours — we have held that the American people would never countenance simply giving money to people, and we have thus left aside that portion of the poor which can benefit only from money. I think for reasons like this it is becoming time, perhaps even political time, for income maintenance, and I am quite critical of the liberal manpower experts who still try to separate the "deserving" sheep from the "undeserving" goats. I think we need a new classification of liberalism — we used to have "liberals" and 19th century liberals; now we need liberals, 19th century liberals, and 1930's liberals. "Liberal" manpower experts who are still worried about other people's Puritan consciences, and other people's ability to work, should reconsider the question of substitutability between income maintenance and manpower programs.

My third general comment is that there are really two interrelated objectives in the war on poverty. One of the objectives is reducing poverty defined as low income — income below some arbitrary poverty line. The other objective is the elimination of inequality of opportunity among groups, primarily but not exclusively racial groups. This inequality extends the whole length of the income distribution. The original history of the poverty program contains both these elements: many of the programs discussed are programs designed for someone who is not below the poverty line, but who needs training and occupational upgrading. It is a well known phenomenon that an educated negro does more poorly than an educated white, but usually neither is poor in terms of income. So far, the war on poverty has concentrated almost entirely on the low income concept of poverty. I think there have been good reasons for this. In the past, so called anti-poverty programs without some income limit have immediately floated up to the higher end of the income distribution of a disadvantaged group. They have started off as programs for the poor but have ended up as programs for the not-so-poor. Many of the farm programs of the 1930's fall into the category: they were presented as anti-poverty programs but nowadays they are obviously not. Some of the housing and urban renewal programs were in the same category. We in the Office of Economic Opportunity felt rather strongly that in order to prevent this happening to the poverty program it was necessary to fix a family income ceiling — to maintain the equity objective of helping those most in need.

The equity objective, however, may contradict an effectiveness objective — the objective of aiming at those who will most benefit. It may be, for example, that those who will most benefit from manpower training programs are not primarily the poor in need of entry-level training but rather those who are already in "dead-end" jobs and need a break into the upward ladder. I think that there is an increasing feeling that this is where a lot of programs can be most effective. To spend Federal money there, however, would be to take it away from those most in need. It seems to me that a negative income tax is the only solution to this equity/effectiveness dilemma. A good income maintenance program, providing a reasonable income floor, can take care of the equity consideration for the lower end of the income distribution. The characteristic of the low income poor is the need for resources; the characteristic of those we enlist in training and education programs is unequal opportunity or the likelihood of unequal opportunity, for example, for children. For such people, we could pay less attention to the poverty line since the poverty objective would have already been reached through income maintenance. In this way we would get away from the kind of position we are in now of providing training programs for the aged because the aged are poor and because training schemes are part of our poverty program. This kind of reasoning makes some sense in terms of equity, but not in terms of effectiveness.

The first part of the anti-poverty recommendation, therefore, is a negative income tax. Part three, which I will not discuss, consists of community action types of programs. Let me now move back to part two — manpower programs. The first point to be made is that it is obvious to those of us here that if the unemployment level rises to a certain level, our manpower programs are dead. I am not sure at what level this would occur: perhaps we would not experience large scale collapse of manpower programs until the unemployment rate rose substantially above 4%, but given the uneven impact of unemployment from group to group and from area to area it may start at a national level lower than that. The assumption underlying my remarks, therefore, is that unemployment remains low.

On this assumption, let me talk about what is, in my opinion, the current main manpower thrust, and one which I am very much in favor of — the JOBS program — Job Opportunities in the Business Sector — sponsored by the National Alliance of Businessmen. This is a program combining exhortation and Federal subsidy in an effort to provide on-the-job training for the poor or deprived, or for those with unequal opportunity (and let me again indicate that these categories are not synonymous). I am still fairly enthusiastic about the JOBS program — I will explain later why I use the word "still". The JOBS program seems to work on a large scale: in the Federally funded portion of the program we are talking in terms of 20 to 30 thousand people, while in the more ethereal but possibly still important free portion of the program — in which training is undertaken by business at no charge to the government — we are talking in terms of hundreds of thousands. Notice, incidentally, by this language how far I have strayed from cost-benefit analysis.

Previous to the JOBS program, manpower training in the United States had taken one of two tacks. Either we had quite good, small, and non-replicable programs, or we had large scale and not very effective manpower programs. An example of the first type is the Opportunities Industrialization Center of Philadelphia. It depends, I think, fairly heavily on the personality of its founder, the Rev. Leon Sullivan, and personality factors are not replicable; the program has worked less well outside of Philadelphia. We have had a few such programs which do not seem to have been replicable on a large scale once they are separated from their charismatic innovators. On the other hand, an example of a large and not very good manpower program is the Concentrated Employment Program — CEP.

Although the JOBS program may not work perfectly, it is a program which seems to be working fairly well in numbers like the tens of thousands or hundreds of thousands, depending on whether you are talking about funded or free jobs. It seems to be approaching the order of magnitude necessary. (The data on which these statements are based, incidentally, are unreliable.) The retention rate in the JOBS program is probably somewhere between a half and two thirds. This may not be a bad performance compared with previous programs.

Let us take a closer look at the JOBS program. One of the most important discouraging factors is that the contracted portion is very small. There has not been a breakthrough in getting business to take contracts for on-the-job training — contracts which make them feel obligated to take the kind of person supplied. Most of the businesses which have joined the program have gone into the free portion of the program where they can select their own trainees. They have been reluctant to take what one of the officials in the National Alliance of Businessmen called the "basket case". The indication, therefore is that people selected for training are not from the hard-core or "basket case" group.

At this point, let me revert to the dichotomy between anti-low-income poverty programs and pro-equal opportunity programs. It may be that the free portions of the JOBS program is concentrating on those who are not hard-core poor but who are in need of opportunity, and it may be that the contracted portion is concentrating on the hard-core poor, although this is not a statement which is subject to quantification at present. If this is the case we may have reached a proper division of the program: a Federally funded program is attacking the problem of hard-core poverty, while a non-Federally funded program is promoting the equal opportunity objective. This may be an over-optimistic interpretation of what is happening. In any case, it is difficult to say what the benefit-cost ratio of the free portion of the program would be; even if the benefits were zero, the costs are zero, and the ratio of zero to zero is difficult to compute.

There are a number of problems which arise if, in fact, the program is going this way. Although it has been advertised as a business participation program designed to break through the bureaucracy which has limited previous manpower training programs, it has still been a negotiated contract program. In this sense it is one step before a tax incentive program where business takes on trainees and tries to take the tax concession: in this case the argument would be after the event with the IRS accountant rather than before the event with the contracting office of the Labor Department. I am not recommending a tax incentive program, but I am suggesting that one way of improving the JOBS program might be to decrease the amount of bureaucratization. In talking to businessmen, I have found that the bureaucratic aspect of dealing with a Federal organization is, rightly or wrongly, regarded as an important obstacle. The JOBS program might be suitable for experimenting with a tax incentive scheme.

The second obstacle to the JOBS program is the cost of finding job slots. The economist's phrase is "there is some price at which": if the average price of a job slot at present is $3,000, perhaps we have set too low a price; if we could do what we wanted for $10,000 or $15,000 per slot, it might be worthwhile. In other words, if the program is not working properly at present in terms of business participation, there may be some price at which it would and this kind of investment might pay off in terms of alternatives.

I have already mentioned the possibility of experimenting with tax incentives in the JOBS program. It seems to me that we also should experiment with a number of different payment concepts. For example, the JOBS program differs from the economist's concept of pricing in that it pays for input rather than output. It might be useful to experiment with payment for output — payment for people trained and employed rather than payment for training done.

This leads me to another kind of experiment which might be undertaken. If business participation in the JOBS program is influenced by the prospect of making a profit or of not making a profit, one of the factors discouraging participation is likely to be uncertainty. What happens to the plant, the equipment, the labor force, when these so called "basket cases" join the firm? Uncertainty, as was suggested yesterday, can be insured against. It may be that various kinds of insurance schemes, supplementing the subsidy scheme, might help to break down some of the institutional barriers to the expansion of the JOBS program.

Despite the difficulties I have outlined, it seems to me that the JOBS program still offers the greatest hope of breaking into successful wholesale operations in the manpower area in terms of training the poor. It seems to be the best way of overcoming the dilemma of choosing between bad large programs and good small ones.

One alternative to JOBS is the so-called JOPS program — Job Opportunities in the Public Sector — and I guess and hope they will change the acronym! It seems quite reasonable that, if business will train and employ people for a price, the public sector should do likewise. Again it is possible that there will be just as much fear of the unknown, hard-core poor in the public sector as in the private sector. Nevertheless, it seems worthwhile trying to bring public employment under a subsidy program.

The question of public employment in general is the last point I want to raise. Let me specify what I mean by public employment. I am not referring to the JOBS program which is a program to train poor people and bring them into the Civil Service, just as the JOBS program trains poor people and brings them into private industry. I am not talking about "New Careers", which is a mystique as much as a program. JOBS, JOPS, and New Careers seem to demand a raw material input in terms of people who have some possibility of succeeding.

In talking about public employment I am not talking about the pool of people who can be made "capable" of filling jobs from a corresponding job-pool, but rather about a residual public employment program for people who are unable to benefit from JOBS, JOPS and New Careers. Basically I am talking about a "make work" program — the public sector would be something like an "employer of last resort". Initially such a program might be started in rural areas since these areas lack the private industrial base necessary for the JOBS program. The program might also take up some urban employment slack as cyclical unemployment moves up to 5%. At full employment in urban areas, however, the program would cater to people of low skill, perhaps of low reliability, perhaps people who simply do not care to go into any other kind of employment. These are people who are not now being recruited for manpower programs or who are not succeeding in these programs, but who might be capable of working. In 1965, on the basis of reports done for the Office of Economic Opportunity, the National Commission on Technology, Automation, and Economic Progress talked of five to six million jobs needed for poor people. This number may be far too high for the program I am outlining — it is an estimate of the needs of the public sector for all sorts of people, not just the residual poor who cannot make it elsewhere — but the true number is still likely to be substantial.

What kind of jobs are we talking about in a public employment program? We are not talking about leaf-raking because it has a bad name, but we are talking of manual labor, of outdoor maintenance, including perhaps even the redistribution of arborial debris! We are talking perhaps about ditch-digging: there was an interesting article in *The Public Interest* magazine about a year ago (and I am not sure how valid the technical end of it was) suggesting that there was a lot of such work to be done — the separation of sewers from other kinds of drainage lines etc.[4] We may be talking about work in the post office — which could hardly be done worse! We are not talking about doctor's aides and teacher's aides: there are and should continue to be programs of this sort but they do not come under the category of residual public employment. The size of the programs? I think we could start a program at around two hundred thousand participants, largely rural. This would give us some idea of the demand for the program.

This brings me to my conclusion. I do not know how to measure the needs of the poor for manpower programs, either in terms of the kind of programs or of the number of slots required. There is just no demographic or any other method of predicting demand, and thus there is no valid current estimate of the need for manpower programs, either for the JOBS and JOPS complex of training programs or for the residual public employment type of program. We have not really tried to learn from experience how many people will apply, how many will be accepted, and how many will drop out.

We must "feel our way". In talking about "feeling our way", I am afraid that I may put my fellow program planners into a state of shock, but I think that this is the only way to proceed. Instead of setting targets

---

4 Roger Starr and James Carlson, "Pollution and Poverty: the Strategy of Cross-Commitment," *The Public Interest* 10 (Winter 1968).

for programs, we should set reasonable initial numbers and start out with a hierarchy of programs. It is fairly clear that JOBS and JOPS are the highest quality programs: for any one who is capable, this is obviously the best course to follow — if someone can reach the initial two or three dollar per hour range in the blue- or white-collar career ladder, that is clearly best for him. This type of program, however, may not be available in all areas, and some people will not enroll and some will drop out. The public employment program should be available as an alternative with a wage of from $1.60 to $2.00 per hour, which is less attractive that JOBS, but far more attractive than the maximum income guarantee under a negative income tax for all but the largest families. A family of six would be guaranteed about $2,500, or $1,25 an hour. The hierarchy concept allows a fall-back from one program to another, and programs can be designed according to the numbers of people likely to fall from one to another.

The keystone of this kind of system is the final fall-back position — the negative income tax. It may be that we are being unrealistic about public employment as we have been in the past about JOBS. It is possible that people will not come into public employment for one reason or another, even although we might predict that the system will work well. If we have a final fall-back position in terms of income maintenance for those who, for one reason or another, have not been able to hold any kind of job, then we can experiment much more freely with improving programs. We have been experimenting over the years with manpower programs and while some have been fairly successful none has been very successful. We are suffering from the arrogance of planners who think that the next idea will be the one which will finally catch.

We planners, and I include myself, have not really been allowing for our own stupidity. We say that this program will work, that program will work; that the nation is not ready, sometimes for income maintenance, sometimes for public employment; that we want to get people into the private market; and the best idea is just over the horizon. Meanwhile there are a lot of poor people waiting around for the idea that works. An income maintenance scheme should work in the sense that simply giving out money should be easiest. I think we have a design by which money can be given out without hurting incentives severely. I think that, given this design, the country can afford to try to find the best manpower and other programs, to fool around with techniques like cost-benefit analysis, but can do so without a lot of people suffering while we flounder on in our own ignorance.

Page One Hundred and Eighty-three

MANPOWER MOBILITY PROGRAMS

ROBERT A. JENNESS

Canada Department of Maanpower and Immigration

THIS paper deals with geographic mobility only. It will not be concerned with other related manpower programs or processes that complement or substitute for geographic movement — these have already been well discussed. Suffice perhaps to say this. Programs that focus on training or on occupational or industrial mobility centre mainly on the breadwinner. They involve a deepening of the human capital component through the acquisition of new skills. Geographic mobility programs on the other hand are not directly intended to deepen human capital, but rather to transfer given skills to places where they generate a higher marginal product. Admittedly, one can carry this distinction too far. The difference between taking a job across town or in another town may be a simple function of the size of the labour market and the speed and cost of daily transportation. Workers moving spatially may indeed learn or apply different sets of attributes in their new place — man is a multivalent creature and no single job commands more than a fraction of his knowledge. Nonetheless, it seems reasonable to distinguish between the two types of programs if only to underscore that the investment that a family makes differs between the two. Occupational or skill upgrading puts the burden on the worker rather than the family, and much of the investment is in foregone earnings. Spatial relocation on the other hand puts the burden on family adjustment, and calls forth considerable financial expenditure to move household effects. Analytically then, a study of geographic mobility programs must focus on the family, not simply the wage-earner.

In most western nations relocation programs form part of the package of government manpower aids to raise worker productivity. By getting people out of depressed areas to centres that are growing due to public or private initiative, such schemes serve both as an alternative and a complement to area development programs. All governments that administer mobility programs aim them primarily at unemployed or underemployed workers; Britain and a few other countries use them too to channel highly skilled manpower to selected areas where their skills are in very short supply. In all these efforts, governments are underwriting some or all of the risks of workers who would not otherwise move, in return for reasonable pay-offs through a more efficient allocation of the labour force. Such a focus is sound, for no economic purposes would be served by subsidizing workers who would move on their own anyway.

The emphasis governments give to mobility programs varies from country to country — among western nations, Canada and Sweden appear to attach the greatest weight to them, and the United States and Germany[1] the least. Several comparative studies have been made of mobility programs by the O.E.C.D. Secretariat and others,[2] and I shall not attempt to replough old fields. It might be useful though in this forum to compare the approaches to mobility adopted by the two North American governments.

Canada has perhaps the most generous and "open" mobility program of all western nations. Any unemployed or underemployed worker who has a permanent job offer in another community is eligible for federal assistance. The only constraints are that there be no suitable jobs locally, and that the worker does not merely contribute to additional unemployment in the area to which he moves. But these considerations aside, the Canadian scheme provides full travel and household removal expenses, resettlement grants of up to $1,000 or more depending on family size, and housing allowances which have recently been increased from $500 to $1,500. Even more important the program is generally free of administrative complications. It is not confined to persons living in or moving to designated areas, it is not administered on a needs or means test basis, nor are workers held tightly accountable after their move. On a per capita

---

1. Note however Germany's heavy expenditures in moving refugees from East Germany, and in maintaining mobility between West Berlin and the rest of Germany.
2. See O.E.C.D., *Government Financial Aids to Geographic Mobility in O.E.C.D. Countries* (Paris, 1967); O.E.C.D., Manpower and Social Affairs Committee, *Replies to Questionnaire M.O. (66) 24;* J. Steiber, *Manpower Adjustments to Automation and Technical Change in Western Europe* (East Lansing: Michigan State University, 1966).

basis, the Canadian government allocates roughly ten times more for its mobility program than does the United States.

The principal United States initiative has been through a $5 million authorization under the Manpower Development and Training Act for Labour Mobility Demonstration Projects. These projects involve moving workers from a few specially depressed areas and implanting them in carefully selected receiving areas where jobs or training facilities are available. The stated objectives of the U.S. program are two-fold — to test the effectiveness of mobility assistance in reducing unemployment, and to examine the operational, economic and social implications of such a program.[3] These objectives contrast with the Canadian and most European programs which put primary emphasis on raising the productivity of workers and capital. The distinction is not simply one of semantics. For a critical examination of the American program soon embroils one in the now hoary issue over the usefulness of manpower programs to remedy structural or cyclical unemployment. In the Canadian and European cases however, it is only necessary to establish that workers and employers have in fact increased their marginal output as a result of the moves. A second difficulty with the American scheme arises from its project approach, which has evoked some negative response by farm and industrial employers in both sending and receiving areas.[4] In the Canadian case, there is no project or clustering effect and no real opposition to the program. Indeed the Canadian mobility program draws support from all quarters of the country.

RECENT STUDIES OF GEOGRAPHIC MOBILITY

There is no dearth of studies with respect to mobility of human resources either within or between national boundaries. Among the more well known are Kuznets' insights into internal migration processes and economic growth, Parnes' 1954 appraisal of research findings in the United States — which remains a classic reference — and the empirical work of Gladys Palmer, Shryock and, more recently, Lansing and

3. Garth Mangum, *Manpower Policies of the 1960's; An Evaluation* (forthcoming).
4. Audrey Freedman, "Labor Mobility Projects for the Unemployed," *Monthly Labor Review* 91 (June 1968): 56-62.

Mueller.[5] The U.S. Bureau of Labor Statistics is a continuing source of information. Several very helpful O.E.C.D. publications deal with mobility.[6] And not long ago, an entire issue of the *Journal of Human Resources* focused on mobility processes, including occupational and international mobility.[7]

Apart from the broad surveys, much of the recent work on mobility can be divided into three streams:

(a) identification of causal forces through multiple regression and related techniques,

(b) statistical prediction models, using path analysis or Markov chain methods with a probability matrix for "movers" and "stayers", and,

(c) investment models that calculate the stream of income differentials to individual workers.

The benefit-cost model outlined later in this paper combines elements of all three techniques.

The most common mobility models feature a series of multiple regressions relating net migration to independent variables covering personal characteristics and economic incentives which include regional income and unemployment differentials, and distance. With one notable exception — which affirmed the weakness of using simple wage data as a proxy for net advantage[8] — the findings tend to confirm orthodox theory.

5. See Herbert S. Parnes, *Research on Labor Mobility: An Appraisal of Research Findings in the United States,* Bulletin 65 (New York: Social Science Research Council, 1954); S. Kuznets, "Introduction," in *Population Redistribution and Economic Growth, United States 1870-1950,* Vol. III, ed. Hope T. Eldrich and Dorothy S. Thomas (Philadelphia: The American Philosophic Society, 1964); S. Kuznets and Dorothy T. Thomas, "Internal Migration and Economic Growth," in *Selected Studies of Migration Since World War II* (New York: Milbank Memorial Fund, 1958); Gladys Palmer, *Labor Mobility in Six Cities; A Report on the Survey of Patterns and Factors in Labor Mobility* (New York: Social Science Research Council, 1954); Henry S. Shryock, *Population Mobility Within the United States* (Chicago: Community and Family Study Center, University of Chicago, 1964); John B. Lansing and Eva Mueller, *The Geographic Mobility of Labor* (Ann Arbor: Institute for Social Research, University of Michigan, 1967).

6. O.E.C.D., Manpower and Social Affairs Directorate, *Urban Worker Mobility* by Laurence C. Hunter and Graham L. Reid (Paris, 1967); *Government Financial Aids to Geographic Mobility in O.E.C.D. Countries* (Paris, 1967); and *Wages and Labour Mobility; A Study of the Relation Between Changes in Wages Differential and the Pattern of Employment* (Paris, 1965).

7. *Journal of Human Resources* 2, no. 4 (Fall 1967).

8. O.E.C.D., *Wages and Labour Mobility, op. cit.*

Workers respond to expected earnings differentials, and distance acts as a barrier to mobility both by raising the costs of moving and by reducing the labour market information available to workers.[9] Personal characteristics such as age and education (and race in the United States), are significant with respect to workers' initial motivations to move or their ability to respond to opportunities. Regional differences in unemployment do not show up strongly although differences between regional and national unemployment levels give a better correlation.[10] In general however, the weakness of this approach for purposes of cost-benefit application is that it generally focusses on *net migration*. The studies tend not to distinguish sharply between factors that bear on the supply side of effort, and factors that reflect working conditions or the demand for worker skills — all tend to be thrown together into the same multivariate pot. Finally, it is open to question whether regional income differentials, however disaggregated by occupation or industry, are suitable proxies for the differential earnings expectations that confront individual workers.

Recently sociologists and statisticians have become interested in the application of path analysis to mobility, and have developed a set of models to describe workers as "movers" or "stayers" whose behaviour can be predicted by the aid of Markov chain methods.[11] Some of these models use a transition probability matrix in which the proportions of workers in each code category are unknown parameters. They usually use

9. See L. Gallaway, R. Gilbert and P. Smith, "The Economics of Labor Mobility: An Empirical Analysis," *Western Economic Journal* 5 (June 1967); L. Gallaway, "Industry Variations in Geographic Labor Mobility Patterns," *Journal of Human Resources* 2 (Fall 1967): 461-474; R. Raimon, "Interstate Migration and Wage Theory," *Review of Economics and Statistics* 44 (1962); H. Robinson, "The Response of Labour to Economic Incentives," in *Studies in the Mobility of Labour,* ed. Makower, Marschak and Robinson, *Oxford Economic Papers* 2 (1939): 70-97; R. Bunting, "A Test of the Theory of Geographic Mobility," *Industrial and Labor Relations Review* 15 (1961-62): 75-82.

10. F. R. Oliver, "Inter-regional Migration and Unemployment, 1951-61," *Journal of the Royal Statistical Society,* Series A, 127, pt. 1 (1964): 42-69; and J. Vanderkamp, "Interregional Mobility in Canada: A Study of the Time Pattern of Migration," *Canadian Journal of Economics* 1 (August 1968): 595-608.

11. See I. Blumen, M. Kogan and P. J. McCarthy, *The Industrial Mobility of Labor as a Probability Process* (Ithaca: Cornell University Press, 1955); Leo Goodman, "Statistical Methods for the Mover-Stayer Model," *Journal of the American Statistical Association,* Dec. 1961; R. W. Hodge, A. Lane and P. Siegel, "Path Analysis of Occupational Mobility: Some Advantages and Illustrative Calculations," and James Coleman, "Demand and Supply Considerations in Mobility" (Papers presented at the Cornell Conference on Human Mobility, Cornell University, Ithaca, New York, Oct.-Nov. 1968).

past statistical frequency distributions as *a priori* expectations that a worker will move or not move, given different options. Then on the assumption that both independent and dependent variables are related in a linear fashion, they predict the likelihood that a worker will wind up in a particular industrial or geographic location. So far, work in this area is in the frontier stages. It requires a high degree of mathematical and statistical sophistication. And as its authors usually admit, the use of the linear assumptions and the presence of interactions between variables seriously limit its application. Nonetheless, the approach offers insights and methods for benefit-cost calculations since these involve *a priori* expectations about the future course of individual workers and families.

Finally, there is the approach pioneered by Sjaastad, which makes individual decisions to move analogous to investment choices in which workers compare the present value of the stream of private benefits against the private costs, suitably discounted.[12] This approach is consistent with much of the work now going forward in the human resources field. It is particularly useful because it puts the decision to move on a plane with other personal investments involving work and leisure, education, skill training or medical care. Although Sjaastad's earlier work dealt primarily with net flows, he recognized here the need for gross migration data, and more specifically for explicit information on individual migration incentives and response rates. Empirical data on gross flows are scarce. Fewer sources yield the kind of individual data required by Sjaastad's model. And even where individual data is available, such as for instance Galloway derived from U.S. Social Security Administration files,[13] one winds up attributing *ex ante* preference functions from *ex post* earnings and migration information. Thus while Sjaastad's work has been recognized as a landmark contribution to the theory and to analytic rigour, his formulation has had little direct application.

In our benefit-cost model though, we draw heavily upon his insights, and encounter some of the same problems.

12. Larry Sjaastad, "The Relationship Between Migration and Income in the United States," *Papers & Proceedings of the Regional Science Association,* vol. 6 (1960); and "The Costs and Returns of Human Migration," *Journal of Political Economy Supplement,* October 1962.
13. L. Gallaway, *Interindustry Labor Mobility in the United States, 1957 to 1960* (Washington: Social Security Administration, 1967).

SOME GENERAL COMMENTS ON APPLYING BENEFIT-COST
ANALYSIS TO MOBILITY PROGRAMS

Human migration is a process. It represents the natural response of workers to day to day economic disequilibria in the market place. All this is perhaps obvious. But it is stressed here because the process of human migration is a dynamic one that arises from varying endowments, rates of growth and returns to factors in one place and another. Benefit-cost analysis is an investment criteria approach based on static partial equilibrium assumptions. To apply benefit-cost analysis to processes of factor adjustment is, therefore, something like using scissors to dissect a liquid flow. Before the two "fit" they must be surrounded by assumptions about the parameters and functional relationships that are often extremely arbitrary.

Cost-benefit studies presuppose some objective function that can be optimized. But whose function? The economy's, the federal government's, the administering department's or the workers' collectively who use the program? Once that is determined, there is the problem of defining the social welfare function. Governments have mixed and mutually interdependent objectives — as for instance maximizing per capita income on the one hand while achieving reasonable regional balance on the other. Mobility programs bear directly on these options through their positive and negative effects in the destination and leaving areas, and on the economy as a whole. Thirdly, there is the measuring problem. Given differing dispatches of opportunity, productive factors and initiative in each region and the many spillovers associated with human migration, how does one get at the real economic and social benefits? Fourthly, there is the difficulty of attribution. The decision to enlist the help of a government mobility program is only one in a series of decisions made by a family that moves. Migration involves new experiences and incentives, new work places and frequently exposure to different production techniques and new skills. Thus, even if it were possible to calculate all the private and public gains and losses associated with a move, how valid is it to attribute them to the single set of decisions and program that facilitated the move?

Quite apart from these conceptual problems lie the differences in academic and government approaches to benefit-cost analysis. The cardinal point is that government departments must make practical decisions daily on allocating resources between programs and on who should or should not qualify for them. Benefit-cost and simulation models are useful to government departments principally as monitoring instruments to help channel programs along acceptable economic and socio-political paths. For purposes of efficiently allocating public services, then, one-shot studies are not sufficient, at least in the manpower field. This means, for our mobility model that it:

(1) Accommodate a continuing flow of endogenous data on the characteristics of workers, and subsequently combine this information with feedback on the disposition of the workers after their moves.

(2) Accommodate also a concurrent flow of exogenous data about different labour markets, alternative programs, changes in factor returns, etc. that are germane to the mobility issue.

(3) Have practical application. The proxies and assumptions must be reasonable and the variables subject to measurement. It is not enough simply to cite the significant factors and offer a mathematical formula that fails because of lack of adequate yardsticks. Conceptual purity is important, but not if it results in a dead end.

(4) Yield a steady flow of incremental and aggregate results that have meaning for decision-makers. It should, for instance, continually demonstrate which kinds of clients have the best likelihood of success, what destination jobs or areas seem riskiest, what sub-activities are the costliest or where does the program appear to be inefficiently administered.

In our manpower mobility benefit-cost analysis, we try to meet these requirements. The model is a working apparatus.

MANPOWER MOBILITY BENEFIT-COST MODEL

The benefit-cost model described here is also a predictive instrument. It combines information on each client entering the program with a set of *a priori* expectations drawn from a scanning of the characteristics of the individual workers and from exogenous sources, to yield an estimated benefit-cost value for each worker using the scheme. Subsequently, these *a priori* expectations are replaced by *a posteriori* estimates derived from follow-up data, and the original benefit-cost ratios are revised. As the program continues, and the model becomes more refined, the predicted incremental benefits and costs associated with each client should therefore come closer to the true mark. Table I illustrates the type of information that goes into the model, and the manner in which it is used to facilitate departmental and government decision-making.

Our frame of reference is the economy. This is consistent with the stated objectives of the Manpower Mobility Program, which in substance state that it should contribute to increased GNP and accelerated economic growth by more efficiently allocating the economy's stock of human resources to areas of higher productivity.

A key assumption is that the *family*, not the individual client is the immediate unit for which we must measure benefit. Usually, a move to a more favourable labour market will have positive effects for all family members. But there may be instances where negative gains to dependents offset the positive gains to the worker. In these cases, the family is not likely to move. A second assumption that severely constrains the model is that what is good for the worker and his family is normally of net benefit to the economy as a whole. This implies:

(a) That the inter-dependencies are positive — that a worker's change of location does not simply displace someone else who remains idle,

(b) that the taxes used to move the worker and his family do not impose a greater disincentive elsewhere,

(c) that the secondary and psychological benefits and costs roughly balance off,[14] and,

---

14. This assumption is probably excessively conservative. Among those taking out manpower mobility grants there is a net movement from declining regions which carry a more than proportionate share of subsidies to natural growth areas that require relatively less subsidy. Subsidies may take the form of federal equalization tax transfers to "have-not" provinces, shared-cost social overhead programs, special tax exemptions to individuals or firms, or direct payments or similar incentives to employers. All have the effect of artificially raising the stock of private or social capital in the net recipient regions and artificially inflating the marginal productivity of the workers who live there. The usual easy assumption that a worker's wages roughly equal his marginal real product ignores this distortion effect. Thus when workers move out of depressed and highly subsidized areas or — more precisely — areas that would have to be more heavily subsidized were workers to remain there, the net real gain to the economy is substantially greater than revealed simply by subtracting their foregone wages from the wages earned after the moves. Given however the complexity of tax and subsidy arrangements in any nation, the difficulties in measuring this extra differential are acute. (I am indebted to Gosta Rehn for these insights.)

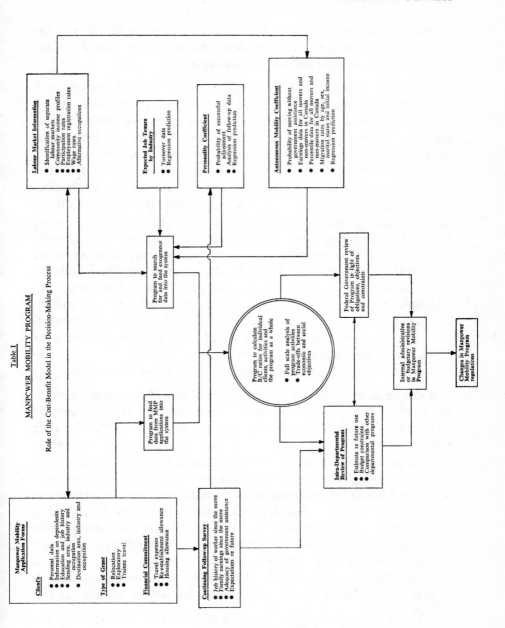

Table I

MANPOWER MOBILITY PROGRAM

Role of the Cost-Benefit Model in the Decision-Making Process

(d) that the returns to the other factors roughly cancel out, i.e., the gain for the owner of capital in the destination area roughly offsets the loss on idle capital in the leaving area.

With these assumptions we are already at some distance from the real world. We are ruling out, for instance, cases of gross discrepancy between the private benefits and costs of workers who move, and public benefits and costs. Even where families succeed in capturing their real incremental product, they may have less discretionary income because of higher housing or food costs. Where these extra real earnings go as rent to a landlord or profit to an entrepreneur the nation benefits, but the families may personally feel worse off. In other cases, they may be better off but only by virtue of higher real costs borne by taxpayers elsewhere — as for example when they move to a frontier area requiring heavy government investments to promote settlement. Analytically, these situations can be interpreted either as a difference between private and social returns, or an income distribution problem. The point here is that because of substantial disparities between private and public benefits, and the redistribution effects, an optimal transfer of labour from lower to higher productivity areas may not occur, even with the Mobility Program. And in terms of the model, measurements of family income differentials will not necessarily yield a true index of the Mobility Program's benefits or costs.

A change in residence imparts psychological as well as financial costs to the family. Traditional investment theory rules out psychic costs on grounds that workers take these into account anyway in calculating their marginal rates of substitution of work for leisure, saving for consuming, etc. It follows that mobility incentives that are concerned with overcoming psychological costs in fact upset the necessary optimizing condition.[15] But this line of reasoning blurs the distinction between *ex ante* and *ex post* satisfactions. Families undoubtedly have high psychological attachment to familiar areas — but once they move and establish new roots and familiarities, their sentiments and preference functions change. Mobility incentives over and above the real costs of travel, removal and risk, may thus be well justified. Analytically, however, this is difficult to prove. It is the old Scitovsky-Kaldor double welfare criterion in new

15. This for instance is Sjaastad's view in his 1962 *J. P. E. Supp.* study "The Costs and Returns of Human Migration," p. 85.

garb.[16] Suffice perhaps that we recognize these incentives as costs, but because of our inability to measure psychic benefits before and after, acknowledge that we cannot relate these extra costs to individual satisfactions.

Table II clearly demonstrates the limitations of the mobility model we have constructed. Virtually all secondary, social and psychic benefits are ignored. Nor do we attempt to gauge the spill-over effects or the impact of the program on regions through the multiplier processes, or indeed upon the aggregate trade-off between unemployment and inflation. These remain areas open to further work.

Thus acknowledging our many shortcomings, let us go on to the methodology and to the model itself.

Methodology

The procedures adopted in developing the benefit-cost model included:

(1) Obtaining each workers' personal and family information, job and unemployment histories and estimated wages in the leaving and destination communities from their Mobility Program application forms.

(2) Matching the individual data against separate estimates of worker tenure by industry, and regressing it against a model predicting the probability of moving successfully as a function of personal and job history characteristics.

(3) Obtaining income frequency distributions for each separate labour market from Federal National Revenue Income Tax files; identifying therein the median income for men and women, disaggregated by age and marital status; and establishing the income percentile each applicant occupies in the leaving and destination labour markets.

(4) Again from National Revenue files, obtaining gross migration rates between separate labour markets, broken out according to absolute and relative income differentials and absolute and relative "percentile" differentials.

---

16. See N. Kaldor, "A Note on Tariffs and the Terms of Trade," *Economica* 7 (Nov. 1940): 377-380, and T. Scitovsky, "A Note on Welfare Propositions in Economics," *Review of Economic Studies* 9 (Nov. 1941): 77-88, and the general discussion in W. Baumol, *Economic Theory and Operations Analysis* (Englewood Cliffs: Prentice-Hall, 1965), p. 267.

Table II

MANPOWER MOBILITY PROGRAM

PRIMARY OR DIRECT BENEFITS

	Code
Real output attributable to workers moved into the new job in the destination area	XP
Real output attributable to workers in subsequent jobs in the destination labour market	AP
Real output attributable to their (i) wives, (ii) children in destination market	A
Additional real output attributable to the owners of capital employing the (i) workers, (ii) wives, (iii) children who moved	—

SECONDARY OR INDIRECT BENEFITS

	Code
"Multiplier Effect" stimuli to destination areas	—
Economies of scale in destination areas	—
Unemployed in leaving areas can fill the jobs vacated	—
Reduction in the demand for social overhead capital in leaving areas	—
Less pressure on price increases due to faster filling of vacancies	—
Better productivity, international competitiveness and foreign exchange earnings	—

PSYCHIC OR SOCIAL BENEFITS

	Code
Greater overall sense of family security	—
Job satisfaction and permanent employment	—
Positive encouragement to new investment	—
Social dynamism due to interchange of ideas, and productive methods	—

PRIMARY OR DIRECT COSTS

	Code
Travel and removal expenditures	X
Administrative costs of Mobility Program	X
Real output attributable to the workers in their old job	XA
Real output attributable to workers in subsequent occupations in the old area	A
Real output attributable to their (i) wives, (ii) children in immediate or potential employment in the old labour market	A
Additional real output attributable to the owners of capital employing the (i) workers, (ii) wives, (iii) children who moved	—

SECONDARY OR INDIRECT COSTS

	Code
Negative "Multiplier Effect" in leaving areas	—
Reduced economies of scale in leaving areas	—
Reduced job vacancies for unemployed in leaving areas	—
Increased demand for social overhead capital facilities in destination areas	—
Possible interference with normal free market forces and individual incentives	—

PSYCHIC OR SOCIAL COSTS

	Code
Greater family uncertainty	—
Job dissatisfaction and heightened likelihood of additional unemployment	—
Negative impact on employers' investment plans	—
Social tension due to increased congestion, pollution, and urban over-crowding	—

CODE
X Actual figures available through the Manpower Mobility Program information system
P Predicted from equations within the model
A Attributed, drawing on exogenous labour market information
— Not considered or assumed to have an insignificant or neutral effect.

A discussion of the methods and sub-models used in these derivations follows shortly.

The income frequency distributions disaggregated by labour market, sex, age, marital status, movers and non-movers, are stored on magnetic tape. As each worker's characteristics are coded and programmed, their absolute and relative incomes, and absolute and relative "percentiles" in the destination and leaving areas are computed, and matched against stored data for all movers and non-movers in the economy. By a simple regression we obtain a migration rate value for each worker, which with some adjustment provides us with a reasonable measure of probability that given the income incentives confronting him, the worker would have moved independently of the Mobility Program. We can then gauge how much of the net benefits (or losses) to attribute to the Program. Thus, if for instance, the probability is .10 that a worker *with a given expected annual income differential* would in one year have moved on his own, it is then only reasonable that we attribute .90 of his family's incremental gains in the first year to the Mobility Program. In the second year, if the differential stays the same, the attributed amount would be $.90^2$, and so on.

Once this data is assembled, the calculation of benefit-cost ratios for the Manpower Mobility Program is relatively simple. It involves merely aggregating the differential benefits of:

(1) the worker in his first job in the destination area,

(2) the worker in subsequent jobs,

(3) the wife during the same time period, and,

(4) other dependents during a calculated time period,

subjecting these to the probability function for the worker moving autonomously and relating the aggregate estimate to the mobility grant and overhead costs associated with the worker's move.

The key variables and formulae take the following form:

(I) *Present value of worker's net differential in the first job in the destinattion area.*

$$\overline{Y}_i = \sum_{t=0}^{t=T} \left(k_{(t+a)} \left\{ \frac{(Y_{ij})_1 - (Y_i)_0}{(1+r)^t} \right\} \prod_{t=0}^{t=t} b_{\left[(t+a),\ i,\ d\right]} \right) \tag{I}$$

where,

i = Worker designation

j = Industry to which the worker moves

t = 0, 1, 2 . . . . . .

T = Expected length of employment in the new job, which in turn is determined by α_{ij}, the normal turnover period of industry j, and η_i, the worker's personality coefficient based on past job history, education, marital status etc.

The functional relationship is simply

$$T = \text{closest integer} < \eta_i \cdot \alpha_{ij}$$

and is described in the two sub-models set out in the next section.

$(Y_{ij})_1$ = Annual wages of the worker in his new destination job

$(Y_i)_0$ = Imputed annual wages of the worker in his old area[17]

r = Rate of discount

a = Worker's age when he moved under the Mobility Program

k = Life expectancy for 1 more year

d = Worker's annual wage differential in year $(t + a)$ and,

b = Autonomous mobility coefficient, i.e., the proportion of the worker's net differential income attributable to the Mobility program, derived from the sub-model that measures the probability of workers moving on their own.

(II) *Present value of the worker's net differential in subsequent employment in the destination area.*

$$\overline{Y}_i^1 = Z_i \left(\sum_{t=T+1}^{t=s-a} \left\{ k_{(t+a)} \left(\frac{(Y_i)_{11} - (Y_i)_0}{(1+r)^t} \right)_{t=T+1}^{t=t} b_{(t+a), i, d} \right\} \right) \quad \text{(II)}$$

where,

s = Terminal age for the worker (i.e., 65 years)

$s - a$ = Worker's expected remaining work life

$(Y_i)_{11}$ = Worker's expected annual wages in all subsequent jobs. What

---

17. We used the mean of the worker's highest and lowest wage during the preceding three years, despite the fact that most workers moving under the Mobility Program are unemployed with no apparent prospects of getting work locally. Our definition of $(Y_i)_0$ thus nullifies any accusation of under-estimating opportunity costs, and thus inflating the benefit-cost ratio.

the worker ultimately earns, and where he goes after the first job is of course open to speculation. If we assume that he moved to his best chance in the new area, $(Y_i)_{11}$ becomes a measure of the next best job. Ruling out any skill increases derived from his first job, it seems reasonable to suppose that each worker in his second or subsequent jobs in the new area will occupy the same percentile of the income curve as he occupied when earning $(Y_i)_0$ in the leaving area. This assumption offers several attractions. It requires minimal extra data and provides a conservative estimate of differential benefits. Perhaps even more important, this measure coincides generally with the realities of the alternatives, i.e., $(Y_i)_{11} > (Y_i)_0$ when the destination labour market offers better paying alternatives at all levels of income, and $(Y_i)_{11} < (Y_i)_0$ when it offers poorer paying alternatives.

$Z = $ A labour market variable that varies between 0 and 1 depending on the alternative job opportunities in the labour market to which the worker initially relocates. If there are no second-best employment prospects in the destination area $Z = 0$, and the workers are removed from the benefit stream. This procedure eliminates double counting if they move again with a second mobility grant. The value of Z may be arbitrarily determined according to changing labour market information, or may simply be set as a function of labour market size.

(III) *Present value of wife's imputed differential.*

$$X_i = \sum_{t=0}^{t=T} \left(k_{(t+m)} \left\{ \frac{B_i(x_i)_1 - (x_i)_0}{(1+r)^t} \right\}_{t=0}^{t=t} \quad b_{(t+a), i, d} \right)$$

$$+ Z_1 \left[\sum_{t=T+1}^{t=s-a} \left(k_{(t+m)} \left\{ \frac{B_i(x_i)_1 - (x_i)_0}{(1+r)^t} \right\}_{t=T+1}^{t=t} b_{(t+a), i, d} \right) \right] \quad \text{(III)}$$

where,

$m = $ Wife's age (assumed to equal the husband's)

$(x_i)_1$ = Median female earnings in the destination labour market

$(x_i)_0$ = Median female earnings in the leaving labour market

B_i = A measure of the wife's probability of working relative to her situation in the leaving area. The destination area may offer, for instance, much better or worse demand prospects for female employment. Or the wife may be more or less strongly motivated to work. While recognizing the inter-dependencies, we used female participation and unplaced registrations rates derived from Canada Manpower Centres, and a method developed by Sylvia Ostry[18] to regress age, region and husband's income on female participation rates, to derive the following formulation for B_i:

$$B_i = \frac{(p^c_{1m} D_1) - f_1}{(p^c_{0m} D_0) - f_0} \cdot \frac{D_0}{D_1} \tag{IIIa}$$

where,

$P_{0, 1}$ = Female participation rates in sending and destination areas for married women age m computed by the Ostry formula

$D_{0, 1}$ = Female populations over 15 years of age in sending and destination areas

$F_{0, 1}$ = Unplaced female registrants reported by Canada Manpower Centres in the sending and destination areas

c = Proportion of females in the labour force who seek work through Canada Manpower Centres (assumed constant).

(IV) *Present value of differential for dependent children.*

$$Q_i = Z_i \left[\sum_{w=1}^{w=n_i} k_{(18-g_{wi})} \sum_{t=g_{wi}}^{t=(g_{wi}+e)} \left\{ k_{(t+a)} \left\{ \frac{(q_{wi})_1 - (q_{wi})_0}{(1+r)^t} \right\} \prod_{t=g_{wi}}^{t=t} b \left((t+a), i, d \right) \right\} \right] \tag{IV}$$

where,

n_i = Number of children of worker i

a = Age of the child w

---

18. Sylvia Ostry, *The Female Worker in Canada*, Dominion Bureau of Statistics, 1961 Census Monagraph Programme (Ottawa: Queen's Printer, 1968), p. 51.

g = Estimated number of years until each child starts working (we assume children enter the labour force at age 18)

e = Estimated working life of each child over which differentials may be attributed to the Mobility Program. The choice here is judgmental, based on how soon each child moves away from the family household and the area. Probability estimates could be derived either from migration rates by age category or from marriage data.

$(q_{wi})_1$ = imputed annual wage for dependent w in the destination labour market

$(q_{wi})_0$ = Imputed annual wage for dependents in the leaving labour market.

Logically the two imputed wages should be functionally related to different educational expectations in each labour market. Such information is not available, and the $(q_{wi})_{0, 1}$, estimates are simply the median incomes, by age and sex, taken from the tax files for each labour market.

The present value of income differentials for the entire family then is simply the summation $\overline{Y}_i + \overline{Y}_i^1 + X_i + Q_i$.

On the cost side, since the opportunity costs have been calculated in the numerator, the only other direct expenditures for moving each family are the relocation grants themselves, G_i — which we assume cover full travel and removal costs, plus imputed risks and motivational incentives — and the departmental overhead costs C_i. Aggregating the benefits and costs for all families then we get simply:

$$\frac{B}{C} = \sum_{i=1}^{i=N} \left(\overline{Y}_i + \overline{Y}_i^1 + X_i + Q_i \middle/ G_i + C_i \right)$$

where,

N = The total number of workers moved under the Manpower Mobility Program during any given period.

Computations and aggregation of family benefits are all very well, but not unusual. They simply follow traditional analytic paths. However, the considerations that determine $T_i = \eta_i \propto_i$ — the best estimate of how long each worker will stay in his new job — are important. And even more useful are the insights drawn from analyzing gross migration patterns and estimating the autonomous mobility coefficient b_i, which sets the portion of each family's stream of net benefits attributable to the Mobility Program. It is here that we have had to break new ground.

The Sub-models[19]

(I) *Expected tenure of workers in Canadian industries (derivation of α_i).*

Our hypothesis is simply this:

> The probability of employees leaving a firm is functionally related to the length of service they have already put in. Because working conditions vary so much among different industries, there will be substantial differences in quit rates during the first month. For new employees therefore, the first month serves as a pivot, setting subsequent levels of survival. But after that the expected rate of survival is a simple function of the time an employee will put in on the job. And this initial functional relationship (i.e., slope of the expected survival curve) is the same for every industry.

If our hypothesis proves right, we could set a regression to the one month pivot point, and obtain an expected value α_i, the length of time an average worker will remain with an employing firm in an industry. For our mobility model, then, we could combine this expected value α_i with each individual worker's "personality coefficient" η_i (see sub-model II) to get a best estimate T_i for his expected length of employment in his first job in the destination area.

Very little research has been done on survival rates among cohorts of new employees in Canadian industries. We drew therefore on some empirical findings of the British Institute of Management, in 1951,[20] and fitted a series of regressions to employee survival rates in 17 industries, allowing the intercept term to equal the survival rate after one month. The best fitting regression took the following form:

$$(S_i)_t = T + \beta \log t + E; \quad t = 1, 3, 12 \text{ and } 60 \text{ months}$$
$$i = 1, 2, \ldots 17$$

---

19. A more detailed report on each of these sub-models is available on request.
20. British Institute of Management, *Labour Turnover Analysis 1949-50* (London, 1951).

where $(S_i)_t$ = survival rate for industry i at time t
E = error term.

The results were:

coefficient (β): -39.6 (significant at 1% level)
coefficient of determination (R^2): .88 (significant at 1% level).

We then got a pooled "beta" estimate by averaging the seventeen slopes, and tested to see whether the pooled estimate could be used as a valid proxy for the "beta" coefficients of each industry separately. As Table III shows, the improvement from using separate slopes for each industry is not significant. We therefore concluded that except for the first month after joining a firm, workers in one industry will likely leave at the same rate as workers in any other industry.

Table III

17 INDUSTRIES

Source of Variation	d. f.	Sum of Squares	Mean Square	F. Ratio	Significance
Single line regression	1	47,269	47,269		
Residual term	66	6,511	98.7		
—Amount of residual explained by fitting regression lines with same slope to each industry	16	3520.2	220.0	2.23	Significant at $\propto$ = .01
—Increment in amount of residual explained by fitting regression lines with different slopes rather than same slopes	16	1253.1	78.2	.79	N.S.
—Amount of residual still not explained	34	1737.7	51.1		
TOTAL —	67	53,780			

We then used the same predictive equation for workers in similar U.S. industries, on the view that if the regression could significantly simulate survival rates among U.S. workers, there would be a good case for adopting it in Canada. The principle sources of U.S. job tenure information were various Special Labour Force Reports published in the B.L.S. *Monthly Labor Review*.[21] Although these involve a cross-sectional cut of employed workers as against the longitudinal cohort view taken by the British study, by taking several of the simplifying assumptions from Lane and Andrews' 1955 study[22] we were able to compare the two sets of data. Our findings confirmed that subject to differences in the number of first month dropouts, survival rates among U.S. workers were similar to those in the United Kingdom; we therefore felt justified in applying the single pooled regression to Canadian turnover data.[23]

The result is a set of best estimates $\propto_i$ for how long an average new employee will stay with a firm in a specified industry in Canada. These estimates are listed in the Appendix. They indicate that the average Canadian worker stays with new employer less than sixteen months, and in industries subject to seasonal swings the tenure expectation is less than eight months. As workers stay longer and acquire more experience and seniority, of course, their tenure expectations become more elastic. But since the Manpower Mobility Program helps workers to move into a new job, it is these initial tenure expectations $\propto_i$ that are relevant to our calculations.

(II) *The personality coefficient (derivation of η_i).*

Having found $\propto_i$, we must now make allowances for the stochastic individuality of each worker using the Mobility Program. There are those older and those younger than the average, some married and some single, with more or less training, with stable and unstable job histories and so on. If we can quantify these characteristics to yield a success probability for each worker, we can then transform this probability into a "personality

---

21. See Seymour Wolfbein, "Job Tenure of American Workers," *Monthly Labor Review* 75 (Sept. 1952): 257-262; H. Hamel, "Job Tenure of American Workers January 1963," *Monthly Labor Review* 86 (Oct. 1963): 1145-1152, and "Job Tenure of American Workers January 1966," *Monthly Labor Review* 90 (Jan. 1967): 31-37.

22. K. Lane and J. Andrews, "A Method of Turnover Analysis," *Journal of the Royal Statistical Society* 18, pt. 3 (1955).

23. Using turnover data of course yields probabilities of leaving from stocks that are being replenished, whereas we need probabilities from unreplenished stocks of employees all hired simultaneously. However, the discrepancy at the one month pivot point is probably not very large.

coefficient" η_i and arrive at a best estimate of each individual's survival expectations T_i in his destination job. The hypothesis is therefore:

> The success or non-success of a relocation is a function of age, marital status, number of dependents, formal education, specific training, past job history, distance of move, and other personal and environmental characteristics, all of which can be represented by a linear multiple regression equation.

To test this hypothesis, we conducted a sample follow-up of 200 workers across Canada.[24] We defined a successful relocation as one in which the worker was employed in the relocation area at the time of follow-up, i.e., 6-9 months after the move. A non-successful relocation was one where the worker had either returned home, was unemployed, or had left his job and his whereabouts were unknown. We left open the category of movers who were employed in a third area — since we could not gauge whether the initial move had or had not contributed to their finding their subsequent jobs.

We then set up a series of contingency tables and identified the variables significant to the success or failure of the moves. Having done this, we constructed a regression model with a dichotomous dependent variable (success, failure) representative by 0 and 1 values. Following Orcutt[25] we also represented the independent variables by a set of 0/1 dummies. The variables are listed in the Appendix. The regression took the usual form

$$Y = a + \sum_{i=1}^{k} b_i X_{ij}; \quad j = 1, 2 \ldots n$$

where, k = number of independent variables
and n = number of observations.

We ran a number of regressions of this type, and the best results are given in Table IV. Here there are four significant variables — marital status, incidences of unemployment, employment in the manufacturing industry before the move, and employment in primary or unskilled occupations before the move. Several other variables are close to being significant. The R^2 is highly significant at the 99% level. The standard error is extremely low at 0.204.

Although the R^2 is not very high, we had deliberately looked at only the supply side of effort and ignored the demand side variables (since these we

---

24. We recognize of course the limitations of small samples when testing the significance of many variables. A systematic follow-up procedure on every mover is now incorporated into the Manpower Mobility Program.
25. G. Orcutt, *Microanalysis of Socioeconomic Systems: A Simulation Study* (New York: Harper & Row, 1961), pp. 216-231.

Table IV

PERSONALITY COEFFICIENT

Results from Regressing Variables Listed Below on Success/Failure
of a Move

$R^2 = .2060^{**}$; Standard error $= .2038$; $F(14,188) = 3.483$

Major Headings for Variables	Order in which Variables were Introduced	R^2	Increase in R^2
EMPLOYMENT HISTORY			
(1) Industrial Attachment	(i) Employed in the fishing, forestry, trapping or mining industry before the move	.0046	.0046
	(ii) Employed in the manufacturing industry before the move	.0386	.0339
	(iii) Employed in printing, publishing and allied industries before the move	.0393	.0007
	(iv) Employed in the construction or transportation industry before the move	.0570	.0177
(2) Occupational Attachment	(i) Employed in an agricultural, fisheries and forestry or unskilled occupation before the move	.0894	.0324
	(ii) Employed in a professional and managerial or a skilled occupation before the move	.0894	.0001
(3) Unemployment	Incidences of unemployment in the 3 years before the move	.1264	.0370
PERSONAL CHARACTERISTICS			
(1) Marital Status	Married, single or other	.1454	.0189
(2) Formal Education	(i) Completed grade 8 or less	.1728	.0275
	(ii) Completed grade 11 or more	.1810	.0082
(3) Other Skill Training	Vocational training, apprenticeship courses, etc.	.1880	.0070
(4) Age	(i) Under 25 years	.1990	.0110
	(ii) 25 - 34 years	.2057	.0068
	(iii) 35 - 44 years	.2060	.0002

assumed were covered by the $\propto_i$ term). At best therefore, we could not expect an R^2 much higher than 50%. There was of course also a high degree of multicollinearity among the independent variables, even with interaction terms. How much was not clear since dummy variables do not lend themselves to meaningful matrices of correlation coefficients. However, since we are using the regression as a predictor rather than as an explanatory instrument, this is not too serious a matter. Since the personality coefficient *per se* serves as a scalar for the expected tenure variable $\propto_i$, the last step was to set up a one to one correspondence between the predicted probability of moving successfully and the continuous 0 to 2 η value arbitrarily assigned to the personality coefficient.

(III) *Autonomous mobility coefficient (derivation of b_i).*

Through an examination of the reported earnings and location of tax filers in two successive years, it should be possible to identify a migration rate for workers in response to observable income and "status" differentials, where "status" is defined as the percentile one occupies on the income cumulant of one's community. We focused primarily on families who by moving voluntarily increased their real income and, by assumption, their marginal productivity. (Where families move in response to negative differentials, it seems reasonable to assume that their motives are non-economic.) Under several severe but necessary assumptions,[26] we can regress migration rates against the income and percentile differentials, and if the results are significant, use this information to predict the probability that a worker will move autonomously in response to observed opportunities. The hypothesis is that:

> The higher the expected absolute and relative income differentials, and the higher the expected absolute and relative percentile gain, the greater the probability that workers will move voluntarily to a more favourable labour market within the year. If a migration rate M_1 represents the probability that a worker will move voluntarily within the year, then $(1 - M_i)$ equals the probability that he will not move in that time. If this hypothesis is valid, then for each worker taking out a mobility grant, we can calculate expected diff-

---

26. i.e., (i) that filers in the same locations did not move during the year, and those in different locations moved only once.

    (ii) that *ex post* reported income differentials coincide with *ex ante* differentials expectations.

    (iii) that income expectations for filers who do not move coincides with the average increase in wages and earnings in their region.

erentials and predict the probability of his not moving had he not received the grant. Since he did move, we may attribute $(1 - M_i)$ of his family income differential to the Program.

Employing the full Canadian income tax file for 1965-66, and coding the earnings data in $200 intervals, we developed a program which:

(a) Sorted filers reporting in both years by age, sex, marital status, labour market and initial income class.

(b) Sorted into movers and non-movers, identifying all movers and a 10 per cent systematic sample of the non-movers.

(c) Calculated for each of the movers their absolute and relative income differentials (adjusted to take account of annual wage increases), and their absolute and relative percentile differentials.

For each labour market, then, there is an income distribution curve by age, sex and marital status in the computer ready to be matched against the inflow of data on each worker using the Manpower Mobility Program.

The second step was to calculate the migration rates for each sex, age and marital status group, for each of the income classes, and relate these to the absolute income differential (A.I.D.) relative income differential (R.I.D.) absolute percentile differential (A.P.D.) and relative percentile differential (R.P.D.). (See Appendix, Examples A and B.)

The last step was to carry out for each age, sex and marital group the following regressions:

$$M_i = a + b_1 X_{1i} + b_2 X_{2i} + b_3 P_{1i} + b_4 P_{2i}$$

where,

M_1 = Migration rate/income group; $i = 1, 2, \ldots 13$ for movers with a positive income differential.

X_{1i} = Mean absolute income differential/income group,

X_{2i} = Mean relative income differential/income group,

P_{1i} = Mean absolute percentile differential/income group,

P_{2i} = Mean relative percentile differential/income group.

The results are given in the Appendix. Despite the high degree of multicollinearity between the variables (see the accompanying Table of Correlation Coefficients), most results are highly significant. We appear justified therefore in using the formulae to assign an expected migration rate M_i to each of the workers moving under the Manpower Mobility Program.

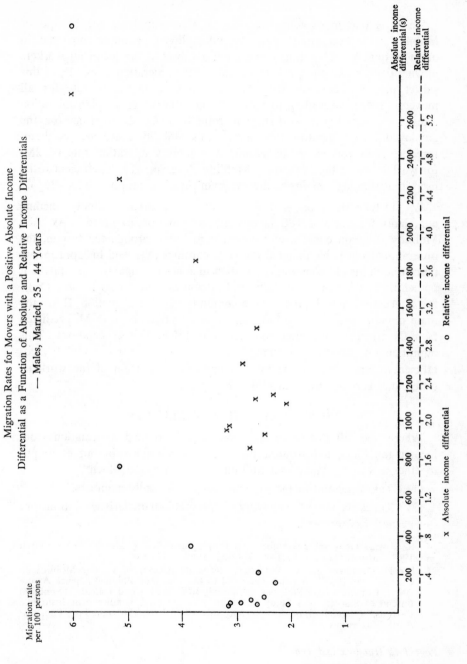

Migration Rates for Movers with a Positive Absolute Income
Differential as a Function of Absolute and Relative Income Differentials
— Males, Married, 35 - 44 Years —

There is one more consideration. Workers applying for Manpower Mobility relocation grants must be unemployed or under-employed in order to qualify. They thus come from a subset of the set of all workers moving between labour markets annually. The migration rates M^1_i of this subset may not coincide with M_i the expected migration rate for all movers. Indeed according to Saben [27] and others[28] geographic migration rates for unemployed workers are roughly twice as high as for the employed. In computing the autonomous mobility coefficient b_i therefore, it seems reasonable to assume a voluntary migration rate of $2M_i$ for workers using the Manpower Mobility Program. The coefficient to be used in attributing benefits to the Program thus becomes $b_i = (1 - 2M_i)$.

Let us take stock of what we are now able to do. Firstly, income cumulants for each of 180 labour markets are programmed. As each Mobility Program client's information card flows through the system, the program calculates his imputed foregone earnings $(Y_i)_0$ and his appropriate percentile in his old community. It then matches this against the equivilent percentile in the new community and attributes a next best income $(Y_i)_{11}$ for alternative jobs in the new community, as per Equation II of the main model. Secondly, we have an expected migration rate M_i predicted from the client's own income and percentile differentials expectations. This migration rate can then be transformed into the autonomous mobility coefficient b_i and used to attribute an appropriate portion of the worker's differential earnings to the Mobility Program.

SUMMARY AND CONCLUSION

Where does all this leave us? We have combined information from income tax filers, industrial turnover data and follow-up sources to put together a working Manpower Mobility Program model which:

(1) Takes account of the expectations of all family members,

(2) Takes account of each worker's personal characteristics, job history and environment,

27. S. Saben, "Geographic Mobility and Employment Status, March 1962 - March 1963," *Monthly Labor Review* 87 (Aug. 1964): 873-881.

28. See H. Greenway and G. Wheatley, "Regional Aspects of Labour Mobility in Canada 1956-1959" (A paper delivered to the Canadian Political Science Association, Conference on Statistics, Montreal, June 1961); and Canada, Dominion Bureau of Statistics, "A Study of Mobility Based on Unemployment Insurance Records," *Canadian Statistical Review*, July 1960, Nov. 1961 and Jan., Feb. and April 1962 issues.

(3) Gives a reasonable estimate of the period over which we can compute his initial earnings differential,

(4) Gives a relatively conservative estimate of the earnings differentials in alternative employment in the destination community,

(5) Removes him altogether from the Program calculations if the destination market has few alternatives,

(6) Through the use of the autonomous mobility coefficient b_1, provides a measure of benefits that is consistent with the Mobility Program's main economic purpose — i.e., to move workers who would not otherwise have moved to more productive opportunities.

The proof of the pudding is in the eating. Let us run an example through the model:

John Smith, age 29, married with a wife and child aged 6, moves from Halifax to Winnipeg. He has Grade 11 education, no vocational training, and has been unemployed twice in the previous three years. He is semi-skilled and moving from and to firms in the Misc. Mfg. Industry. His unweighted high-low average annual earnings in Halifax were $3,000; his reported annual earnings in Winnipeg will be $4,500. Median wages for women in Halifax are $2,000, in Winnipeg $2,400; and for males under 25 years of age, they are currently $3,000 in Halifax and $3,500 in Winnipeg. Interest rate: 10%.

Costs involve:

(a) Travel and removal expenses	$750
(b) Re-establishment grant	400
(c) Overhead	50
	$1200

The pertinent calculations for this client are:

(1) Personality coefficient: $\eta_i = 1.98$

(2) Expected tenure in Misc. Mfg. Ind.: $\alpha_j = 12.8$ months

(3) Client's expected initial job tenure: $T = 2$

(4) Autonomous mobility coefficient
    (a) During first job $b_i = (1 - 2 \times .05) = .90$
    (b) In alternative occupation $b_i = (1 - 2 \times .02) = .96$

(5) Wife's working probability in Winnipeg relative to Halifax:
$B_1 = .89$

Given these parameters, the Present Value of family benefits are roughly: $\overline{Y}_i = \$2,300$; $\overline{Y}_i{}^1 = \$1,500$; $X_1 = \$700$; $Q_1 = \$200$
Present Value, Total Benefits $= \$4,700$
Benefit-Cost Ratio $= \dfrac{4.7}{1.2} = 3.9$

We postulated a fairly extreme example, where the worker's absolute and relative differentials in the first job were $1,500 and 50% respectively. This is high — the Canada Mobility Program so far shows first job differentials of about $1,000 and 20% respectively. But the example demonstrates two things —

(a) that the model is workable, and,

(b) the results it yields will be in line with reasonable expectations for the Program.

APPENDIX

JOB TENURE BY INDUSTRY
CANADA

Industry	Average Monthly Turnover 1964-1966 (Per cent)	Expected Length of Job Tenure* (Months)
Forestry (mainly logging)	29.8	3.3
Mining	5.6	13.5
Metals	5.1	13.9
Fuels	6.1	13.1
Non-metals	4.3	14.5
Quarrying	9.6	10.7
Manufacturing	5.2	13.8
Foods, etc.	7.6	12.0
Tobacco	6.1	13.1
Rubber	3.9	14.9
Leather	4.9	14.1
Textiles	4.2	14.6
Clothing	6.1	13.1
Wood	8.0	11.7
Paper	3.5	15.2
Printing	3.8	15.0
Iron and steel	4.8	14.1
Transportation equipment	4.8	14.1
Non-ferrous metal products	4.3	14.5
Electrical apparatus	3.8	15.0
Non-metallic mineral products	6.1	13.1
Petroleum and coal products	2.0	16.6
Chemicals	3.3	15.4
Misc. Mfg.	6.5	12.8
Construction	16.0	7.3
General contractors	18.1	6.5
Subcontractors	12.7	8.9
Transportation, etc.	3.4	15.3
Transportation	3.5	15.2
Storage	4.9	14.1
Communication	2.5	16.2
Public Utility Operation	2.9	15.8
Trade	5.3	13.7
Wholesale	4.8	14.1
Retail	5.7	13.4
Finance, etc.	4.0	14.8
Service, except government	5.8	13.3
Community	2.8	15.9
Recreation	10.7	10.0
Business	5.7	13.4
Personal	9.1	11.0

Source: DBS, "Hirings and Separations".

* Expected length of job tenure = antilog $\left[\dfrac{50.0 - (100.0 - \text{average monthly turnover})}{-39.3} \right]$

VARIABLES FOR REGRESSION ON SUCCESSFUL AND UNSUCCESSFUL RELOCATEES

Personally Coefficient

Age

$X_1 = 0$ if client is other than under 25
$\quad = 1$ if client is under 25

$X_2 = 0$ if client is other than 25-34
$\quad = 1$ if client is 25-34

$X_3 = 0$ if client is other than 35-44
$\quad = 1$ if client is 35-44

Marital Status

$X_4 = 0$ if client is married
$\quad = 1$ if client is single, widowed, separated or divorced

Education

$X_5 = 0$ if client has other than grade 8 or less
$\quad = 1$ if client has grade 8 or less

$X_6 = 0$ if client has other than grade 11 or more
$\quad = 1$ if client has grade 11 or more

Vocational Training

$X_7 = 0$ if client has no vocational training
$\quad = 1$ if client has some vocational training

Incidences of Unemployment

$X_8 = 0$ if client has other than 3 incidences
$\quad = 1$ if client has 3 or more incidences

Industry Before the Move

$X_9 = 0$ if client was employed in an industry other than fishing, forestry, trapping and mining before the move
$\quad = 1$ if client was employed in the fishing, forestry, trapping or mining industry before the move

Page Two Hundred and Fourteen

Industry Before the Move (continued)

$X_{10} = 0$ if client was employed in an industry other than manufacturing before the move

    $= 1$ if client was employed in the manufacturing industry before the move

$X_{11} = 0$ if client was employed in an industry other than printing, publishing and allied industries before the move

    $= 1$ if client was employed in the printing, publishing and allied industries before the move

$X_{12} = 0$ if client was employed in an industry other than construction and transportation before the move

    $= 1$ if client was employed in the construction or transportation industry before the move

Occupation Before the Move

$X_{13} = 0$ if client was employed in an occupation other than agriculture, fisheries and forestry or an unskilled occupation before the move

    $= 1$ if client was employed in an agricultural, fisheries and forestry, or an unskilled occupation before the move

$X_{14} = 0$ if client was employed in an occupation other than professional and managerial or a skilled occupation before the move

    $= 1$ if client was employed in a professional and managerial or a skilled occupation before the move

AUTONOMOUS MOBILITY COEFFICIENT
EXAMPLE A
All Males, Married, 19 Years

Income	Movers	Non-Movers	Y Times Non-Movers	Movers + Y Times Non-Movers	Movers + Y Times Non-Movers	Cumulative Per Cent*	Migration Rate**
	(Number)	(Number)	(Number)	(Number)	(Cumulative)		
< 1,000	a_1	b_1	$Y(b_1)$	$a_1 + Y(b_1)$	$a_1 + Y(b_1)$	P_1	M_1
1,000 - 1,999	a_2	b_2	$Y(b_2)$	$a_2 + Y(b_2)$	$\sum_{i=1}^{2} a_i + Y(b_i)$	P_2	M_2
2,000 - 2,999	a_3	b_3	$Y(b_3)$	$a_3 + Y(b_3)$	$\sum_{i=1}^{3} a_i + Y(b_i)$	P_3	M_3
3,000 - 3,999	a_4	b_4	$Y(b_4)$	$a_4 + Y(b_4)$	$\sum_{i=1}^{4} a_i + Y(b_i)$	P_4	M_4
4,000 - 4,999	a_5	b_5	$Y(b_5)$	$a_5 + Y(b_5)$	$\sum_{i=1}^{5} a_i + Y(b_i)$	P_5	M_5
5,000 - 5,999	a_6	b_6	$Y(b_6)$	$a_6 + Y(b_6)$	$\sum_{i=1}^{6} a_i + Y(b_i)$	P_6	M_6
6,000 - 6,999	a_7	b_7	$Y(b_7)$	$a_7 + Y(b_7)$	$\sum_{i=1}^{7} a_i + Y(b_i)$	P_7	M_7
7,000 - 7,999	a_8	b_8	$Y(b_8)$	$a_8 + Y(b_8)$	$\sum_{i=1}^{8} a_i + Y(b_i)$	P_8	M_8
8,000 - 8,999	a_9	b_9	$Y(b_9)$	$a_9 + Y(b_9)$	$\sum_{i=1}^{9} a_i + Y(b_i)$	P_9	M_9
9,000 - 9,999	a_{10}	b_{10}	$Y(b_{10})$	$a_{10} + Y(b_{10})$	$\sum_{i=1}^{10} a_i + Y(b_i)$	P_{10}	M_{10}
10,000 - 11,999	a_{11}	b_{11}	$Y(b_{11})$	$a_{11} + Y(b_{11})$	$\sum_{i=1}^{11} a_i + Y(b_i)$	P_{11}	M_{11}
12,000 - 14,999	a_{12}	b_{12}	$Y(b_{12})$	$a_{12} + Y(b_{12})$	$\sum_{i=1}^{12} a_i + Y(b_i)$	P_{12}	M_{12}
15,000 +	a_{13}	b_{13}	$Y(b_{13})$	$a_{13} + Y(b_{13})$	$\sum_{i=1}^{13} a_i + Y(b_i)$	P_{13}	M_{13}
Total	A	B	$Y(B)$	$A + Y(B)$			

$$* \ P_1 \ = \ \frac{a_1 + Y(b_1)}{A + Y(B)} \ \times \ 100$$

$$P_2 \ = \ \frac{\sum_{i=1}^{2} a_i + Y(b_i)}{A + Y(B)} \ \times \ 100$$

$$\circ$$
$$\circ$$
$$\circ$$

$$P_{13} \ = \ \frac{A + Y(B)}{A + Y(B)} \ \times \ 100 \ = \ 100\%$$

**Migration Rate:

$$M_1 \ = \ \frac{a_1}{a_1 + Y(b_1)}$$

$$M_2 \ = \ \frac{a_2}{a_2 + Y(b_2)}$$

$$\circ$$
$$\circ$$
$$\circ$$

$$M_{13} \ = \ \frac{a_{13}}{a_{13} + Y(b_{13})}$$

EXAMPLE B
Male, Married, Age — 35 to 44

Income	Movers with +VE Aid	Movers with —VE Aid	10 Times Non Movers	Movers Plus CCL 3	Mig'n Rate +VE	Mig'n Rate —VE	Mean Aid Movers +VE Aid	Mean APD Movers —VE Aid	Mean RID Movers +VE Aid	Mean RPD Movers —VE Aid	Mean APD Movers +VE Aid	Mean RPD Movers +VE Aid
< 1000	633	177	9490	10300	0.0615	0.0172	2829.93	1.9153	5.70	0.6841	87.4377	11.4035
1000 - 1999	962	247	17160	18369	0.0524	0.0135	2271.43	—20.3805	1.48	—0.3243	86.0606	2.6355
2000 - 2999	1321	484	34340	36145	0.0366	0.0134	1858.03	—32.3347	0.73	—0.3259	68.1515	0.9985
3000 - 3999	1638	890	60730	63258	0.0259	0.0141	1499.93	—47.1034	0.41	—0.3035	43.0494	0.3845
4000 - 4999	2274	1463	98180	101917	0.0224	0.0144	1157.07	—42.0930	0.25	0.0473	27.6953	0.4439
5000 - 5999	2900	1751	111500	116151	0.0250	0.0151	947.90	—29.0495	0.16	0.1204	23.6712	0.4253
6000 - 6999	2990	1500	87660	91750	0.0283	0.0164	882.79	—14.6705	0.14	0.4432	16.0718	0.5919
7000 - 7999	1702	963	51180	53845	0.0317	0.0179	981.52	—7.6313	0.13	0.3238	9.0976	0.4335
8000 - 8999	1006	660	29550	31216	0.0323	0.0212	981.19	—10.9333	0.11	0.2969	9.9295	0.4077
9000 - 9999	456	454	15860	16770	0.0272	0.0271	1124.43	—4.0770	0.11	0.3154	—1.0131	0.3282
10000 - 11999	465	319	15140	15924	0.0293	0.0201	1298.62	—21.5046	0.12	0.1592	7.2109	0.4151
12000 - 14999	181	161	8170	8512	0.0213	0.0190	1113.18	—28.5092	0.09	0.1973	10.8068	0.4615
15000 +	0	157	8570	8727	0.0000	0.0180	0.0	—14.0699	0.0	0.3291	0.0	0.0

REGRESSION RELATING MIGRATION RATES TO INCOME AND
PERCENTILE DIFFERENTIALS

Model	Constant	Absolute Income Differential	Relative Income Differential	Absolute Percentile Differential	Relative Percentile Differential	D-W	R²
(i) Males, married, under 25	-.0166	.00007 (5.792)				.6353	.7474**
	.00001	.00005 (3.221)	.0130 (2.086)			1.0977	.8108**
	.0191	.00002 (2.104)	.00415 (1.230)	.00199 (5.587)		2.5897	.9566ʳ
	.0195	.00001 (.854)	.0375 (.399)	.00199 (5.252)	-.0157 (-.355)	2.6531	.9513**
(ii) Males, married, 25-34	-.00944	.00005 (3.036)				1.0454	.4276*
	.0202	.00002 (.949)	.0110 (1.614)			1.2079	.5067*
	.0288	.000001 (.057)	.00565 (.911)	.00096 (2.211)		1.4886	.6555**
	.0574	-.00003 (-1.520)	.1859 (3.085)	.00031 (.838)	-.0717 (-2.999)	1.4691	.8277**
(iii) Males, married, 35-44	.00737	.00002 (6.503)				.7708	.7897**
	.0137	.00001 (2.204)	.00257 (1.225)			1.1672	.7997**
	.0154	.00001 (.937)	.00277 (1.168)	.00004 (.237)		1.1450	.7762**
	.00504	.00002 (1.507)	-.0388 (-1.423)	.00017 (1.030)	.0191 (1.529)	.8804	.8083**
(iv) Males, married, 45-64	.00278	.000008 (3.960)				.4129	.5717**
	.0143	-.000003 (-.554)	.00820 (1.989)			.4950	.6694**
	-.00207	.00002 (2.152)	.00280 (.849)	-.00020 (-3.279)		1.5189	.8413**
	.00505	.000009 (1.435)	.0227 (2.746)	-.00028 (-4.928)	-.00432 (-2.530)	2.0582	.9053**

REGRESSION RELATING MIGRATION RATES TO INCOME AND PERCENTILE DIFFERENTIALS

Model	Constant	Absolute Income Differential	Relative Income Differential	Absolute Percentile Differential	Relative Percentile Differential	D-W	R^2
(v) Males, single, under 25	.0390	.0000004 (.076)				.8394	-.0994[N.S.]
	.0353	-.0000004 (-.085)	.00830 (1.665)			1.3571	.0662[N.S.]
	.0230	.000008 (.841)	.00619 (1.155)	.00044 (1.037)		1.1748	.0739[N.S.]
	.0307	.000002 (.143)	.00904 (1.462)	.00008 (.136)	-.00393 (-.944)	1.2872	.0611[N.S.]
(vi) Males, single, 25-34	-.0196	.00006 (5.544)				1.5530	.7300**
	-.0100	.00005 (3.103)	.00442 (.906)			1.3332	.7251**
	-.0184	.00005 (3.919)	.00559 (1.284)	-.00026 (-1.886)		1.3009	.7859**
	-.0167	.00006 (6.149)	-.00355 (-.850)	-.00011 (-1.069)	.0138 (3.140)	2.7005	.8984**
(vii) Males, single, 35-44	-.00635	.00003 (4.501)				1.2066	.6364**
	.00821	.00002 (1.832)	.00528 (1.602)			1.5196	.6856**
	.00754	.00002 (1.771)	.00554 (1.565)	-.00004 (-.366)		1.6390	.6522**
	.0103	.00002 (1.410)	.00559 (1.485)	-.00004 (-.325)	.00021 (.303)	1.6379	.6076*
(viii) Males, single, 45-64	.0185	.0000001 (.064)				.3522	-.0995[N.S.]
	.0132	-.000002 (-3.427)	.0168 (9.130)			(1.6188)	.8809**
	.0135	-.000002 (-3.059)	.0176 (6.430)	-.00002 (-.444)		1.6181	.8693**
	.0118	-.0000008 (-.687)	.0101 (1.495)	-.00002 (.557)	.00885 (1.211)	2.1904	.8765**

CORRELATION COEFFICIENTS —MALES, MARRIED, UNDER 25

	Migration Rate	Absolute Income Differential	Relative Income Differential	Absolute Percentile Differential	Relative Percentile Differential
Migration Rate	1.0000	.8777	.8166	.9689	.7958
Absolute Income Differential		1.0000	.7112	.8135	.6792
Relative Income Differential			1.0000	.7701	.9987
Absolute Percentile Differential				1.0000	.7518
Relative Percentile Differential					1.0000

CORRELATION COEFFICIENTS — MALES, MARRIED, 25-34

	Migration Rate	Absolute Income Differential	Relative Income Differential	Absolute Percentile Differential	Relative Percentile Differential
Migration Rate	1.0000	.6926	.7457	.8455	.7026
Absolute Income Differential		1.0000	.7501	.7461	.7160
Relative Income Differential			1.0000	.7323	.9971
Absolute Percentile Differential				1.0000	.6951
Relative Percentile Differential					1.0000

CORRELATION COEFFICIENTS — MALES, MARRIED, 35-44

	Migration Rate	Absolute Income Differential	Relative Income Differential	Absolute Percentile Differential	Relative Percentile Differential
Migration Rate	1.0000	.8993	.8647	.8145	.8484
Absolute Income Differential		1.0000	.8713	.9175	.8342
Relative Income Differential			1.0000	.7304	.9965
Absolute Percentile Differential				1.0000	.6787
Relative Percentile Differential					1.0000

CORRELATION COEFFICIENTS — MALES, MARRIED, 45-64

	Migration Rate	Absolute Income Differential	Relative Income Differential	Absolute Percentile Differential	Relative Percentile Differential
Migration Rate	1.0000	.7815	.8487	.5118	.8444
Absolute Income Differential		1.0000	.9545	.9170	.8565
Relative Income Differential			1.0000	.8158	.9647
Absolute Percentile Differential				1.0000	.6571
Relative Percentile Differential					1.0000

DISCUSSION: MANPOWER MOBILITY PROGRAMS

HERBERT S. PARNES
Ohio State University

MR. Jenness is to be congratulated for having developed an intriguing model for the study of geographic mobility. For reasons that I hope to make clear below, however, I should be reluctant to assume that this model — or probably any other, for that matter — can provide a measure of the benefit-cost ratio of the Canadian Mobility Program sufficiently precise to justify its use as a basis for policy decisions. The model will permit the testing of a number of hypotheses relating to the process of geographic mobility, at least among those who apply for grants under the Canadian program, and will also yield data that should provide useful guidelines for evaluating several aspects of the operation of the program. For example, data called for by the model will allow analyses of the characteristics of mobility grant applicants, the direction of migration under the program, and the economic consequences of movement so far as the earnings of the movers are concerned. It will be possible to ascertain what characteristics of labor markets and what characteristics of individuals are associated with varying probabilities of successful movement. Mr. Jenness correctly observes that the entire family of a worker is involved to a considerably greater extent in a geographic job change than in other types of labor market transactions. An important feature of the model, therefore, is that it provides a means of studying the effects of migration on the labor market activity of the total family. However, for this purpose, it would seem desirable to collect information on the labor market activity of other family members prior to the move. Such information, which could readily be obtained on the application form for the mobility grant, would not only provide a better basis for examining the effect of migration on the labor market status of family members, but would eliminate the necessity of using probabilistic measures as a basis for computing the effect of the move on total family earnings. Perhaps the most appealing aspect of the model is its flexibility. Predictions based upon the existing version can be readily checked, with the possibility of introducing modification or refinements that the empirical data suggest.

In addition to its general usefulness for the aforementioned purposes, the model has the merit of some rather ingenious approaches to several of the difficult problems involved in measuring the benefits of the mobility grant program. For example, in order to avoid overstating the benefits of the program by attributing to it geographic moves which would have occurred even in its absence, the model uses the characteristics of the worker as well as those of the labor market of origin to calculate a probability that the move would have occurred irrespective of the program. Another imaginative aspect of the model is the attempt to predict the length of time the migrant will stay in his first job in the new area and to estimate his earnings in subsequent jobs. In this case, however, I am troubled by the assumption that after the first month of service there are no inter-industry differences in the relation between length of service and probability of separation. It seems reasonable to suppose that differences in sensitivity to cyclical movements would cause layoff rates to differ substantially among industries with respect to workers having comparable tenure. Moreover, there are also reasons for expecting inter-industry differences in quit rates by length of service. If there is anything at all to the notion that voluntary mobility is inhibited by such factors as formal seniority provisions and non-vested pensions, then long service workers in industries where such arrangements are prevalent should have lower probabilities of leaving their jobs than workers with equal tenure in industries where these arrangements are less likely.

However useful the mobility model may be for some purposes, and despite the ingenuity of certain aspects of it, I nevertheless would have serious reservations about using the benefit-cost ratio it yields as a basis for evaluating the Canadian Mobility Program. These reservations do not stem primarily from inadequacies that are unique to the model presented here, but rather arise from what I consider to be the basic limitation inherent in the benefit-cost approach to evaluating social welfare programs, namely, the impossibility of measuring accurately all of the benefits and costs involved and the consequent ambiguity of the calculated ratio.

I am sure that Mr. Jenness is aware of most of the problems that I see in the model. Many of them, as a matter of fact, he explicitly acknowledges. For example, in Table 2, he lists a host of "secondary or indirect" benefits or costs that the model completely ignores. It is doubtful that even this is an exhaustive list. For instance, it seems plausible that one of the economic benefits of migration is better education of the migrant's children that may result both because the quality of schools is likely to be better in areas of high opportunity and also because of the greater financial ability of the parents to keep the children in school.

Not only are there elements of benefit and cost that the model does not include, but the estimates for some of the factors that are included are necessarily extremely crude. As an example, consider the way in which the opportunity cost of migrating is measured. The imputed annual wages of the worker in the area of origin are estimated by the arithmetic mean of the highest and lowest wage during the preceding three years. As the author acknowledges, this is despite the fact that most of the workers who apply for grants under the mobility program are unemployed "with no apparent prospects of getting work locally". The measure almost certainly, therefore, overstates the opportunity costs of the move, and thus under- states the economic benefits accruing therefrom. Mr. Jenness' motive in making this very conservative assumption is, from one point of view, laudable: to avoid inflating the estimated benefit-cost ratio. While it is understandable that the administrative agency responsible for the program should be somewhat sensitive to possible accusations that it is overstating the value of the program, it is not at all clear that from the standpoint of social policy it is any greater sin to underestimate than to overestimate the benefit-cost ratio of manpower programs, particularly if benefit-cost ratios are to be used as a means of selecting among alternate programs. The theoretical rationale for benefit-cost analysis, after all, is that it permits one to make choices among alternatives on the basis of the returns that they promise at the margin. This, in my view, implies a degree of precision which, unfortunately, is not attainable. Moreover, given the fact that so much goes unmeasured in the typical benefit-cost study and that some of what is measured is so palpably imprecise, one wonders what sense it makes to attempt elaborate refinements in the case of those variables where they happen to be possible.

Lest I be misunderstood, I am not asserting that benefit-cost analysis in general or the model presented here in particular are not useful for some kinds of program evaluation. Indeed, Dr. Dymond has pointed out in his talk during the luncheon session yesterday that policy decisions have already been based upon the application of the model. For example, emphasis is being placed on serving older married workers because they have been shown to be least likely to move on their own and to be most likely to settle successfully after a move. As another example, efforts are being made to avoid directing migrating workers to areas of high labor turnover. While both of these are interesting illustrations of the way in which data from the model may be usefully applied in guiding the operation of the program, it is noteworthy that neither of them depends upon formal benefit-cost calculations.

So far as benefit-cost analysis *per se* is concerned, it seems to me that its chief contribution to sound policy decisions lies in the comprehensive view of the issue that it engenders. Benefit-cost analysis is a way of thinking about programs that compels one to consider systematically all of the factors that are relevant to a decision. This is an advantage that is not to be belittled, for even if not all of the relevant factors can be measured, their systematic consideration is likely to lead to better policy decisions than would otherwise be made. Moreover, it may even be possible to arrive at admittedly crude measurements that will either point to a policy decision or perhaps enhance one's confidence in a decision that has been arrived at on other grounds. Be that as it may, my principal point is that the very nature of the problem, as illustrated by the present paper, precludes a precise quantification of a benefit-cost ratio and that we should perhaps be better off if we did not strain so hard to arrive at one. The chief danger is not that the effort will have been wasted; it is that the expenditure of so much effort may cause us to want to use the result.

GRAEME H. McKECHNIE
York University

MR. Jenness presented a most interesting and informative paper. His model is an attempt to introduce new concepts into the analysis of geographic mobility. This endeavour has been needed for some time. Too often, analysts are content with traditional variables such as age, marital status and home ownership, and fail to inquire into geographic movements in sufficient depth to provide guidelines for appropriate policy formulation.

I will divide my comments into four main sections: (1) the program itself, (2) the model, (3) the sub-models and (4) the data requirements.

The Manpower Mobility Program

The author states that the Canadian program differs significantly from that of the United States in a variety of ways. Setting aside the monetary considerations and number of persons relocated, the major difference stated by Jenness is the goal of the program — "primary emphasis on raising the productivity of workers and capital". The author states that the program in the U.S. is more concentrated toward the solution of structural unemployment.

A closer investigation of the criteria for selection used by both countries reveals that there is in fact very little difference. In Canada, a person must be unemployed or underemployed to qualify for selection. In the United States, the worker must reside in an economically distressed area and move to an area of labour demand. This is not a stated criterion in Canada. However, in Canada, in addition to the unemployment or underemployment criterion, there must be no suitable job for the individual locally. These criteria thus are very similar to the U.S., and, in fact, denote the existence of structural unemployment. This statement does not mean that increased productivity should not be a major goal, but I feel that we should not place undue emphasis on this without recognizing our structural problems.

The statement that ". . . workers (are not) held tightly accountable after their move" is somewhat confusing. As the author suggests, the program is free of stringent administrative constraints. It is the degree of freedom in such a program that is important. The goal of the program is to allocate labour as efficiently as possible. The existence of the program implies that the market mechanism is not operating optimally. Thus, the government must have designated specific areas that it considers as surplus areas and others where demand for labour is greater than supply. The movement of workers therefore must be controlled so that optimal allocation will result. This control means that freedom of movement will have to be somewhat constrained and the activities of the workers, after relocation, monitored.

The above are comments rather than criticisms since in the main body of the paper, Mr. Jenness does give the impression that the worker is directed and, further proposes, that follow-up studies be made so that the experiences of the relocatees can be studied, presumably with a view to directing their movement to areas where they are needed.

The Model

Mr. Jenness has presented a model which is a good step in the lengthy process of analysis of relocation programs. Three areas of analysis appear to present problems.

The model is established as a comprehensive analytical tool. The use of the family as the appropriate unit of analysis is excellent. However, the author excludes certain variables from his analysis that would appear crucial to the success or failure of the relocation. He states: "Virtually all secondary, social and psychic benefits are ignored. Nor do we attempt to gauge the spillover effects, or the impact of the program on regions through the multiplier processes . . .". These omissions are serious. They are omissions traditionally made by economists when studying human resource programs; however, this gap must be closed. Researchers should attempt to analyze the process of moving from the standpoint of the non-monetary costs borne by the family, the readjustment problems encountered in the new area and the non-monetary benefits.

The impact of these variables on the relocation process will aid in the determination of future policy. Research now being conducted at the University of Wisconsin has shown a number of problems arising from the non-monetary variables. Unemployed workers often will respond positively to the suggestion that relocation be undertaken to improve their labour force position. However, when required to make a final and binding decision to move, workers often revise their earlier position. These changes are based more on fear of the new area than on financial problems, since jobs have been guaranteed.

Problems with adjustment to the destination area can be very serious. Often the worker is satisfied with the job, including the wages, but the family situation is the source of problems. In the Wisconsin project, 20% of the relocatees had returned to their home area within the first six months, mainly for non-monetary reasons.

These costs, and the benefits of new areas, must not be left out of the analysis, especially when this model is considering the family unit, not only the breadwinner. Perhaps the economist is not ideally suited to this type of analysis. The involvement of other disciplines, particularly Psychology and Sociology, is advisable so that proper scales can be designed to provide answers and insights into these problems.

The second area of concern is the author's use of regional income differentials. He states, ". . . it is open to question whether regional income differentials . . . are suitable proxies for the differential earnings expectations that confront individual workers." Yet, Mr. Jenness does in fact use regional income differentials. These differentials are utilized in computing the migration rate value and the probability of moving.

Finally, the model loses the precision it attempts to develop through the use of a great many averages, imputed averages, expected wages and probabilities computed from averages. The use of these averages would not be necessary if a reliable control group were present. The author only refers to a possible control group in connection with one of the submodels; however, the group used does not have the same profile as the relocatee group.

Benefit-cost analysis can be performed either in terms of before/after comparisons or with/without comparisons. The author has presented a model using the former. The latter technique — comparing actual experiences with experiences that would have occurred if no relocation program was present — is more accurate. Experiences during the period of relocation can also be compared to analyze the process of adjustment. The control group should be identical to the study group for optimum results, but this is seldom possible. A large number of similar characteristics in each group is usually the only alternative, and, as a result, there will be problems with the lack of complete comparability. One variable that presents the greatest difficulty with respect to measurement and comparability is initiative. It is very difficult to tell whether the relocatees had more initiative, and, if so, how much more than the non-relocatees.

Problems in the use of control groups are not as serious, in my opinion, as those generated through the use of before/after analysis, and the use of averages and imputed quantities. Two control groups can be used for the analysis of relocation programs: those persons who were accepted into the program, but who refused to move; and those who were not accepted into the program.

The Sub-Models
The personality coefficient has been established to aid in the prediction of the degree of success or failure an individual will experience in the destination area. The variables used and results obtained from the analysis

do not appear to provide this information. The sub-model appears to measure only the job tenure of a worker. That is, the analysis did not utilize mobility determinants to any degree. Age, education and marital status were considered; however, only marital status provided significant results. The results obtained appear to confirm what might be estimated *a priori* — in manufacturing industries, the workers who had tenure provisions (perhaps through a union) and the married breadwinners are more likely to be stable and long-term employees. What is needed is a combination of this information, mobility determinants, and adjustment expectations (non-job oriented).

The autonomous mobility coefficient is used to determine propensity to move. If so, its place in this model is unclear. The best use of this coefficient would seem to be as a screening device, rather than a tool of the cost-benefit analysis of an operating program.

The assumption made in such programs, and stated on pages 184-85 of paper is that the workers would not otherwise move except through the Manpower Mobility Program. If this is so, this coefficient of autonomous mobility should be 1 in every case. If it is not 1, the person would have moved on his own initiative. Therefore. rather than assigning costs and benefits, the administrators should begin determining cut-off scores or coefficients that will help them decide whether a person requires relocation, monetary assistance or some "package" of services.

Data Problems

There are no data presented in the paper except the one example given in the concluding section. This perhaps is the time to raise the issue of the goals of the analysis. Benefit-cost analysis should enable the administering body to determine the ratio of benefits to costs of an entire program and the various parts of the program. In this way, the ability of the program and its sections to "pay off" can be noted. Mr. Jenness has presented a model that appears to do more than this. Yet, some of the variables used lend themselves more as predictive devices than devices to measure costs and benefits.

Through the use of "expected occurrences" and "propensities", administrators could screen out those individuals who do not need the full range of services or any services of the program. Then, having eliminated these factors, the cost-benefit ratios would determine the effectiveness of the program for those who need it most.

The data problem faced by Mr. Jenness is severe. His use of "imputed" and "expected" averages is not specific enough to merit confidence in the results. Many of the problems, especially those connected with wages of succeeding jobs, could be alleviated and perhaps solved by using more extensive follow-up procedures and control groups.

In conclusion, the model presented by Mr. Jenness is an exciting one because it does extend our present method of analysis beyond the usual age, education horizon. The deficiencies are mainly in the data and these problems can be eliminated as the program progresses. The model, hopefully, can be used both as a predictor and as a measure of "payoff". In this way, the effectiveness of the Manpower Mobility Program can be increased.

SOME FURTHER THOUGHTS ON THE CONCEPT
OF HUMAN CAPITAL

NEIL W. CHAMBERLAIN
Columbia University

NOT long ago I was discussing the concept of human capital with an economist friend, attempting to convey to him the qualms I felt concerning its use. His response was one neither of agreement nor disagreement. He simply said, "Why take it so seriously? When it comes right down to a policy issue, human capital theory won't make any difference."

In effect, my friend was suggesting that the human capital approach is just another of the many fads which have struck the economics profession over the changing years. The present preoccupation with it would in time give way to other preoccupations. In the meantime, it would be an amusement of no harm to anyone.

I venture no guesses as to how long the concept of human capital will be around. It has a geneology which can be traced beyond Professor Schultz, whom we often honor as its father, certainly to Alfred Marshall and I suspect also to Jeremy Bentham. That suggests it is something more than a fad. In any event, I take the concept as seriously as do its adherents, though in my judgment the potential is one more of harm than good.

As I see it, the central issue on which the validity and desirability of the human capital concept turns is how far the pecuniary calculus can be extended to embrace people in their roles as producers. Once we conceive of people as capital goods, valued economically according to their productive contributions, we presumably place them in the same category as plant and machines. Not that we value them only in this way; for other social purposes we appreciate them by different standards. But with respect to their function as factors of production we treat them as part of society's capital stock, from which streams of services issue, some more specialized than others, whose value can be increased by appropriate investment policies. The question, then, is whether we are prepared to accept the implications of this conception of human beings as capital.

There is a specific subsidiary issue to which I propose to devote some attention. If people can be viewed as capital, then training and education can be looked at as an investment in human capital. It is true that some part of education can also be regarded as a consumption item, wanted for its own sake, producing nothing more valuable than the satisfaction derived by the person being educated. There is a troublesome problem of separating out education as consumption from education as investment, which human capital theorists are the first to admit, but conceptually the distinction seems clear. It is most evident in educational programs which train people for particular jobs, where the training would not even have been undertaken were it not for the economic objective. In examining the validity and desirability of treating education as investment, I shall not be much concerned with how to distinguish it from the consumer variety, or whether the distinction is as clear as it seems. I shall chiefly be interested in whether it is reasonable to value that portion of the educational process which makes a contribution to people's productive functions by how much it increases their capital value. To put the matter more simply, should we value an investment in education according to its rate of return?[1]

Put in this form, one can readily discern some relationship between human capital theory and cost-benefit analysis, which have enjoyed a simultaneous development. The rate of return on an investment in education can be looked at as the ratio of the economic costs and benefits of an educational program, appropriately discounted. Of course cost-benefit analysis has numerous other applications unrelated to the human capital concept, with which I shall not be concerned in this paper. Despite the fact that I remain skeptical of many of the attempted cost-benefit uses, because of problems of measurability and incommensurability, I do recognize it as a valid and worthwhile technique for certain kinds of problems, whereas I am opposed in principle to the concept of human capital.

---

1. I have dealt with this and related issues in "Some Second Thoughts on the Concept of Human Capital," in *Proceedings of the Twentieth Annual Winter Meeting: The Development and Use of Manpower* (Madison: Industrial Relations Research Association, 1967), pp. 1-13. In this paper I have partly sought to elaborate certain of the ideas advanced there but also to add to them.

Now let me get down to the meat of the matter.

The human capital approach is designed to extend the area of applicability of economic analysis. By taking a coolly scientific attitude towards human beings as they engage in the production process, by quantifying the value of their productive contributions and the returns on investments made in them as producers, economists of this persuasion seek to extend the scope of capital theory, providing objectively valid criteria for a significant range of social decisions. Until now, many types of social expenditures have been made as acts of faith or of ignorance. By clarifying the purposes of these social investments and relating the pecuniary outputs to the inputs, economists can provide a rate of return which acts as the same reliable guide to social decisions as a businessman has in making his investment choices.

Indeed, there is a presumption that the rate of return which may be imputed to education as investment in human capital can be laid alongside rates of return on other forms of investment, public or private, to determine priorities. If an educational program designed to improve the productive capacity of a given number of people returns a lower yield than an investment in highways or a supersonic transport or a sports arena, it faces a presumption that these others are preferable forms of investment.

The Subcommittee on Economy in Government of the Joint Economic Committee, chaired by Senator William Proxmire, only last year recommended "that no public investment be deemed 'economic' or 'efficient' if it fails to yield overall benefits which are at least as great as those which the same resources would have produced if left in the private sector."

That presumption may of course be rebutted by non-economic considerations, in the form of reasons why the educational program is wanted even though it cannot carry its economic weight. Human capitalists, like cost-benefit analysts, are always quick to point out that all they seek to provide is information, which the decision-makers are free to ignore on whatever grounds they choose. Nevertheless, the whole point of the exercise is to affect judgment; there is the economist's presumption that economic values are important, and the calculated rates of return on education and health programs and other forms of investment in humans are intended to have their influence on the decision — else why bother to compute them?

But why should one worry as long as the computation is objectively valid? If the rate of return *is* taken into account, that is the province of the decision-maker, not the economist who computes it. The latter is a purveyor of facts, not of a point of view. He offers only data, not a philosophy or an ideology. He assembles information which can be used by people of any persuasion, and he does so without fear or favor or ulterior motive. He takes other people's tastes as beyond his province, and provides a scientific analysis which is taste-less.

It is the implicit ethical foundation for this supposedly objective formulation which bothers me. While purporting to be ethic and value free, in the sense that it takes purposes and preferences as given and confines itself to drawing conclusions on the strength of the price and income data which are generated, human capital analysis harbors certain ethical persuasions. One derives from its own disciplinary preoccupation with economic rationality, looking with single and specialized detachment to the efficient performance of the economic system, with individuals regarded as means. All capital is functional, including human capital, once that notion is accepted. Capital, including human capital, is integrated into a production system and controlled for purposes which lie outside of itself. We do not concern ourselves with the welfare of capital stock, except in the sense of keeping it in good running order or perhaps updating it; we do not think of capital as having wishes and needs which are independent of the production process of which it is a part. People as producers, if they are viewed as capital in a scientific and conceptual rather than an allegorical or analogical sense, must be regarded in the same light.

It is at this point that my friend's comment has pertinence. *Is* the concept of human capital intended only as a picturesque figure of speech, suggestive but not to be taken too seriously? Or is the concept intended to have precise analytical relevance to the generic concept of producer capital? As I read the literature, it is this latter intent which comes through the printed page, and it is this latter intent that concerns me.

We are in danger here of repeating the intellectual excesses of the scientific management movement of the turn of the century. Under the leadership of Frederick Taylor, it treated workers purely as instruments in a production process where efficiency in an input-output sense was the criterion to be served. The consequence was ultimately an explosion of worker protest which led to Congressional inquiry and action. We have now moved beyond the individual firm to the economy as a whole, and are seeking to organize that more encompassing system of relationships on the same discredited criterion of engineering efficiency. Once again, the individual is seen as subordinated to the production process, an educational investment in him is to be guided importantly by the pecuniary returns which it produces for the system. The educational process is seen as consisting, in substantial if uncertain measure, as a training ground for the production function. And once again all of this is justified on the grounds that it is of primary benefit to the individuals who are trained.

Of course there is a sense in which education necessarily prepares one for economic roles, as for any other kind of human endeavor. Education is part of the socializing process, and instructs its participants in the technical skills of reading, writing, and measurement, which are germane to the producer role as well as to other roles. But the human capital approach must mean more than this if it is to add anything to our analytical economics. It seeks to value some forms of education or some *parts* of education as having a specific and identifiable pecuniary value, whose magnitude is instructive in determining how much of an investment should be made in human capital in contrast to, for example, other forms of capital. The whole approach is designed to incorporate investment in human beings in the analytical apparatus which treats maximizing as the ultimate principle, and goods and services as the ultimate object of maximization.

Of course, economists recognize that nonmaterial satisfactions have their value and are to be given full weight in economic decision. The only problem is one of measurement. We find difficulty in imputing quantities of value to things that are not subjected to market valuation. The consequence is that, just as Bentham and Marshall before them, contemporary economists tend to treat the pecuniary measure as the most generally valid measure of value. The recognition that other values exist, while given verbal recognition, drops out of the *measurement* process, which is designed to guide judgment. Well might the measurement-minded echo the words of the great old man of the Felicific Calculus: "I beg a truce here of our man of sentiment and feeling while from necessity, and it is only from necessity, I speak and prompt mankind to speak a mercenary language. . . . Money is the instrument for measuring the quantity of pain or pleasure. Those who are not satisfied with the accuracy of this instrument must find out some other that shall be more accurate, or bid adieu to Politics and Morals."

Of course, in societies which border on the subsistence level the utilitarian approach of treating each person as a producer and of exacting efficient performance from him as the price of his own subsistance is understandable. I do think there is a difference here between societies which are barely surviving and those which are relatively affluent. At lower standards of living a kind of military austerity may be relevant to social policy, and the maximization of economic product may be an appropriate social end. But in the more industrialized societies, certainly in our own, I fail to see the imperialistic necessity of maximizing output, and conforming social programs to a standard of economic efficiency.

There is one other aspect to this crude economic rationality which purports to provide a guide to social investment policy which I note in passing — the insistence on a discounting approach to the streams of costs incurred on behalf of the human capital as well as the income produced by it. We feel it necessary to apply some discount since we are dealing with the future, and we know as a point of doctrine that the present is worth more than the future. We are convinced of this even though we find it difficult to decide what rate of discount to apply.

The uncertainty is not surprising. We move from the realm of private investment, where understandably the individual has a present preference and a future discount, which creates a market for money, to the realm of social investment, where a similar time prejudice is much less applicable. For it is not the case that the "now" generation, so to speak, or the generation at Time T_0 or T_1, to use the familiar notation, has collectively the same present preference as, individually, it has in its private affairs. Otherwise we should as a society be engaging in behavior similar to that which Henry Simons, in one of his weaker moments, ascribed to labor unions, namely, investing and consuming in such a way that social investment would be totally consumed when the last member of the given generation expired. If the suggestion appears fanciful, it is no more so than the view that society should invest in its future only to the extent that the streams of income accruing to future generations, when properly discounted down to the present, should bear some relationship to the costs borne by the present generation. Since that abstraction, society, with its overlapping generations, tends to function at least as much with a sense of history, including the future as history, as with a psychology that discounts its future, it is understandably hard to determine what rate to impute to its calculations. It certainly is not the rate which prevails in the private money markets, since a society can itself amend that rate.

C. West Churchman once suggested that an orientation to future generations was a teleologic basis for optimal social decisions, and while I find some difficulty with that rather startling conclusion, and he advanced only a tentative formulation, at least it underscores vividly how a society constitutes more than the sum of its present citizens, and why future discounting is not as applicable to it as to an individual with a finite life. But I return to the mainstream of my remarks.

I suggested previously that the human capital theorists tend to treat people as instruments of the production process. Perhaps they would remonstrate with that interpretation, which seems to ascribe to them some peculiar aberrant view, claiming that this ignores the fact that the productive activities of people in any society must *necessarily* be directed to some purpose, and hence must *necessarily* be viewed as the means to some end. To speak of people themselves as the instruments or means, rather than the purpose for which the production process exists, is — they might say — to commit the naive fallacy of confusing the services which people provide with the people who provide the services. The purpose or the end of economic activity is consumption. The people who produce also consume. The object of the economic game is to minimize their input of effort or — the same thing — to maximize their output of consumption goods. All that is intended is to channel *necessary* activity along lines that achieve more efficiently whatever consumption goals society has set for itself — again, a value-free approach, since no ends are given priority over others by the economic analyst. The choice lies with others.

But what is not said, and what is perhaps more to the point, is that in a real sense the choice has already been made by others, before the economist begins his presumably value-free analysis. How value free is an analysis which has value built into the very data on which it rests?

Let me interrupt myself at this point for just a brief aside. In speaking of the deficiencies of the data for the purpose of value-free estimates directed to efficient economic performance, I will waive the significant consideration that the uncertainty effects arising from futurity make the very notion of efficiency and maximization dubious in investment matters, whether public or private. The uncertainty of the values which will take shape over a future time stream renders attempts at maximizing present values less than persuasive. The future value of a present education, for example, depends on a future whose contours can only be guessed at. By invoking Delphic principles, or their equivalent, some may feel greater assurances in their guesses, but there is no way of removing the speculative nature. If one seeks to take account of this by providing a range of estimated rates, varying according to the assumptions on which the estimates are based, he would come up with an enormous number of estimates from among which to choose if he went no farther than a "5 per cent level of confidence," if I may use that term loosely to make a point — I simply mean the estimation of values of a given investment based on all the changes in the future environment which are conceived of as possible by as many as 5 per cent of the professions involved.

But this is a consideration which applies to investment in physical capital no less than human capital, and, as I say, I waive it as an element in my argument. I am less concerned at this point with economic presumption than with ethical assumption.

Even accepting, hypothetically, the efficiency criterion as valid for investment, it is valid only insofar as one accepts the whole system of social, legal, and political relations which produce the very valuations which are intended to guide choice. By taking price and income data as "given," one also accepts as given the existing distribution of property, wealth, and income, as well as the existing distribution of bargaining power and positions of influence and control. It is out of this complex of existing social and political relations that emerges the stream of particular goods and services and the values which attach to them, values which create the rates of return on any investment in human capital. It is the existing specifications of the organization of society which produce the pecuniary valuations which lead to judgments as to which investments are more productive than others, and the form which human capital should take if it is to produce maximum returns.

Nor can we identify producers with consumers, as though they were the same people, and hence themselves the ends of their own efforts as means. Just as Keynes pointed out the obvious fact that the people who invest are not the same people who save, so should we recognize the equally obvious fact that the people who produce a bundle of goods are not the same people who consume it, so that to maximize their output is not to maximize their benefit, in any objective sense. Indeed, we could go farther. The value of the bundle of goods a person receives for his efforts is in no objective sense equal to the value of the bundle of goods he produces. Rewards are distributed by a social process which ultimately derives from that complex intermixture of power, tradition, and institution of which I spoke. The efficient economic performance, deriving in part from educational investment, on which rates of return are based, is an efficiency which is geared to the advantage of some more than others. It could hardly be otherwise, regardless of the political configuration of a society, since there is always some group which at a point in time possesses a greater equity in a society than do others, or — if we choose to extend A. A. Berle's thesis that control is more important than equity — some group which possesses a dominant position. Although this is hardly news to any of us, we sometimes forget it because of its familiarity. We then consider ourselves objective and value-free, as scholars, even as we accept the values given by the system inside which we operate as members of society.

It would not be too extreme to suggest that the effect of the human capitalists is to channel social investment (and we are particularly interested in investment in education) along the lines which tend to serve those whom the economic system as a whole serves best. This is not to argue that others are not benefitted in the process. But to the extent that rate-of-return analysis guides social choice, and that analysis is based on price and income data deriving from a particular distribution of power and property, it can hardly be termed value-free. An educational program calculated to yield a 5 per cent rate of return does so not because of any "objective" considerations but because the worker so educated finds his appropriate place in an economic system whose built-in values are "set" to yield 5 per cent on the money invested in him. The economic analyst who totes up the returns on investment in education is performing the same accounting function on behalf of the existing system as the investment analyst who does the same for a business firm.

The value of any investment in education, in the human capital sense, is given by the existing social and political relationships. A different education, given the same relationships, would yield a different value. The same education, given a different set of relationships, would yield another. The economist believes he is leaving choice to others, providing only objective data, but in fact the data with which he works are loaded with value considerations carried over from the past, affecting the magnitudes of his calculations, and thereby influencing — insofar as his calculations do influence — choices among investments.

Perhaps I can restate my proposition by posing a hypothetical question. If an economist were to begin a cost-benefit analysis with respect to some educational program, or a rate-of-return analysis on human capital, under one government, and a revolution occurred while he was in progress, could that economist complete that same analysis under the new government, simply carrying on from where he had started, making use of his original data? More specifically, would a cost-benefit analysis of an educational or training program use the same data and reach the same values under a Trujillo as under a Castro? If not, why not, if only objective considerations enter?

But is not this kind of built-in ethical orientation the same type of phenomenon as futurity uncertainty to which I referred a few paragraphs back, and which I was willing to waive since it applies to capital of all kinds, physical as well as human? Are not the values which undergird a society part of the same inescapable human condition as the uncertainty which shrouds the future? I think there is a difference in kind here. Investment in human capital has a special role, in that it involves not just the direction of inanimate capital but more particularly *human* capital to ends which are chosen because they serve others especially well. Once again we are back to our treatment of people as instruments for the production of certain selected values (not just any values), rather than themselves constituting the values which production should serve.

Perhaps all this sounds like a re-run of Ruskin romanticism. No system can be viewed as either perfect or self-denying. With whatever imperfections, it seeks to perpetuate itself. If a society, whose values the economist shares, seeks to perpetuate itself, no less than do other societies, who is the economist to say that he is somehow above all this? Is not an exposé of such an alignment of interests as somehow defective in terms of the purported standard of objectivity a straining at gnats? Let me develop the reasons why I think there are more than gnats in the picture.

The social scientist is torn between two purposes. On the one hand, he seeks to serve an integrated society and to improve its functioning. On the other hand, he cannot fail to recognize that within his society there are contentious interests, some of them seeking — from their own point of view, quite legitimately — to disintegrate and reintegrate society along lines more to their liking. In confronting these conflicting tendencies to integration and disintegration he is no different from other individuals in his society, except that he carries a double load of tension, in that he is not only a participant in but a student of the phenomena involved.

The pull in the direction of seeing society as an integrated system is a strong one. It satisfies the social scientist's sense of orderliness and design. It more readily permits theoretical development. By concentrating on the forces making for equilibrium, the economist can more readily systematize and quantify his concepts.

This sense of system has, indeed, run through the main stream of economics since the days of Adam Smith. I introduce his name not accidentally but quite selectively, since few of the great names of our field have had as strong and explicit a sense of system and design as he. Some years ago I satisfied myself on this score by tracing his views on this matter back to an early essay on astronomy, written prior to his *Theory of Moral Sentiments* and long before *The Wealth of Nations*. I will not be tempted into a pleasant bypath by dilating further on the way in which this remarkable man tied together the whole of his body of writings by his sense and conception of system. I mention it only to underscore the strength of this persistent pull which has characterized the study of economics over the years, and along with it the continuing attraction of the notion of system equilibrium.

In recent years we have all become systems analysts. The idea which has run like a thread through the major writings of the great theorists, even though often kept out of view, has now become a stout cord which binds us all together. It is the rare piece of economic reasoning which, these days, does not start by making its initial reference to a systems approach.

Now this has a special relevance to my subject. Once one adopts a systems approach to human affairs, he can scarcely escape the issue of purpose. What are the objectives or functions of the particular social system which concerns him? It is necessary to know in order to understand and appraise its functioning. The teleological approach comes naturally in the case of human society. We invest our systems with purpose, and we study the functioning of their parts with respect to that purpose. For many economists, purpose becomes translated into maximizing certain values.

It is also axiomatic among all of us who find this systems approach rewarding that virtually all systems can be aggregated into supersystems or disaggregated into subsystems. This is true for all except the very largest and the very smallest of human units — the world society, at one extreme, and the individual at the other.

But once the economist identifies the unit with which he is concerned, and imputes to it a certain purpose, he tends to evaluate all its component parts — all the subsystems of which it is made up — in terms of the overarching system objective, not their own more specialized and particularistic objectives. From the viewpoint of the system with which he is concerned, whether a corporation or a national society, the subunits are all teleologically oriented towards the overall purpose of the system which they jointly compose.

The fact of the matter is, however, as we all know, that individuals and groups, even if part of a larger system, do have their own purposes and values, which differ in some respects from those of the larger system which they help to form. Inducements are held out to such cooperating individuals and groups to secure their more effective functioning, such as subsidies or avoidance of penalties, or conditional grants or tax concessions. These are part of the costs which must be measured in computing a rate of return on a particular program, on a social investment.

Nevertheless, it is the teleological approach to the system as a whole which governs. The purpose of the larger system controls our view of the desirable forms of behavior of the component groups. Any efficiency which we seek, whatever maximization is attempted, runs in terms of the system as a whole. We cannot simultaneously maximize some value for it and other values for each and all of its components.

But it is precisely for this reason that an ethical choice confronts the analyst. If he is concerned with the system and its values, he applies a monistic standard, efficiency from *its* point of view, maximization of *its* present values. This involves his acceptance of the values of the system as a whole and an exclusion of any competing values of the groups of which it is composed. At least it requires that choice if he is to come up with a rate of return on the proposed investment.

In an effort to rationalize this necessary choice, the analyst may fall back on the argument that in fact the competing interests of the groups composing a society have led to some present political compromise, a form of social compact, and it is that combined interest of all the subordinate groups which he serves. But the escape can only be partial at best. However compromised at the moment, the conflict of goals remains. The interests of certain groups are less well served by the existing political and social arrangements than are the interests of other groups. There is always a pulling and hauling below the surface to change the system of relationships.

For social scientists who are attuned to this conflict of groups and who, despite the valid and inescapable appeal of systems analysis, concern themselves as well with the divergent purposes of interest groups, social values are pluralistic rather than monistic. Rate-of-return analysis cannot be based on system-oriented valuations. No fan of estimates based on varying assumptions will satisfy, unless such estimates relate to the disparate and divergent objectives of the relevant interest groups. And in this case there are no estimates which the future will prove right or wrong; waiving the question of futurity-uncertainty, all estimates would be right though different from each other, in the sense that each would reflect the costs and benefits to a particular interest group.

To put the matter another way, the same system which he takes as given, representing a compromise of values, which he would like to see operate more efficiently in terms of maximizing criterion, thus more nearly achieving its goals and more nearly approaching an equilibrium condition, that same system is always in danger if not actually in process of being fragmented and re-assembled with a different configuration of economic and social relationships, conforming to changes in the balance of power among the contesting interests. That continuing contest generates its own interest to the social scientist. If he responds to it, he finds himself looking at social issues and proposed social programs from the point of view, not of the system as a whole but of its major contentious interests. When he computes a rate of return, he cannot evade the question, "Return to whom?" For him, it is unlikely that there will be some objective return on an impartial investment.

Both of these are powerful pulls, the pull towards analysis of an integrated system with monistic values, and the pull towards analysis of a conflict-full society with pluralistic values. A belief that decisions can be based on a rate-of-return analysis which provides objective data for all the decision-makers, whoever they may be, responds to only one of those pulls.

Perhaps I can illustrate my point with reference to an issue which recently arose on the Columbia campus. It concerned the role of the Naval Reserve Officer Training Corps — was it to be accorded space on campus, were its offerings to be given academic credit, were its instructors to be given faculty status? Let us assume we approach this from a cost-benefit point of view, seeking to ascertain the value of the NROTC program. Would we not first have to inquire, costs and benefits to whom? The valuation would produce one result if measured from the Navy's point of view, a different result if viewed by the university, still another from the student's point of view.

Can these somehow all be subsumed into some single analysis which simultaneously considers the effects on alternative and competing lines of social expenditure of maintaining a Navy as economically as possible, the effects on the educational system of accepting military training as equivalent to any other form of instruction, the effects on some students who are induced to accept officer training as a means of financing their education, and on other students who see this as reflecting a national style of life which they are intent on changing? Is not the heart of the problem precisely the ethical conflicts, which cannot be smothered beneath some homogenizing form of systems analysis?

I suppose the rebuttal to my rhetorical question would run in terms of confining the areas of ethical conflict in some pen labelled "incommensurable values," restricting the objective analysis to those pecuniary measures which all parties in interest could accept. I cannot myself accept this view, since the pecuniary measures themselves derive, as I have said, from a system of existing power relationships, not the system of relationships which some would like to put in their place, which would cast up a different set of pecuniary values. But further, whatever of objective measure may remain is certain, in this case, to be so swamped by non-pecuniary considerations as to offer little assistance in joint decision-making.

The same problem exists with expenditures on human capital, such as industry-operated training programs. The cost and benefits of particular programs differ depending on whether one looks at them from the point of view of the individuals being trained, the firm providing the training, or a government agency with program responsibility, to name at least three parties in interest. Admittedly all such interests must be considered in arriving at a decision, but the process is one of reconciling and accommodating divergent interests, in a political decision. Even if one accepts price data as valid, it involves not one but at least three cost-benefit analyses, which cannot possibly be homogenized. To proceed as though some encompassing analysis is possible is to proceed from some implicit institutional or system position with its related (monistic) ethical view. It implies that all that impedes a clearcut conclusion is the immeasurability of certain items, but that if these could be measured and put on the scale, an objective decision would emerge.

It is true that incommensurability can be said to be at the root of the problem, but it is incommensurability of a particular kind — not springing simply from the differing tastes of people, such as whether it is better for a government to support the performing arts or cleaner streets, or to put its recreational funds into urban parks or rural retreats. It is an incommensurability that arises out of clashes of more fundamental interests, which define each person's place in society, interests so fundamental and opposed (opposed in part because of the scarcity condition which especially concerns economists) that they are incapable of anything except short-run compromise.

I would suggest that such incommensurability takes two forms. Type A consists of certain phenomena which can have no accepted or common means of valuation because the value which each of us would impute to them would be too high to permit any exchange or compromise or trade-off. They would be absolute rather than relative. We could never agree on the value of a life or of good health, because we would necessarily then be setting a finite value on our own lives and good health, to which we understandably attach infinite value, since all other values depend on these.

Parenthetically, I suspect that one reason for some of our most serious present problems on campus and in the ghetto lies precisely in the fact that some things to which a majority in society used to apply market values have been moved by larger and larger minority groups into the Type A category of matters so intimate and integral to the person's existence that he cannot allow others to set a value on them which he is obliged to accept — things like self respect, to which we have tended to give a market value in terms of the pecuniary worth of an hour or an occupation or a level of education, whatever the effect on the individual. Previously when a job was offered, carrying its own rate, we tended to ignore the job content or the job significance, assuming that the money payment sufficed for the transaction. We now find that money no longer performs the function so well.

Type B incommensurability arises out of an identification with a class or interest group or status category. In this case we are unlikely to feel that our very existence is tied up in such identifications, since we can and do transfer group allegiance or change identities, but the identification does define the whole style of our lives. (Type A values would usually persist even with a change in an individual's Type B alignment, though at times the two merge, as when an individual is willing to lay down his life for his country or become a martyr to a cause; but the two seldom go hand in hand, as witness the current preoccupation with "alienation.")

Type B incommensurabilities thus relate to clashes of partisan interests; people in contending positions could hardly be expected to value equally things that they perceive differently. Here is the basis for the clash of labor and management, of black power versus white supremacy, of the upcoming generation against the established generation, of one nation versus another. The political stance provides a unique scale of valuation. We are, then, precluded from using a common scale.

When either Type A or Type B incommensurabilities are present, I cannot understand the logic of attempting to calculate some rate of return which has "objective" power. I cannot share the faith that even though such incommensurabilities emerge or are highlighted by the analysis, the act of valuing all that can be valued on a common pecuniary scale carries us closer to some conclusion. The presense of incommensuralibities of such significance in any part of the problem precludes solution by means relying on impersonal measurement. Only a personal or political decision is possible. A monistic approach cannot serve pluralistic ends.

Cost-benefit analysis can be useful, it seems to me, where Type A and Type B incommensurabilities are absent or weak, but human capital analysis cuts too close to personal integrity and life style to win my acceptance. Even if the individuals who are being treated as capital do not themselves react adversely to such treatment, I cannot accept the analyst's role of making such vital assumptions on their behalf.

How can we talk about the economic value of education without inquiring who it is who decides what kind of education the individual will be offered, what its implications are for his personal integrity, what will be the effects on present income and power distributions of a more egalitarian educational system, how the privacy of business enterprise will be affected? Any notion that incommensurable values of this sort can somehow be accommodated in an objective, non-ethical, non-political analysis strikes me as quixotic however well-intentioned.

What are the returns on an education under school decentralization as against one under present centrally-controlled procedures? Returns to whom? Returns to those with more of a stake in the economic system as it has evolved, to whom community control may carry threats to system control? Returns to those who for whatever reason have been excluded from effective participation in the economic system and who are looking for a subsystem which they can more effectively control? Returns to those with political responsibility for making *some* educational program work but who for that reason are not devoid of political preference? Even the identical program would have different values for those in differing circumstances.

Even if one descends from such lofty political issues to more pedestrian forms of education, such as on-the-job training, one does not escape such issues. Many managements, as we know, are now refining and expanding their company's training and education programs. For the most part, they talk in terms of improving or upgrading their manpower. But the very term "manpower" reflects the utilitarian approach, the objective of increasing the employee's value to the company. In the process, of course, the employee can be expected to benefit himself; by increasing his productiveness to the company, he increases his own earnings.

But it is not far-fetched, as campus activities have taught us, to conceive that sooner or later employees may choose to take a look at corporate educational programs in other than manpower terms. They may ask why companies, in addition to treating employees as parts of the production process, should not also treat them as individuals with their own intellectual interests, not necessarily related to turning out trucks or tinplate, or servicing telephone equipment or computer installations. A response that this is not in the company's interest may not be satisfactory if it is in the employees' interests. What omnipotent authority decrees that corporate resources should not be used for such a purpose? And where, in this case, lies the public interest? How can we calculate a rate-of-return even on OJT which will be viewed as in some sense "objective" by the parties in interest?

This last consideration leads directly to my final point, the impossibility of calculating the return on an investment in human capital whose underlying purpose is to change the shape of society. I will not dwell for more than a moment on the fallaciousness of attempting to separate educational expenditures into a productive investment category and a consumption category. Where, in such a dichotomous approach, is there room for the individual or interest group or coalition to invest in particular forms of education not to make people more marketable, or to make them a superior capital good, but in order to effect changes in society in ways unrelated or only partially related to the economic marketplace?

Such purposive programs, by attempting to shift the very scales by which we value, preclude the calculation of a rate of return based on present values. This, I venture to affirm, is not likely to be a trivial consideration. In the ongoing political contest, disequilibrating in our society even as we struggle to achieve some equilibrium, educational programs are an increasingly important arena of the contest.

To the extent that present manpower programs are geared to private business needs, that is, to economic opportunities as created by a business-oriented society, and to the extent that society is moving away from so exclusive a concern with private profit and private accumulation and is becoming more involved with the collective environment, both physical and social, to that extent will there be an unpredictable change in the valuation of costs and benefits deriving from investment in education.

I close with a troublesome question. If my preceding comments imply an answer, it is much less certain even in my own mind than my sometimes dogmatic assertions would suggest.

Economists — whether working in the U.S. or the U.S.S.R. — can say that they take values as given and work within that framework. But there is a legitimate question as to whether policy recommendations extending beyond the near future (or even presumably non-policy formulations like a calculated rate of return which, however, are intended to carry policy implications) *should* take values as given. There is a question whether the economist, in taking them as given, is not faced with the same dilemma, though perhaps on a less horrendous scale, as the scientist working in nuclear weaponry or biological warfare who also eschews value considerations.

To some extent the intellectuals of a period would be remiss if they did not contribute to the integration of their society. They have a social function which extends beyond the production of new knowledge. But to some extent they are also the challengers of an existing system by exploring it more objectively than others who are more directly caught up in the value premises and illusions of their age. They are both part of their times and above their times.

The need for social conformity gets expressed in the style of an epoch, the rationality principles which are accepted, the value systems. But how does the need for nonconformity get expressed? How but by a continued questioning of the very rationality principles and value systems with which we work?

APPENDIX A

NORTH AMERICAN CONFERENCE ON COST-BENEFIT ANALYSIS OF MANPOWER POLICIES

CONFERENCE PROGRAM

WEDNESDAY, MAY 14, 1969

THEORETICAL ASPECTS OF COST-BENEFIT ANALYSIS

8:30-9:00 a.m.   **Registration at the Wisconsin Center**

9:00 a.m.   **Morning Session, 210 Wisconsin Center**

Chairman: GERALD G. SOMERS
Chairman, Department of Economics
The University of Wisconsin

"Benefits: Theoretical and Methodological Issues"
BURTON A. WEISBROD
Professor of Economics
The University of Wisconsin

"Costs: Theoretical and Methodological Issues"
RICHARD W. JUDY
Professor of Political Economy
University of Toronto

Discussants:

JOHN S. MacDONALD
Faculty of Social Sciences
University of the West Indies

ANDRE RAYNAULD
Professor of Economics
University of Montreal

12:15 p.m. Luncheon in the Wisconsin Center Dining Room

Chairman: J. KENNETH LITTLE
Co-Director, Center for Studies in Vocational and
Technical Education
The University of Wisconsin

"The Role of Cost-Benefit Analysis in Formulating
Manpower Policy"
WILLIAM R. DYMOND
Assistant Deputy Minister
Canadian Department of Manpower and
Immigration

2:30 p.m. Afternoon Session, 210 Wisconsin Center

Chairman: W. DONALD WOOD
Director, Industrial Relations Centre
Queen's University

"The Social Discount Rate"
KENNETH J. ARROW
Professor of Economics
Harvard University

Discussants:

ARNOLD C. HARBERGER
Professor of Economics
University of Chicago

GRANT L. REUBER
Head, Department of Economics
University of Western Ontario

**5:00 p.m. Reception and Social Hour in the Alumni Lounge,
Wisconsin Center**

THURSDAY, MAY 15, 1969

APPLICATION OF COST-BENEFIT ANALYSIS TO MANPOWER PROGRAMS

9:00 a.m. **Morning Session, 210 Wisconsin Center**

Chairman: DUNCAN R. CAMPBELL
Planning and Evaluation Branch
Canadian Department of Manpower and Immigration

"Occupational Training and Retraining Programs"
EINAR HARDIN
Professor of Economics
Michigan State University

"Evaluating Manpower Programs for the Disadvantaged"
GLEN G. CAIN
ROBINSON G. HOLLISTER
Associate Professors of Economics
The University of Wisconsin

Discussants:

ERNST W. STROMSDORFER
Associate Professor of Economics
Pennsylvania State University

DAVID O. SEWELL
Assistant Professor of Economics
Queen's University

12:15 p.m. **Luncheon in the Wisconsin Center Dining Room**

Chairman: ROBERT J. LAMPMAN
Bascom Professor of Economics
The University of Wisconsin

"Manpower Programs in the War on Poverty"
ROBERT A. LEVINE
Urban Institute

2:30 p.m.   Afternoon Session, 210 Wisconsin Center

Chairman: BETTI GOLDWASSER
Manpower Administration
U.S. Department of Labor

"Manpower and Employment Service Operations"
FRANK H. CASSELL*
Frank H. Cassell, Consultants
Chicago, Illinois

"Manpower Mobility Programs"
ROBERT A. JENNESS
Planning and Evaluation Branch
Canadian Department of Manpower and Immigration

Discussants:

HERBERT S. PARNES
Professor of Economics
Ohio State University

GRAEME H. McKECHNIE
Assistant Professor of Economics
York University

5:30 p.m.   Reception in the Alumni Lounge, the Wisconsin Center

6:30 p.m.   Banquet in the Dining Room of the Wisconsin Center

Chairman: Representative
U.S. Department of Labor

"Some Second Thoughts on Cost-Benefit Analysis"
NEIL W. CHAMBERLAIN
Graduate School of Business
Columbia University

* Due to illness, Mr. Cassell was unable to present his paper.

APPENDIX B

CONFERENCE PARTICIPANTS

I **Canadian Participants**

ADEL-CZLOWIEKOWSKI, I. J., Department of Economics, University of Lethbridge.

ALLEN, DONALD, Unemployment Insurance Commission, Government of Canada.

ANDERSON, RONALD, Economics and Business Section, *The Globe and Mail* (Toronto).

BARRON, JUNITH, Office of Institutional Research, University of Toronto.

BECK, R. G., Department of Economics, University of Saskatchewan.

BERNIER, JEAN, Faculty of Social Sciences, Laval University.

BLACK, E., Manpower Programs Committee — Council of Ministers of Education, Province of Manitoba.

BODKIN, R. G., Department of Economics, University of Western Ontario.

BOTHAM, G. C., Treasury Board, Government of Canada.

BOWLES, K., Department of Indian Affairs and Northern Development, Government of Canada.

BRAULT, F., Department of Economics, University of Ottawa.

BROWN, MURRAY G., Department of Economics and Political Science, University of New Brunswick.

BYRNE, D. J., Department of Health and Welfare, Government of Canada.

CAMPBELL, DUNCAN R., Planning and Evaluation Branch, Department of Manpower and Immigration, Government of Canada.

CAMPBELL, HARRY, Industrial Relations Centre, Queen's University.

CELOVSKY, B., Department of Manpower and Immigration, Government of Canada.

CROWLEY, RONALD W., Department of Economics, Queen's University.

DEMAKEAS, JOHN, Planning, Programming and Budgetary Task Force, Department of Labour, Government of Canada.

DODGE, DAVID A., Department of Economics, Queen's University.

DYMOND, WILLIAM R., Department of Manpower and Immigration, Government of Canada.

FAY, P. B., Department of Manpower and Immigration, Government of Canada.

FISH, D. G., Association of Universities and Colleges of Canada.

GREEN, ALAN G., Department of Economics, Queen's University.

HOLLAND, JOHN W., The Ontario Institute for Studies in Education.

HOUSEGO, IAN, Alberta Human Resources Research Council.

JENNESS, R. A., Planning and Evaluation Branch, Department of Manpower and Immigration, Government of Canada.

JOHNSON, CASWELL L., Department of Economics, Carleton University.

JOHNSON, MRS. IRENE, Department of Finance, Government of Canada.

JOHNSTON, L. M., Department of Education, Province of Ontario.

JUDY, R. W., Department of Political Economy, University of Toronto.

KERRIDGE, E. L., Applied Arts and Technology Branch, Department of Education, Province of Ontario.

KINLEY, JOHN R., Research Branch, Department of Labour, Province of Ontario.

KITCHEN, HARRY M., Department of Economics, Trent University.

LANE, J. R., Department of Regional Economic Expansion, Government of Canada.

MAKI, DENNIS R., Department of Economics, Simon Fraser University.

MARSHALL, R. H., Department of Manpower and Immigration, Government of Canada.

MARTEN, PETER C., Department of Indian Affairs and Northern Development, Government of Canada.

MARTENS, ANDRE, Department of Economics, Sir George Williams University.

McKECHNIE, GRAEME H., Department of Economics, York University.

McMILLAN, MELVILLE, Alberta Human Resources Research Council.

McNEIL, JEAN, Ecole des Hautes Etudes Commerciales, University of Montreal.

McNEIL, JEANNINE, Ecole des Hautes Etudes Commerciales, University of Montreal.

MELTZ, NOAH M., Department of Economics, University of Toronto.

MENSINKAI, S. S., Department of Economics, Memorial University of Newfoundland.

MITCHELL, J. P., Department of Education, Province of Alberta.

MORRISON, J. A., Program Planning and Budgeting, Department of Secretary of State, Government of Canada.

NEEDHAM, W. ROBERT, Department of Economics, University of Waterloo.

OSTRY, MRS. SYLVIA, Economic Council of Canada.

PAINE, DOUGLAS W., Treasury Board, Government of Canada.

PAQUET, GILLES, Department of Economics, Carleton University.

PENZ, PETER, Department of Manpower and Immigration, Government of Canada.

PROULX, PIERRE-PAUL, Conference of Rectors and Principals of Quebec Universities.

RAYNAULD, ANDRE, Department of Economics, University of Montreal.

REUBER, GRANT L., Department of Economics, University of Western Ontario.

SALISBURY, MRS. HELEN, Economic Planning Branch, Department of Treasury and Economics, Province of Ontario.

SAUER, WARREN, Science Council of Canada.

SCHREINER, J. A., Editorial Department, *Financial Post* (Toronto).

SEWELL, DAVID O., Department of Economics, Queen's University.

SIMONS, R. L. Department of Indian Affairs and Northern Development, Government of Canada.

SISCO, N. A., Applied Arts and Technology Branch, Department of Education, Province of Ontario.

SPENCER, BYRON G., Department of Economics, McMaster University.

STELCNER, MORTON, Department of Economics, Sir George Williams University.

STRANG, ALAN T., Research Branch, Department of Labour, Province of Ontario.

SUNGA, P., Privy Council of Canada.

SWIDINSKY, R., University of British Columbia.

TANGRI, BEVERLY, Department of Economics, University of Manitoba.

UPEX, F. D., Department of Manpower and Immigration, Government of Canada.

WEICK, EDWARD R., Department of Indian Affairs and Northern Development, Government of Canada.

WEIR, JOHN A., Department of Economics, Waterloo Lutheran University.

WHITTINGHAM, FRANK, Research Branch, Department of Labour, Province of Ontario.

WILSON, B. A., Program Review Branch, Treasury Board Secretariat, Province of Ontario.

WINTER, J. R., Department of Economics, Acadia University.

WOOD, W. DONALD, Industrial Relations Centre, Queen's University.

YOON, TAE-HEE, Department of Manpower and Immigration, Government of Canada.

II United States Participants

APPLETON, LESLIE, Manpower Administration, U.S. Department of Labor.

ARROW, KENNETH J., Project on Efficiency of Decision Making in Economic Systems, Harvard University.

BACKUS, FRANZ, Wisconsin State Employment Service.

BAROCCI, THOMAS, Industrial Relations Research Institute, University of Wisconsin.

BERGSMAN, JOEL, Orinda, California.

BOELAERT, REMI, University of Wisconsin.

BORTON, PAUL, Manpower Administration, U.S. Department of Labor.

BORUS, MICHAEL, Adelphi, Maryland.

BOWMAN, MARY JEAN, Department of Economics, University of Chicago.

BRANDON, GEORGE L., American Vocational Association.

CAIN, GLEN, Department of Economics, University of Wisconsin.

CHAMBERLAIN, NEIL, Graduate School of Business, Columbia University.

CHAPLIN, DAVID, Department of Sociology, University of Wisconsin.

CHRISTENSEN, L. R., Law School, University of Wisconsin.

CHRISTENSEN, SANDRA, University of Wisconsin.

CIBARICH, AUGUST, University of Wisconsin.

COLOSI, JOSEPH, University of Wisconsin.

CONANT, EATON H., Industrial Relations Institute, University of Oregon.

CRONIN, MARY JANE, U.S. Department of Health, Education and Welfare.

DAVID, MARTIN, Department of Economics, University of Wisconsin.

EARL, LEWIS H., Bethesda, Maryland.

FELLER, IRWIN, Department of Economics, Pennsylvania State University.

FERNBACH, SUSAN, Industrial Relations Research Institute, University of Wisconsin.

FEYD, GERALD, Manpower Administration, U.S. Department of Labor.

FISHER, JOHN, Planning Branch, Job Corps, U.S. Department of Labor.

FRANCIS, WALTON, Bureau of the Budget, U.S. Office of the President.

GIBBS, JEFFREY, Industrial Relations Research Institute, University of Wisconsin.

GOLDWASSER, BETTI, Manpower Administration, U.S. Department of Labor.

GOLLADAY, FREDERICH, Department of Economics, University of Wisconsin.

GRAMZA, KEN ROBERT, Resource Management Corporation, Bethesda, Maryland.

HAMBLETON, JOHN W., University of Wisconsin.

HARBERGER, ARNOLD, Department of Economics, University of Chicago.

HARDIN, EINAR, Department of Economics, Michigan State University.

HARRIS, HORACE T., Industrial Relations Research Institute, University of Wisconsin.

HEINES, A. J., Department of Economics, University of Wisconsin.

HOLLISTER, ROBINSON, Department of Economics, University of Wisconsin.

HOLT, CHARLES C., Urban Institute, Washington, D.C.

HU, TEH-WEI, Department of Economics, Pennsylvania State University.

INSEL, BARBARA, Operation Research Corporation, Silver Spring, Maryland.

JACOBSON, WILLIAM O., Office of Economic Opportunity, U.S. Office of the President.

JAIN, HARISH C., Industrial Relations Research Institute, University of Wisconsin.

KOLBERG, WILLIAM, Manpower Administration, U.S. Department of Labor.

KOSHEL, MRS. PATRICIA, Office of Economic Opportunity, U.S. Office of the President.

LAMPMAN, ROBERT, Department of Economics, University of Wisconsin.

LARSEN, HANS, Department of Economics, Michigan State University.

LaWALL, CAROLINE, Manpower Administration, U.S. Department of Labor.

LEE, LEANNA, University of Wisconsin.

LEININGER, W. J., Operations Research Corporation, Silver Spring, Maryland.

LEVINE, LOUIS, Institute for Research on Human Resources, Pennsylvania State University.

LEVINE, ROBERT, Urban Institute, Washington, D.C.

LEVITAN, SAR A., Center for Manpower Policy Studies, Washington, D.C.

LEWIS, FRANK L., Alexandria, Virginia.

LITTLE, J. KENNETH, Center for Studies in Vocational and Technical Education, University of Wisconsin.

LURIE, MELVIN, Department of Economics, University of Wisconsin — Milwaukee.

MacDONALD, JOHN, Department of Economics, University of the West Indies.

MAHONEY, BETTE S., Reston, Virginia.

MAHONEY, WILLIAM M., Reston, Virginia.

MACONICK, ROGER, Department of Economics, University of Wisconsin.

MARKETTI, JAMES, Industrial Relations Research Institute, University of Wisconsin.

MORSE, STUART, University of Wisconsin.

MUELLER, RALPH R., Washington, D.C.

NEAGLE, KENNETH H., Bureau of Prisons, U.S. Department of Justice.

PARNES, HERBERT S., Department of Economics, Ohio State University.

PERLMAN, RICHARD, Department of Economics, University of Wisconsin — Milwaukee.

REGELSON, LILLIAN, Office of Economic Opportunity, U.S. Office of the President.

REHN, GOSTA, O.E.C.D., Paris, France.

REVZAN, LARRY, Operations Research Corporation, Silver Spring, Maryland.

RIGGS, ROBERT J., Planning Research Corporation, Washington, D.C.

ROOMKIN, MYRON, Industrial Relations Research Institute, University of Wisconsin.

ROWLATT, DON, Department of Economics, Princeton University.

SAHAKIAN, HAROLD, Wisconsin Board of Vocational, Technical and Adult Education.

SCHILBERG, MARGARET, University of Wisconsin.

SCHRAMM, CARL, Industrial Relations Research Institute, University of Wisconsin.

SEKHON, ISHER S., University of Wisconsin.

SMITH, RALPH E., Urban Institute, Washington, D.C.

SOMERS, GERALD G., Center for Studies in Vocational and Technical Education, University of Wisconsin.

STAHLER ABRAHAM, Silver Spring, Maryland.

STEVENS, DAVID W., College of Business, Oklahoma State University.

STRAUSS, BOB, University of Wisconsin.

STROMSDORFER, ERNST (Pennsylvania State University), Department of Economics, University of Wisconsin (1968-69).

SZALOCZI, JEAN K., U.S. Department of Health, Education and Welfare.

THIELER, DONALD, Madison, Wisconsin.

TOIKKA, RICHARD, University of Wisconsin.

TOMEY, E. ALLAN, Center for Urban Programs, St. Louis University.

TRUMBLE, ROBERT, Operations Research Corporation, Silver Spring, Maryland.

TSANTIS, ANDREAS, University of Wisconsin.

TUCKMAN, HOWARD, Department of Economics, University of Wisconsin.

VANTHIELEN, WALTER, University of Wisconsin.

WALDMAN, MICHAEL, Operations Research Corporation, Silver Spring, Maryland.

WALKER, RALPH S., McLean, Virginia.

WEISBROD, BURTON, Department of Economics, University of Wisconsin.

WHEELER, GILMORE, Office of Economic Opportunity, U.S. Office of the President.

WILLIAMS, WALTER, National Manpower Policy Task Force, Washington, D.C.

INDEX

Absenteeism, 142
Administrators: use of mobility model, xv; reaction to cost-benefit analysis, 30, 37, 44, 50, 51, 53, 55, 128-129, 130-131, 144-145, 149, 151; collecting data, 145
Adult Occupational Training Program. See Occupational Training for Adults Program
Age: in training programs, 53; and earnings after training, 107; measuring program outcomes, 134, 140; and mobility, 188, 205, 206, 228, 229.
Alienation, 142, 245
Allocative efficiency. See Efficiency
Andrews, J.: job tenure information, 204
Anti-poverty programs: participants, 13, 176-178; and social cost-benefit analysis, 36-37; in Canada, 40; role, 175; and income maintenance, 175-176, 178, 183; objectives, 176-178; equity vs. effectiveness, 176-180 passim; current emphasis, 177; and farm programs, 177; and level of training, 177-178; in the private sector, 178-181; in the public sector, 181-182; different types summarized, 182-183; mentioned, xiii, 119. See also Community action programs; Income maintenance; Negative income tax; Poverty; Social action programs.
Apprenticeship, 48, 52
ARA. See Area Redevelopment Administration
Area Redevelopment Administration: supported training programs, xiii, 97, 98; cost-benefit analysis studies, 160; and employment effects of training, 164; and work relocation programs, 184-185
Arrow, Kenneth, 149

Behavior: factors producing, 35; affected by transfer payments, 41; affected by interest rates, 78; affected by prices, 78; measurement difficulties, 122, 123, 139-140; statistical model to evaluate changes, 131-132; of disadvantaged workers, 142; of "movers" and "stayers", 188-189
Benefit-cost analysis. See Cost-benefit analysis
"Benefit cost estimates for Job Corps", 171
Benefit-cost ratio. See Cost-benefit ratio
Bentham, Jeremy, 230, 234

Berle, A. A., 238
Beroulli, Daniel, 73
Borus, Michael E.: studied retraining in Connecticut, 98, 105; studied retraining in Michigan, 98; defines social economic benefits and costs, 99-100; wage effects, 100-101, 166-167; individual trainee's economic benefits and costs, 102-103, 115; studied disposable income, 103; government economic benefits and costs, 103-104, 116, 117; used control groups, 105-106, 107, 161; estimated training effects, 107-108; statistical approach, 109, 111; response rate, 110; data quality, 111; cost-benefit ratio, 112-113, 114, 158-159, 163
British Institute of Management: studied employee turnover, 202-203
Bureaucracy: in manpower programs, 180
Business. See Private sector

Cain, Glen: studied retraining in West Virginia, 97; social economic benefits and costs, 99, 100, 112; private economic benefits and costs, 102, 103, 115-116; governmental economic benefits and costs, 103; used control groups, 104; estimated training effect, 107, 112, 171, 172-173; statistical approach, 111; studied Job Corps 171, 172-173, 174
Canada: income distribution, 28-29, 39, 93; unemployment, 39, 40; manpower programs, 40, 44, 46-47; mobility program, 40, 185-186, 205-207, 225; discount rate, 89; output/capital ratio, 93; corporate taxes, 93; effect of foreign borrowing on lending, 94; job tenure, 202-204, 213. See also Canada. Federal Department of Energy, Mines and Resources; Canada Manpower Centres; Occupational Training for Adults Program; Ontario, Canada; Toronto. University
Canada. Federal Department of Energy, Mines and Resources, 18
Canada Manpower Centres, 200
Capital: opportunity costs, xii, 56, 80, 82, 84-86; marginal productivity, xii, 68-71, 76-77, 78-79, 82, 90, 93; discount rate, 57, 74, 80, 82, 91; defined, 59; and investment, 59, 237; publicly optimal policy, 63-66, 76-77; and in-

23, 28-29, 57, 137, 154; of capital, xii, 56, 80, 82, 84-86; of foreign exchange, xii, 82, 83, 85; of training, 6, 158, 159, 163; in cost-benefit analysis, 20-21, 86; in education, 20-21, 137, 139; avoidable vs. fixed costs, 24; affects decision-making, 27; measurement, 56, 137-138, 154; and discount rate, 80; model, 84-85; and earnings, 137, 138; compared to capital costs, 152-153; and capital recovery factor, 154; of migration, 223; mentioned, 81, 170

Costs, social, 56, 156-157

David, Martin, 164-165
Decision-making: and cost-benefit analysis, viii, xiv-xv, 16, 19, 37, 42, 45-46, 47, 50, 55, 81, 102, 170-171, 223-224, 233; economists' views, 16, 233-239; determining objectives, 16, 17; determining constraints, 16, 17-19, 26-27; considering alternatives, 16, 19, 26-27; paradigm of choice, 16-19; and uncertainty, 27; and opportunity costs, 27; by governments, 42, 44, 58-59, 81, 190-191; and investments, 58-59, 60, 235; and level, 128, 130-131, 143; and replicability criterion, 128-131; from manpower evaluations, 145, 149-150, 151; from mobility model, 189, 191, 192, 221; effect of human capital theory, 230, 232-233, 236, 241-244; in education, 246

Demand. *See* Supply and demand
Disadvantaged workers: in manpower programs, xv, 10-11, 119, 142, 160-162, 169, 176-177; and income distribution, 4; risks in training, 10-11; problem in program analysis, 140-141; cause problems, 142; mentioned, xiii

Discount rate: investments, viii, 56-60 *passim*, 71, 74, 80, 86-92 *passim*, 116, 235-236; use, x-xii, 88-89; measurement, xii, 81-88 *passim*, 91-92; problems in identifying, 57; model, 60-63, 77; criterion function, 61-62, 76, 78-79; publicly optimal policy, 63-66, 76-77; in a mixed economy, 66-71; rate of return, 72-74; and savings, 74; causes summarized, 74; and market imperfections, 74, 85-86; and discount rate, 77, 82, 89; and opportunity costs, 80; definition, 82; in Canada, 89; and consumption, 89, 91; effect when lowered, 90; in capital and growth theory, 91; in cost-benefit ratios, 112-114;

mentioned, 56, 112. *See also* Interest rate
Displacement effect: and employment effect, xiii-xiv; and production, 100-101, 102, 103; criticized, 117, 159; causes, 163; needs to be studied, 163-164; mentioned, 53, 114
Distributional criteria. *See* Equity criteria
Domar, Evsey D., 69
Douglas, Paul H.: production function, 78, 79, 93
Dropouts, 46-47, 114

Earnings: effect of training on, xiii, 6-7, 49, 100-103, 112-115, 132-133, 139, 159, 162-169, 176, 183, 210; and productivity, 9-10, 100, 101, 164-167, 246; compared to income maintenance programs, 13-14, 175-176, 183; effect on labor supply, 22-23, 101; and opportunity costs, 22-23, 137, 138; of university faculty, 25-26; and shadow pricing, 36; difficult to obtain data on, 49, 106, 110, 111, 126, 140, 141, 171; projected from cost-benefit analysis, 52; and age, 107; and education, 107, 164-165, 171, 172-173; related to duration of training, 114-118; affected by disadvantaged workers, 142; definition, 164; and wage effect, 164-169; employment effect, 164-169; influenced by job placement, 166; studies, 166-167; as objective of anti-poverty programs, 176-178; effect of mobility programs, 197-198, 211-212, 217-220, 222, 223, 226, 227. *See also* Income; Wage differentials; Wage effects; Wage rates
Economics: defined, vii; and cost-benefit analysis, vii, ix, 30-37 *passim*, 53, 135-136; views on decision-making, 16, 238-239; and consumption, 30, 31-32; compared to political science, 32-33; relationship to sociology, 34-35; Tinbergen's theory of policy, 58-59; and non-measurable objectives, 122-123, 238-239, 247-248; view of experimentation, 146; and systems analysis, 241-242. *See also* Micro-economics; Welfare economics
Education: costs, xvii, 20-23, 25-26, 99-100, 123, 137, 139, 152-156 *passim*, 238-239, 246-247; effect on earnings, 28, 107, 164-165, 171, 172-173; for dropouts, 46-47; effect on productivity, 48-49, 119; measurement in pro-